Willa Cather
and the Myth of
American Migration

Willa Cather and the Myth of American Migration

Joseph R. Urgo

University of Illinois Press
Urbana and Chicago

This book is printed on acid-free paper.

Library of Congress Cataloging-in-Publication Data
Urgo, Joseph R.
    Willa Cather and the myth of American migration / Joseph R. Urgo.
        p.   cm.
    Includes bibliographical references (p.) and index.
    ISBN 0-252-02187-8. — ISBN 0-252-06481-x (pbk.)
    1. Cather, Willa, 1873-1947 — Political and social views.
2. Literature and society — United States — History — 20th century.
3. Women and literature — United States — History — 20th century.
4. National characteristics, American, in literature.
5. Migration, Internal — United States — Historiography.
6. Migration, Internal, in literature.   7. United States — In literature.
8. Myth in literature.   I. Title.
PS3505.A87Z891995
813'.52 — dc20   95-5730
                                                         CIP

IN MEMORIAM:

Anna and Rocco Urgo
Mary and Frank Zito
who made the crossing

Contents

Acknowledgments

I would like first of all to thank Lesley Dretar, who gave me a copy of *My Mortal Enemy* before we were married by way of introduction to Willa Cather and other matters.

My professional debts begin with Susan Rosowski. I thank her for her initial support and for a continuing exchange of ideas. The thesis for this study has its roots in a classroom in León, Spain, where I was a Fulbright Lecturer, teaching *A Lost Lady* with a map of the United States on the wall, pointing out the distance from Colorado to the Black Hills, the path of the railroad to California, and, as an aside, the various places I had lived. One student said, "You are a lost professor!" and the whole design (as Professor St. Peter might have said) appeared before me.

This book has improved owing to some careful preliminary readings, and I acknowledge the vital critical interventions of Roger Anderson, James Hurt, and Cecelia Tichi. Karen Hewitt, at the University of Illinois Press, is a patient and discerning editor, and I thank her for it. This book was copyedited by Bruce Bethell. Thanks also to the students in my Willa Cather seminar at Bryant College, who heard all this and made it better by questioning and demanding clarification. These interlocutors cannot be held accountable for any persisting errors.

Bryant College provided release time and technical support for research and writing. I thank in particular Vice President for Academic Affairs Michael Patterson for his unwavering support for the business of scholarly activities at Bryant. Colleagues Earl Briden and Paulo de Medeiros offered very useful responses to these ideas in conversation. Thanks also to Colleen Anderson, Connie Cameron, and Tom Magill for interlibrary loan and research assistance and to Chris Briggs for getting me out of some word-processing predicaments. Jackie David, in Faculty Suite F, is the best faculty coordinator in the world.

This book is dedicated to those who make the crossing.

In Transit

WILLA CATHER
December 7, 1876–April 14, 1947

THE TRUTH AND CHARITY OF HER GREAT
SPIRIT WILL LIVE ON IN THE WORK
WHICH IS HER ENDURING GIFT TO HER
COUNTRY AND ALL ITS PEOPLE

". . . that is happiness, to be dissolved
into something complete and great"

FROM *My Ántonia*
—WILLA CATHER HEADSTONE

A dialectic between migration and settlement informs New World history at every stage, from the age of exploration, encounter, and colonization through the eras of transcontinental expansion, transatlantic crossings, and late twentieth-century corporate transfers. American literary history, as well, reflects the interplay of rootedness and migrancy, settlement and escape. The nineteenth-century figures Hawthorne and Melville may be perceived as forming an essential duality: Hawthorne and the house versus Melville and the ship. The indigenous American slave narrative marks the epitome of this national predicament. Frederick Douglass, prior to his escape from "the wretchedness of slavery," records in his *Narrative* that he held regrets only in "the thought of being separated" from the people he loved in Baltimore, where he was enslaved. "It is my opinion that thousands would escape from slavery," Douglass concludes, "but for the strong cords of affection that bind them to their friends" (105). Presaging the postmodern corporate era, Douglass cuts those ties and relocates: "It was to me the starting-point of a new existence" (113).

American writers in the nineteenth century attempted to synthesize the relation between home and boat, or raft, as in the case of Mark Twain: "it was rough living in the house all the time," Huck says, "and so when I couldn't stand it no longer, I lit out" (1). Twain had his Connecticut home designed to resemble a riverboat, and there it remains, to this day, next door to Harriet Beecher Stowe's cottage on historic Nook Farm in Hartford. Stowe, of course, set forth the principles of domestic science in *The American Woman's Home* (1869), coauthored with Catherine Beecher. Nonetheless, Stowe knew and immortalized the function of outbound transit in the United States. When Eliza escapes from Uncle Tom's cabin, "every familiar object . . . seemed to speak reproachfully to her, and ask her whither could she go from a home like that." Stowe challenges her readers to imagine their children taken away by a slave trader and asks, "how fast could *you* walk?" (104–5). Flight was a matter of desperation to Stowe's Eliza, as desperate an act as settling down was in the mind of Twain's Huckleberry Finn: "We said there warn't no home like a raft, after all." Twain's synthesis kept the ideal home in transit. "Other places do seem so cramped up and smothery, but a raft don't. You feel mighty free and easy and comfortable on a raft" (155).

Twentieth-century literary studies are equally influenced by the facts of settlement and migration, paralleled in this century not by westward expansion or the flight of fugitive slaves but by waves of transatlantic crossings. In the 1920s and 1930s the modernist literary canon was constructed around the phenomenon of the "lost generation," a term that signaled the sense of detachment, both physical and intellectual, shared by American writers. A journey to Europe was considered essential for the aspiring writer, the necessary prerequisite to serious work, to broaden the mind and ensure an escape from the provincialism of U.S. culture. Historically, then, as millions of immigrants were traversing the Atlantic to improve their livelihoods, intellectuals in the United States found it necessary to backtrack along the same routes. The odd thing is that this literary generation has been considered exceptional in its restlessness, its need to light out, and its sense of detachment.

In this book I suggest that we have not fully comprehended the intellectual effects of the one material circumstance that is shared across class, race, and gender categorizations in the United States, transcending regional and historical markers. Blind to this material reality, we have as well not fully comprehended writers who have spoken directly to it. Migration has more often been thought of as a rite of passage—something done once and done with—producing little intellectual residue save some colorful stories about the old people. Immigration was Italians and Irish and Germans, and today is Haitians and Vietnamese and Eastern Europeans, but literary critics take these movements to be the subject matter of history and sociology. The sense of exile felt by the first-generation immigrant has seldom been linked to the sense of alienation felt by third-, fourth-, and fifth-generation intellectuals. Nevertheless, assimilation, acculturation, and even ethnic pride are symptoms of the consciousness produced by migratory existence, and each is rooted in a sense of having landed at some distance from one's source.

I think that the twin sensibilities of exile, both actual and abstract, are parallel enactments of a constant in U.S. culture. To cross from one physical place to another, to find oneself in a strange location surrounded by people who think, speak, and act in ways that underscore one's own sense of difference, and to seek out those who think, speak, and act in the peculiar fashion that one finds familiar—these phenomena are not the exclusive purview of the newly arrived immigrant. What begins as a physical consequence of migration endures as a cultural style. Detachment is the sine qua non of intellectual existence in America, as is the sense of exile, of living in a strange land, of claiming incomprehension before the habits and proclivities of mainstream society.

In the United States migration begins as a physical act and is transformed into a mode of consciousness. An agricultural community will construct cyclical notions of time based on the recurring phenomena of the harvest. Repetition, quite naturally, is valued more highly than is singularity, and ritualistic cultural forms ensure cosmic regularity. An industrial society, on the other hand, will demarcate the historical record of its own productivity, seeing time accumulate like goods in the warehouse. Singular acts that provide benchmarks in the passage of time are valued more highly than are repeatable experiences that obscure the essentials of linearity.

A migratory society, building on its experience, thinks spatially about existence. Time is not cyclical, because seasonal realities alter in transit. An energetic migrant can escape the harvest. Time is not linear, because each destination contains a new historical record that overrides that of the "old home" through the simple fact of its immediacy. If one moves, say, from Virginia to Nebraska, the southern past is made less important than prairie history—but not necessarily, and southerners-as-migrants may suspect this, despite the evidence. Their own memories will insist that their histories unravel elsewhere, away from where they happen to exist at the moment. An ambitious imagination might then conclude that history may quite comfortably exist here, or there, or *anywhere*. The migratory mind knows the spatial and the historical in true simultaneity: one's autobiography is marked out by a succession of places, while each site possesses a distinctive history, altering with time and migration. In transit there is no place one has to be or be from, no exclusive past one has to bear or overcome.

Much of what is superficial about U.S. culture is designed to alleviate the disorienting effects of migration. The thousands of identical commercial strips, as well as the identical iterations of McDonald's, Wal-Mart, Kmart, or Holiday Inn that they contain, provide the transparent sense of being at home that migratory people demand. Uniform housing on U.S. military bases across the globe eases the domestic upheaval that accompanies the regular transfer of personnel and their families. Much of what is profound in American society is meant equally to duplicate familiarity. Constitutional history reflects the need to protect migrancy. The Fourteenth Amendment's equal protection clause privileges migration over home, ensuring that people who move from one state to another do not lose any rights in doing so. The defeat of the primacy of state's rights in the American Civil War, the dismembering of a plantation economy, and the subsequent "incorporation of America," in Alan Trachtenberg's phrase, ensured the future of a migratory American culture. The defeat of the South was marked by the arrival of northern carpetbaggers and the transformation of perpetual, place-bound slaves into potentially migratory tenants.

Nonetheless, the modern American literary canon might suggest that migration is an aberration of some sort: an adventure at best, a displacement at worst. Melville cast his tales of migration onto the ocean; Faulkner attended to migratory consciousness through a distinctively intrusive clan, the Snopes family. Literary scholars who write and teach miles from the postage stamp of their own native soil (to evoke Faulkner) have perpetuated the myth of origins in American history, naturalizing the idea of rootedness and making the notion of migrancy aberrant or marginal. Literary genres such as southern, New England, and Great Plains fiction perpetuate a mythology of place-bound existence, whereas genres such as travel and "on the road" literature attach a mythology of exoticism to migration. More recent genres, cast along ethnic and racial lines (Chicano, African American, Asian) or by sexuality (gay and lesbian), deny the sexual and genetic migrancy that has animated and variegated the social order. Such literary categorizations are meant to clarify but instead work to obscure essential continuities in American culture.

On this matter literary critics have missed the boat. We have failed to recognize that the central theme, the overarching myth, the single experience, that defines American culture at its core is migration: unrelenting, incessant, and psychic mobility across spatial, historical, and imaginative planes of existence. In the twentieth century one writer continuously and throughout her extensive body of work articulates the cultural mode of thought produced by migratory consciousness. Willa Cather felt neither alienated nor detached by displacement but in fact marked intellectual bounty by her own spatial mobility. In this study I focus solely on her writing instead of picking and choosing among a number of authors because Cather is a comprehensive resource for the demarcation of an empire of migration in U.S. culture. She is the one major American writer whose body of work is substantial enough to redirect American literary history in the twenty-first century by showing how thoroughly transit has marked Americans. Willa Cather worked to bring this into focus; it is her self-conscious gift, according to the Jaffrey Center headstone, at once enduring and dissolved, like a previous address.

A cemetery in Red Cloud, Nebraska, is the resting place for members of Willa Cather's immediate family. There is a space between the Cather graves where one might expect to find the famous Nebraska author's remains. If you tour Red Cloud, you might visit Willa Cather's childhood home (on the national register of historic places), see the opera house where she wrote her name on the stage wall, or visit the nearby town of Franklin, where some cousins lived. On all roads leading to Red Cloud there are "Catherland" signs pointing out the boundaries of Nebraska's claim to Willa Cather. You may also visit the house in which the real-life models for Ántonia Shimerda's family lived (this building is also on the national register), see Dr. Archie's office, and spend time on the Willa Cather Memorial Prairie.

When you visit the Red Cloud burial grounds, however, you will not find a stone marked "Willa Cather." To do that you will have to travel east about one thousand miles to Jaffrey, New Hampshire. Cather spent summers in Jaffrey and is buried, by her choice, in the Jaffrey Center historical cemetery. Her grave marks her birth year as 1876, the centennial of the United States, and makes clear "her enduring gift to her country and all its people." Cather was actually born in 1873, but a centennial birth year was, it seems, more appealing to her. For the novelist who wrote so thoroughly about the migratory culture of the United States, to be born in 1876 was a happiness equal to that of dissolution "into something complete and great."

There are no Catherland signs in New Hampshire. The Shattuck Inn, where Cather stayed and wrote many of her novels, is now empty. A modern addition houses the pro shop of a beautiful but distinctly nonliterary golf course. (Although golf, a migratory pastime, is not inconsistent with Cather's aesthetics.) The original Shattuck Inn has been abandoned, leaving no museum, no relics, no historical markers. A few miles away there is only the single gravestone and its mate, that of Edith Lewis, Cather's lifelong companion. The graveyard is in Jaffrey Center; even the town of Jaffrey has moved up the road a few miles.

Cather did not spend whole summers in Jaffrey but traveled as well to Grand Manan Island in Canada and to Northeast Harbor in Maine. Winters she spent in New York City. And throughout her life there were trips to Nebraska, the Southwest, all over North America, and Europe. To know Cather, to know the life she lived, one must migrate around the country. One must remain in transit. The places she knew are disappearing quickly, but then again, these sites were important not as destinations but as stopping points, places to stop and write, to rest and gain strength, before moving on. One can make a pilgrimage to Oxford, Mississippi, and see Faulkner's adult home, his grave, the stores he frequented, the university he attended for a while. Cather, however, lived and wrote another story. Pilgrims to Red Cloud have only begun to "visit" Cather. There are other home addresses: the birthplace in Back Creek Valley (near Winchester), Virginia; 1180 Murray Hill Avenue, Pittsburgh; Washington Square in New York City; Jaffrey, New Hampshire; Grand Manan Island in New Brunswick; Northeast Harbor, Maine. And then there are the places Cather liked to visit: Walnut Canyon, Arizona; Santa Fe, New Mexico; Boston Garden; Manchester, Massachusetts; Cos Cob, Connecticut; Quebec City; and, of course, back to Nebraska, often. There is, then, no such place as Catherland; there is, however, a Cather Trail (or perhaps the Catherland Trail). Reading the texts that were produced by the migratory novelist means exploring the world as it emerges from an imagination in continual transposition.

For a generation after her death Willa Cather was considered to be a minor writer. Occasionally mentioned along with Hemingway, Fitzgerald, and Faulkner, Cather was more likely to be placed along the periphery of any circle of U.S. novelists. The center of that circle during the cold war, for example, was occupied by Hawthorne in nineteenth-century studies and by Faulkner in twentieth-century literary studies. The cultural center in American literature, however, has shifted at the end of the twentieth century—or rather, the culture itself has been decentered. Hawthorne and Faulkner provided American readers with a sense of place, the former writing about New England, the starting place, the roots of the emerging nation, and the latter portraying the South, the enduring region, defeated but still there, the nation under siege and prevailing. These attributes, these things "worth writing about," as Faulkner said in his Nobel Prize acceptance speech in 1950, provided a cold war generation with the sense of home and national origins so necessary to intellectual existence in that era. Cather, with her multiple centers, did not fit.

Writing about his own generation of literati in *Exile's Return*, Malcolm Cowley was struck above all else by the condition of homelessness that intellectuals shared in the 1920s. "A whole generation of American writers—and how many others, architects, painters, bond salesmen, professors and their wives, all the more studious and impressionable section of the middle-class youth—had been uprooted, schooled away . . . from their attachment to any locality or local tradition. For years the process continued, through school and college and the war; always they were moving farther from home." The process eventually made some intellectuals feel at home being uprooted. "At last hundreds and thousands of them became veritable exiles, living in Paris or the South of France and adhering to a theory of art which held that the creative artist is absolutely independent of all localities, nations or classes" (206).

The eventual return of these Americans to the United States in the 1930s amounted to "a mass migration," in Cowley's terminology (210). The experience marked their outlook, critical perspective, and creative energies, however. Cowley claims, for example, that the canonization of T. S. Eliot was due to the critical assessment of him as a poet who continually moved from one aesthetic problem to another. "It was part of the general literary atmosphere" that cast "the ideal poet as an explorer, a buffalo hunter pressing westward toward new frontiers" (111-12). This paradigm could be and eventually was applied to Faulkner, Cowley's own literary pioneer.

Willa Cather is mentioned only once in *Exile's Return*, as a member of a previous and by implication more settled generation, along with Sherwood Anderson and Theodore Dreiser. Cowley works hard in his "literary odyssey of the 1920s" to set his generation apart from American traditions, a modernist generation "seeking for something that was no longer there." The literary figure, in Cowley's mind, "could write about" Americans "but not write for them, not resume his part in the common life." The literati of the 1920s "had been uprooted from something more than a birthplace, a country, or a town. Their real exile was from society itself, from any society to which they could honestly contribute and from which they could draw the strength that lived in shared convictions" (214). Given the massive rate of global migration between 1870 and 1914, and continuing throughout the 1920s after World War I, it is not surprising to find such terms as "uprooted," "exile," and "strangers in their own land" in Cowley's vocabulary. What is surprising is that Cowley barely mentions the transatlantic migration that had been shaping his culture for a half-century.

According to social historian Walter Nugent, fifty million human beings crossed the Atlantic Ocean to the Americas between 1871 and 1914. Net migration to the United States alone from 1871 through 1920 amounted to over twenty million (150). The term "net migration" is used to exclude another five to ten million humans who returned to their country of origin or made more than one migration elsewhere. Statistics on these "birds of passage," as they were called, are imprecise because records are kept accurately only on residents, not on transients. Nonetheless, these figures alone indicate that Malcolm Cowley's literary generation was no aberration, no lost generation, if being lost means being left behind somehow, apart from the mainstream. "Looking backward," Cowley writes in 1951, "I feel that our whole training was involuntarily directed . . . toward making us homeless citizens of the world" (27).

Cowley is correct here, but the inference drawn is misdirected. In becoming homeless citizens of the world, Cowley's generation was being incorporated into a great fact of American existence: migratory consciousness. This mode of thought informs a tradition of American culture from origins through contemporary professional mobility. Seventeenth-century Puritan settlers, thinking they could plant themselves in New England, were schooled in the practice of transit by their vulnerability to capture and forced removal by migrant Native Americans. Mary Rowlandson, after her traumatic captivity in 1676, sensed God's greater purpose: "And I hope I can say in some measure, as David did, 'It is good for me that I have been afflicted' " (75). Cowley's generation, in sensing that something was lost, in feeling displaced, homeless, and removed, had found a national experience transcending region and station. It was good for them, too, to be in transit—good for their art and their literary aesthetics.

The literati of the century preceding Cowley's were sharply aware of the material and intellectual realities of transit. At the end of his poem sequence titled *Birds of Passage*, Longfellow's "Song" declares that "those who wander . . . are baffled and beaten and blown about / By the winds of wilderness and doubt." The conclusion, "To stay at home is best" (340), is not far from Mary Rowlandson's final admonition, taken from Exodus: "Stand still and see the salvation of the Lord" (75). Nonetheless, Longfellow's poem sequence opens by clearly aligning the poet's inspiration with the migration of those "swift birds of passage" whose "distant flight" inspires "the sound of winged words" in the mind of the literary artist (185). Furthermore, the *Birds of Passage* poem entitled "Changed" (295) foreshadows the alienation of Cowley's own lost cohort. The poet, as bird of passage, returns to his origins, to his hometown, "now a stranger, looking down" at familiarity:

> Is it changed, or am I changed?
>   Ah! the oaks are fresh and green,
> But the friends with whom I ranged
> Through their thickets are estranged
>   By the years that intervene.

At this point the poet is, in Cowley words, a "homeless citizen of the world." To escape estrangement, Longfellow suggests that one must "stay at home," but to remain at home means to give up "the poet's songs" that the experience of passage produces (185). "The sound of winged words" comes in transit.

Longfellow was America's first international man of letters. Born in Portland, Maine, a classmate of Hawthorne's at Bowdoin College (in the class of 1825), Longfellow created works that dominated the pre-modernist American canon. The biographical sketch included in the 1915 Riverside edition of his poetry makes very clear that this poet and scholar was no homebody but had traveled extensively. Prior to taking a teaching post at Bowdoin, for instance, Longfellow "increased his qualifications by travel and study in Europe," remaining there for three years. In 1835 Longfellow moved to Harvard College "and again went to Europe for preparatory study" (iii). Preparation meant relocation, and Longfellow's mind was schooled in the habits of migration, as declared in *Birds of Passage* and as evidenced by the incessant movement charted throughout his poetry. To Longfellow, Paul Revere's ride marked his country's birth by transit ("The fate of a nation was riding that night"). His poetic translations (from Spanish, Swedish, Danish, German, Anglo-Saxon, French, Italian, Portuguese, Eastern, and Latin sources), furthermore, declare an international or imperial scope—a roll call of contemporary and future migrations to and from the United States. The abandonment of Longfellow in the modernist literary canon resulted from a shift in aesthetic sensibility. The link between intellectual mobility and migratory displacement was lost in the shifting canon or suppressed by the self-conscious, modernist sense of being exceptional, somehow apart from old traditions.

Nugent's study of transatlantic migration places the experience of the United States in a larger, more inclusive context than those achieved in previous studies of migration, which focused on *immigration* only. Nearly half of all U.S. immigrants, for example, eventually emigrated out of the United States. Immigration to the United States existed as but one piece of a tremendous exchange and interchange of human beings between the Old and New Worlds. Furthermore, Nugent suggests that scholars have been misled by an exclusive focus on the nation's frontier experience. The United States' frontier was, in fact, exceptional, but so were the ways in which every "receiver" nation incorporated migrants. "Focusing on migration rather than on the frontier would . . . place the American experience within the broader transatlantic context rather than isolate it as something unique" (27–29). Situating the American experience in this way would also account for Malcolm Cowley's sense of displacement—a sense felt equally strong in Paris and Madrid, Buenos Aires and New York, because it was no aberration, no generational phenomenon, but the major historical movement of the century, the modern age of migration.

Although they were thoroughly enmeshed in a culture of transit,

American writers celebrated in the twentieth century did not, as a rule, write specifically about migration. Hawthorne and Faulkner, as mentioned, were studied for their evocations of place and canonized, I suspect, partially for their defiance of the migratory dimension of American history and culture. Often paired with Hawthorne, Herman Melville has gained steadily in influence in the twentieth century. Melville's sense of homelessness, of wandering and of continual migration, was for Cowley's generation an exotic "other" to Hawthorne's "us." Literary shifts in recent decades have begun to suggest a reversal of fortunes, where Melville may in fact be "ours" and Hawthorne's sense of rootedness a premigratory memory. In twentieth-century studies Faulkner and Cather provide a similar dichotomy, although Faulkner's depiction of the Snopes family's ascendancy indicates that he shared and appreciated the function of migratory consciousness. The Snopes phenomenon cuts across and moves off the map of Faulkner's apocryphal Yoknapatawpha County. In reverse fashion Cather found settled existence to be as phenomenal as Faulkner's Snopeses, as extraordinary as Native American cliff dwellings, Nebraskan sod houses, and Canadian outcroppings.

Cather has always had a cadre of enthusiasts, as has Melville, while the center, marked by critics like Malcolm Cowley, has not voiced full cognizance of her fictional imperatives. For years Cather has been read through a critical lens appropriate to writers of place. As a result she has been seen as nostalgic for the pioneer era, a repository of old virtues. Cather's unconventional life-style, however, the strong possibility of lesbianism, and the experimentation with gender identification in her fiction have made such categorizations of her writing difficult. Also working against Cather is her accessible style, which largely disqualified her from serious consideration by New Criticism. Critical inquiry into Cather cannot be accomplished by writing twenty pages explicating one paragraph of dense language. Her texts do not allow such dwelling. Serious readers of Cather learn to move within the text, from section to section, from inset story to overall plot, for Cather's aesthetics demand a migratory critical acumen. At the same time, less rigorous readings can be accomplished by birds of passage, reading for the good story and then putting the book aside. As Cowley's study demonstrates, however, American intellectuals resist identifying with mass culture. Just as the lost generation would not admit to being the tip of the migratory iceberg, midcentury literary critics would disqualify from serious examination those writers whose texts manage to cross the century's intellectual boundaries. Always searching for "the center of things," as Dos Passos wrote in *Manhattan Transfer,* Cowley's generation nonetheless wanted to set itself apart from connection to the great wave of transatlantic migration.

For all his concern with displacement and exile, then, Cowley saw nothing in Cather's life and literary production that provided a precedent for his own generation's restlessness. Despite the continual migration of U.S. intellectuals across the nation and in and out of the country, Cather has been neglected in favor of writers who have presented the American mind as settled, place-bound in the region of their ancestors. Largely compensatory, as I will suggest in this book, this idea of community has alleviated the anxieties attendant to incessant migration. It has also resulted in influential studies, such as *Exile's Return,* that suggest migration to be something distinctive or strange rather than at the center of things in America. Far from producing lost generations, in other words, migratory consciousness provides the thread that ties together the experience of a vast cross section of twentieth-century Americans, from steamships through fellowships.

Beginning as a massive, global exchange of labor, continuing as an era of intellectual expatriation, obscured by the fixed political tensions of the cold war, the great fact of human migration is now, at the end of the twentieth century, a (mobile) center of consciousness. The literary heirs to the lost generation find that exile is not novel but as common as the material constructing their U-Haul packing boxes. Those who have *not* moved are the exceptional ones. A "found generation" now reads in Willa Cather a writer who knows its secret. Cowley wrote of a generation "lost because it tried to live in exile" (9). Cather's readers today find that the one constant among their cohort is that they succeed and thrive in exile. In *My Ántonia* Jim Burden moves to Nebraska and leaves behind his Virginia home and the gravesite of his dead parents. "I had even left their spirits behind me," he says, as he moves out "over the edge of the world" and "outside man's jurisdiction." A sense of progression, freedom, and self is constructed on Burden's record of flight by readers who are no longer place-bound but liberated as they move on to a succession of superhighways: intercontinental, interstate, and information. The myths that explain Americans today are myths of relocation.

Willa Cather and the Myth of American Migration explicates an American mode of thought that has expanded in this century to the basis of a global empire, an empire of migration. Cather's popularity has increased since her death in 1947, especially in the 1970s and 1980s, when the popular media of the United States began to abandon the illusory values of settled existence as the basis of American mythology. The 1950s icon of the suburban home, the ritual plot of *Leave It to Beaver*, is now the target of ridicule and nostalgia. The United States is a nation of migrants. We move on the average once every five years. Long-distance telephone companies compete for a share of the longings we accumulate as we move away, further and further from our childhood homes. The novelists whom the academy has canonized have valorized those longings more often than they have explored the meaning and implications of our migrations. The sense of place, the mythical counties, the small town dramas, the historical explorations of family and locality, the tremendous sense of loss—these we know as the meat and potatoes of American literature. Nonetheless, Americans keep moving, accumulating hometowns like military campaign medals: I was born here, went to college there, moved there, then there, then here. We do this too often to call it incidental. Migration is paradoxically the keystone of American existence, and migrants gather paradoxes as they move from one "permanent" residence to the next. The picture of life in the United States is a moving picture; our sense of community is in transit; the consciousness we share is migratory. This book explores the implications of this mode of thought as it is manifested in the writing of Willa Cather.

1

Packing Up:
The Culture of Migration

Now he'll tear himself from his native earth.
—SOPHOCLES, *Oedipus Rex*

Have we not stood here like trees in the ground long enough?
—WALT WHITMAN, *Passage to India*

I keep my own suitcases under the bed.
—WILLA CATHER

The Professor's House (1925) is ostensibly concerned with a scholar's re-action to a specific piece of writing and with the definition that the scholar will attach to the man who wrote that text. At stake in the novel is the diary of Tom Outland, which Professor Godfrey St. Peter cannot bring himself to contextualize satisfactorily in a written introduction. Paralleling this blockage is the professor's simultaneous inability to move out of his old study and into the office that he has built in his new house. Everything in the novel seems as if at an impasse because of the professor's physical and intellectual inertia, and Cather plots a series of unresolved issues (Crane's lawsuit, Godfrey's feud with Langtry, ten-sions between the sisters, the St. Peters' strained marriage) that serves to emphasize the book's strong projection of tentativeness. This is a pending and pensive sort of novel, rooted in an inability to finish pack-ing and move.

American culture, as examined through Cather's texts, is rooted in the vigilant maintenance of unsettled lives, impermanent connections, and continuous movements in space and time. What is happening to St. Peter is not extraordinary. In Cather's America the New World is not so much a historical environment (a cosmos, a home) as it is a motion through space (a transformation, a journey). It is difficult, then, to be at home in a Catherian America; it is nearly impossible to consider any part of it as a place to be. Instead, its places are only and always spaces to traverse, to transform the self, the site, or the other. In *The Professor's House* Godfrey St. Peter is a man at the crossroads, an American in resistance to transit. As a result he is in serious trouble. His refusal to migrate is a life-and-death issue in Cather's imagination. The professor's family, given the choice between staying home and going to Europe, chooses traveling over remaining in the United States with husband and father. The need to travel is greater than kinship ties, and out of St. Peter's inability to move emerges the potential disintegration of his family, his career, and his sense of self.

Conflict is endemic to the Catherian social order, but this contention is better understood as a struggle for spatial definition than as a contest over the course of history. The American aversion to historical determinism, or rather, to the consideration of history as an imperative, is less an indication of cultural isolation than it is of the distinctive influence of migratory experience on consciousness. The classic American formulations of starting over, of new frontiers and new beginnings, are often mistaken as simple arguments against history. They are indeed ahistorical utterances, but they are equally rooted in the positive (that is, progressive) ordeal of spatial movement. St. Peter knows that when his family returns from Europe, it is not the past that he must face but his future (258), in the form of his new house and his grandchild. In addition, through the course of his intellectual difficulties concerning Tom Outland's diary, it is not Outland's history but the future of St. Peter's professional career that is most at stake—and his career is tied in the narrative to where his office will be placed in the future. It is this link between physical and psychic migration that makes *The Professor's House* the keystone to Cather's thinking about American transit.

Willa Cather was acutely aware of the continuum between her own sense of homelessness and exile and the waves of immigrants passing through Ellis Island and into New York City and then dispersing across the American continent in the first decades of the twentieth century. The continuum is made clear in comments she made to her friend Elizabeth Shepley Sergeant in 1910. Cather had just met Sergeant in New York, and the two were becoming friends. Sergeant remembers them in Cather's office at *McClure's* discussing the new immigrants, "Italian peasants in New York," and comparing them to the northern or central Europeans whom Cather had known in Nebraska. They also talked of writers, equally migratory people, according to Cather, and the two subjects are conflated in the recounted conversation. Perhaps Cather envied her settled friends, but she never sought to emulate them. " 'I keep my own suitcases under the bed,' she remarked, with a quick, affectionate smile—'Don't like it—would rather be a lucky Bostonian like you, living in a house, or going to Paris where the good hats come from' " (Sergeant 43). Apparently Cather could not even fantasize about living in a house without immediately including a trip to Paris. The psychic connection displayed in her comment is emblematic of narrative links made throughout her fiction. The vision of American culture projected in the novels of Willa Cather is one of continuous movement, of spatial and temporal migrations, of intellectual transmission and physical uprooting. Willa Cather was the one major novelist of her era to recognize that migration links peasant and poet, immigrant and aesthete, into one global pattern of consciousness.

Cather's articulation of this continuum resulted, in the 1920s and 1930s, in her work being labeled sentimental or nostalgic for its apparent continuation of pioneer themes in an urban world. More recent perspectives, however, provide greater clarity. Geographer Edward W. Soja points to "the recognition of a profound restructuring of contemporary life and an explicit consciousness of geographically (not just historically) uneven development," which amounts to "an extraordinary call for a new critical perspective, a different way of seeing the world in which human geography not only 'matters' but provides the most revealing critical perspective" (*Postmodern Geographies* 23). Cather's sense that Italian peasants in New York were linked to the sense of exile among American writers, that the railroad lawyer Jim Burden was "incommunicably" connected to the Bohemian peasant Ántonia Shimerda Cuzak, or that Professor Godfrey St. Peter's intellectual stagnation was linked to his inability to pack his things and move out of his house—and these are only a few of the hundreds of examples in her work—indicates that Cather was cognizant of the simultaneous enactment of cultural forces in widely divergent settings, a perspective available today under postmodernism.

Postmodern assaults on historical consciousness are symptomatic of a more fundamental shift in intellectual focus from an exclusive historicism to a historicism combined with attention to the "geographical or spatial imagination" (Soja, "History" 140) arising from the experience of migration. A resurgence of interest in cartography and diaspora studies, as well as revised studies of immigration patterns, indicates a profound disruption in the idea of history inherited from nineteenth- and early twentieth-century philosophy. One example can be drawn from the modernist phenomenon of territorial nationalism and the de- pendence of national ideologies on historical consciousness. The ex- perience of twentieth-century nation building and national warfare, for instance, has led Eric Hobsbawm to assert that national unity, as a political program, "could be realized only by barbarians, or at least by barbarian means" (*Nations* 134). The political programs of fascist national unification in Germany and Italy during World War II and Soviet attempts to create national entities during the cold war (matched by U.S. efforts to "build nations" in places like South Vietnam) are testimony to the barbaric potential of nationalist imperatives. In the United States the American studies "myth and symbol" school of criti- cism was at its height during the cold war, grappling with the pro- grammatic processes of myth-history construction as a source of cul- tural unity at the national level. The conclusions of the American myth and symbol school are the presuppositions of postmodern comparative studies in nationalism.

Benedict Anderson has defined the nation as "an imagined political community" rather than as a natural or inevitable human construc- tion. Anderson also defines the nation as "inherently limited," or exclu- sive, because "no nation [has] imagined itself coterminous with man- kind." The limits of nationalism are spatial, as all nations have (and have fought over) "finite, if elastic, boundaries, beyond which lie other nations" (6–7). National ideologies are less likely to admit temporal limitations or historical boundaries, however. Israel claims a historical existence in which its 1948 territorial inception is defined, at best, as incidental to its ideological history. The particularly barbaric national programs of fascist Germany and Italy in the 1930s encompassed ex- tensive linear, historical claims to legitimacy. The link between history and territorial boundaries arises when history is used to rationalize the expansion of national borders.

The importance of spatial consciousness in U.S. culture is a com- monplace idea. However, it has only recently been construed so that its metaphoric implications are understood as the foundation of a revised and potentially less barbaric form of nationalism. Lawrence Fuchs, in a recent celebratory study of race and ethnicity in America, provides a succinct formulation, which he labels "voluntary pluralism." I quote from Fuchs at length to introduce this formulation and to demonstrate the way in which temporal and spatial imperatives are conjoined in American nationalism. Voluntary pluralism, according to Fuchs, forms a civic culture

> in which immigrant settlers from Europe and their progeny were free to maintain affection for and loyalty to their ancestral religions and cultures while at the same time claiming an American identity by embracing the founding myths and participating in the political life of the republic. It was a system of pluralism that began, principally, in colonial Pennsylvania, where immigrants of various nationalities and religious backgrounds moved with relative ease into political life. This new invention of Americans—voluntary pluralism—in which individuals were free to express their ancestral affections and sensibilities, to choose to be ethnic, however and whenever they wished or not at all by moving across group boundaries easily, was sanctioned and protected by a unifying civic culture based on the American founding myth, its institutions, heroes, rules, rhetoric. (5)

Fuchs's book is evidence of a resurgence of American nationalism based not solely in historical consciousness but on a distinctive combination of historic rootedness (the American founding myth) with the cultural imperative to move across group boundaries easily.

Considerations of the significance of American mobility, then, can be linked to a conception of American nationalism that does not demand the erasure of past identities but that certainly allows for such erasure, or partial erasure, if so desired. The choice to be ethnic or not produces such peculiar hybrids as Italian Americans who speak no Italian and know nothing of Italian history, culture, or politics and whose forebears emigrated from a place they did not even know as Italy. Anderson's assertion, for example, that the nation is an imagined community may indeed apply to European history, but the intellectual conclusion was made in an encounter with American history. Anderson points out that "nationalism emerged first in the New World, not the Old," and that "from the start the nation was conceived in language, not in blood, and that one could be 'invited into' the imagined community" (145). Efforts to naturalize national identity, as Hobsbawm has argued, have resulted in the catastophic world wars of this century. Furthermore, "in its modern and basically political sense the concept of *nation* is historically very young." The original equivalent was the ethnic unit, "but recent usage rather stressed the notion of political unity and independence" (Hobsbawm, *Nations* 18). Reconsiderations of national identity, then, turn away from historical and genealogical formulas and toward spatial understandings of communities. France is France not solely because of its history but equally for the fact that the people who occupy space within its geographic boundaries imagine themselves at once connected to one another and different from those outside its borders. A tourist who enters France enters not just history but territory.

Fuchs's laudatory tone comes from his sense that American civic culture has enacted a form of nationalism that has incorporated historical consciousness, that is, the consciousness of group *difference*, into a system of national unity. In fact, the imagined community of U.S. culture may depend on what Fuchs calls the "kaleidoscopic" configurations of ethnic interaction, characterized by an "endless variety of variegated patterns" (276) in which ethnic identities come and go over generations of immigration, assimilation, and conscious differentiation. United States culture, in other words, has managed to combine a kaleidoscopic history within its territorial boundaries so that ethnic differences provide the foundation of national unity, not disunity. The American exception, then, to the disruptive effects that ethnicity has had on nations in the late twentieth century is rooted in the migratory consciousness of its people. It is inconceivable, for example, that the Italians on Staten Island would demand a homeland there. Throughout history, demands for an African American homeland within the continental United States have been defeated by majorities of both black and white Americans. The thought of legally confining an ethnic or racial group to a particular place in the United States is antithetical to the national program—and the one exception, that of Native American reservations, only proves the point. Considered in American mythology to have predated both the European discovery of the hemisphere in 1492 and the declaration of nationhood in 1776, Native Americans are thus carefully demarcated as outside the boundaries of the United States, even if they exist within its borders. Limitations on Native American mobility signal that this group is an exception to the civic culture.

American migration has been conceived of and recognized literally, as an aspect of the social condition, but it is less understood as an integral component of a national ideology supported by a body of myths and stories. We know that Americans move often, through initial immigration and then by continued mobility, but our sense of the centrality of these movements to American consciousness is less developed. The literary canon in the American academy has tended to concentrate on writers who represent specific regions (the South, New England, the West) and who were particularly adept at historical projections of particular places. Attempts to assign a home region to Willa Cather, on the other hand, inevitably fail. Through Cather's novels we can see the way in which migratory consciousness directly influences the formulation of American ideology, especially concerning the significance of history, the burden of the future, and the development of the American global empire. Elizabeth Sergeant found Willa Cather to be a bit eccentric because "rapid motion was essential to her." She would pack her suitcases often: "after a few months in the city, she got wildly homesick for the West. She would dash to see her 'family' . . . and the wheat harvest, and then flee back to Pittsburgh to Isabelle McClung—for fear of dying in a cornfield" (48–49). Sergeant implies that all Cather's friends knew when "the need to travel was upon her," at which point she would pack up and leave (119). Cather's personal eccentricities have become contemporary commonplaces of U.S. culture.

Cultural critic Richard Slotkin identifies the present era, the late twentieth century, as a "liminal" one in American history. "We are in the process of giving up a myth/ideology that no longer helps us see our way through the modern world, but lack a comparably authoritative system of beliefs to replace what we have lost" (*Gunfighter Nation* 654). The old American myths, with savage Indians on the border and heroic gunfighters on the frontier, no longer serve to guide us through a new set of complexities in the multicultural United States of the post–cold war era. The myths and ideas that we do need are available to us largely in texts that have gone relatively unread or unexplicated in previous eras. In revisionist projects women's historians, African Americanists, and labor historians have attempted to reconstruct American history so that the challenges of the contemporary era might be comprehensible to future leaders of the state and the culture. We need art, however— stories, pictures, and images—along with history to prop up this new sense of the world. Artists provide us with a way of seeing the world and recasting our role in it.

Cather is a strong resource for Slotkin's motion of an evolving idea of American nationalism. To put this in Cather's own terms, the question here is what sort of pictures Cather creates in the reader's mind or what sort of consciousness is produced by an immersion into her work. By *pictures* I do not mean narrative descriptions. Catherian picture making refers not to what is described on the page but to what is suggested or communicated to the reader without description. In *The Professor's House* Cather makes plain the relation of this literary technique to the construction of consciousness. Cather refers to details of Godfrey St. Peter's past that "had made pictures in him when he was unwilling and unconscious, when his eyes were merely open wide" (21). Those pictures remain with him, forming his adult consciousness. In the novel Cather explores the function of such pictures to get St. Peter through the crises of adulthood and mature disappointment—specifically, to enable him to migrate into a new house and a new way of thinking. St. Peter draws on his experience of past migrations (intellectual movements and physical travel) to cope with future transit. Cather's novels as a whole produce pictures in her readers' minds. Her novels project a mode of consciousness that can provide a useful, powerful set of sustaining beliefs for the inevitable turmoil of millennial transition. She describes such conscious production as "the inexplicable presence of the thing not named," the thing "felt upon the page without being specifically named there" (*Not under Forty* 14).

Critics have addressed Cather's picture making in ways that help to define the idea more precisely. Janis Stout calls them "the artful omissions and gaps in [the] narrative" that may signal areas or aspects of the narrative that Cather "does not want to confront directly" (73). Jo Ann Middleton calls these artful omissions by the biological term *vacuoles* and places them at the center of Cather's poetics. Vacuoles are gaps in the narrative structure, such as "a thirteen-year space between parts of a work, or a minute space between disparate details, or an unexpected space between scenes; however, it is in this space . . . that we experience the insight arising from the juxtapositioning of Cather's often disjointed elements. It is the vacuole that gives the novel its form, arising from the carefully selected material itself; it is the vacuole that sustains the structure of the work without overloading it" (56). The reader fills in these vacuoles unconsciously. If the effort were conscious, one would quickly assess the novels as unfinished or incomplete—a charge rarely leveled at Cather. Instead, the overwhelming sense of completion that comes from reading Cather is due to "the inexplicable presence of the thing not named" and the consequent picture making performed routinely and unconsciously by the reader. The novels arouse the reader's desire and also provide the space, or vacuole, for that desire to enter. Cather writes often of memory and desire, and Mary Beth Ryder identifies the Catherian "alliance of memory and desire" as "the force from which both art and civilization evolve" (160). The process of reading Cather enforces this juxtaposition, as the texts play on the reader's desire for transition and closure.

Cather's poetics, then, invites cultural criticism and debate. When those things that are not named by Cather are named by critics, we begin to learn some things about how the minds of our contemporaries work. In an early and influential study of Cather's work Edward and Lillian Bloom found that each novel "depends for its essential meaning upon a secondary level of interpretation" and thus placed Cather in the allegorist tradition of Dante and Kafka. The novels possess an "exterior impression . . . of simplicity" but also contain an "inner complexity" that cannot be grasped without greater, more intense effort. This inner complexity is communicated by gaps, vacuoles, and pictures left on the reader's unconscious mind. Each novel is animated by a central set of nonnarrated ideas, an "intellectual motif" that provides the pattern for all its disparate elements (14). This intellectual motif is the most powerful of the things not named in Cather's novels.

Coming to grips with these ideas is inevitably an ideological process. Explication of Cather's texts has proceeded in a thorough fashion; her work has attracted talented literary critics. Cultural criticism of Cather has yet to be accomplished, however, largely because in the past she has seemed to lie outside the concerns of politics and social issues. Among her notable vacuoles is the ideological, and without an understanding of Cather's poetics the cultural dimension of her work is unfathomable. Her frontier is not Cooper's, her great war is not Hemingway's, and her sense of history is not Faulkner's. Cather's frontier is a place not of regeneration but of humility and loss. There are, as Edward and Lillian Bloom have pointed out, "no Wild West exploits, lawlessness or melodrama" but rather pioneers "in conflict with a primeval force" that transcends traditional popular legend (21) and approaches a late twentieth-century version of environmental predicament. Her world war is an acceleration of values, not a crisis but a conclusion, an opportunity not for "grace under pressure" but for refuge from impossible conditions. According to literary historian Peter Aichinger, Cather's war is about "the removal of the usual moral restraints" from the American individual (47), projecting a sense of war that is more relevant to the post-Vietnam era in American culture than to the modernist period of the two world wars. Moreover, her sense of history is far from a Faulknerian burden or snare; it is far from Faulkner's "not *was* but *is*." In Cather's idea of history conquests and defeats occur in succession, none of which can possibly interfere with the desire of the present to accomplish its own mission and to avoid, if possible, its own defeat. Eudora Welty saw that "Cather's history was not thus bonded to the present; it did not imprison the present, but instructed it, passed on a meaning" (148). The very logic of Cather's migratory culture mitigates against immuring the present in historical necessity; in fact, it moves in an opposite direction. Cather's imagination was predominantly spatial rather than linear, and her consciousness was migratory.

The animating idea in *The Professor's House* is this: the things with which we surround ourselves, the things we study and look at continually, our natural and familiar environment—these things produce us, produce consciousness. Much of this source material is acquired in the experiences of youth, through socialization and education, but we go on gathering unconscious resources as long as our minds remain acquisitive. Questions follow: Will these resources, the intellectual sources of our production, be sufficient to carry us through a crisis? Will we have what we need to survive in unprecedented situations? More to the point, will these resources sustain us through the successive migrations of body and mind that our profession, our family, and our history demand? On a cultural level the issue is more profound. A culture is formed largely by its origins and by what it believes and chooses to remember and preserve about its origins. But it also must continue to generate ideas about itself, within the space it occupies, and find what it needs to survive, especially in times of transition or crisis. Catastrophic conditions inevitably arise when old ideas will not sustain the culture, when new myths must be generated to instill a fresh sense of purpose and fortitude. To accomplish this rejuvenation the culture depends on the imaginative resources of its individual components, such as that represented by Professor Godfrey St. Peter, historian, editor, and intellectual. In this novel Cather presents no new myths or stories (the purview of other novels) but rather describes the conditions under which such regenerative production can proceed.

The first chapter of *The Professor's House* explains that "the great fact" in Godfrey St. Peter's childhood was Lake Michigan: "It was the first thing one saw in the morning . . . and it ran through the days like the weather, not a thing thought about, but a part of consciousness itself" (20). Aspects of the lake "had made pictures in him when he was unwilling and unconscious, when his eyes were merely open wide" (21). The lake's effect on St. Peter's consciousness is very much like the effect that Tom Outland will have on him, adding something immovable to the mind, informing the way he thinks about and reacts to the world. In Cather's view the great facts of our lives—our natural surroundings, our associations, our removes—are what produce the pictures that we know as our consciousness. Emblematically, these great facts even contribute to the way we appear. St. Peter, although of American and French lineage, is said to resemble a Spaniard "because he had been in Spain a good deal, and was an authority on certain phases of Spanish history." Adopted children often come to resemble their parents; even dogs and their owners are said to tend to look alike if they live together long enough. The things to which we turn our attention and the things that are thrust on us as great facts are the ingredients that produce us, our ideas, projects, and countenances.

Salman Rushdie, perhaps the present era's most recognizable migrant, echoes Cather:

> Given the gift of self-consciousness, we can dream versions of ourselves, new selves for old. Waking as well as sleeping, our response to the world is essentially *imaginative:* that is, picture making. We live in our pictures, our ideas. I mean this literally. We first construct pictures of the world and then we step inside the frames. We come to equate the picture with the world, so that, in certain circumstances, we will even go to war because we find someone else's picture less pleasing than our own. . . . Dreaming is our gift; it may also be our tragic flaw. (377–78)

What are the sources of these pictures? Rushdie says that we construct them, but this begs the question of origins. According to Cather they originate in the great facts of circumstances. In some of her novels the great fact is the remembered landscape; in others it is the relation to another, or it is the past (a memory) or the future (a desire). Throughout her texts Cather is concerned with the ingredients and foundation of conscious life. Our suitcases, in other words, are packed with more than a change of clothing. Those who possess a migratory culture must carry with them what they need to preserve the vitality of their unconscious lives. Whole communities of purpose, family histories, mothers and fathers and children—all these great facts are kept in suitcases under beds. In a migratory culture personal memories cannot bind together local communities because these histories are rarely shared. The past is spatialized within migratory consciousness: childhood was Chicago; education was Boston; marriage was California; children were Tennessee. Recalled images of other places are nonetheless the adhesives of contemporary identity, securing a sense of self to persons who have substituted a spatial conception of history for proximity to its artifacts.

A migratory consciousness is completely susceptible to the lure and power of images, since so much of what it knows as its past is contained within their frames. Rushdie's constructed pictures function as realities: not as mimetic images (because they do not depend on verification by others) but as actuality itself, commanding and necessitating responses. Art historian David Freedberg claims that "the time has come to acknowledge the possibility that our responses to images may be of the same order as our responses to reality." Images created on film and canvas or images created in print share space in human consciousness with immediate reality because these images *are* a form of immediate reality. "In this respect," Freedberg concludes, "representation is exactly the opposite of what it has always supposed to be. Representation is miraculous because it deceives us into thinking it is realistic, but it is also miraculous because it is something other than what it represents" (438). In this sense a painting is never simply a picture of something, a novel never "about" something. Rather, each is always something in addition to the phenomena that it may represent. Out of this space, the space between the image and the representation, comes the picture-in-consciousness that the art form evokes.

Rushdie's insistence on the primacy of the imagination and Cather's understanding of consciousness as picture making make the art historian's conclusions quite useful. The effort to interpret and comprehend images should not be confused with the mere identification of those images. This is the way of thinking about literature that Cather deplores in her essay "The Novel Démeublé," or the *defurnished* novel. In this essay Cather asserts that "realism, more than anything else, [is] an attitude of mind on the part of the writer toward his material" (*Not under Forty* 45). *Realism* is the name for one type of picture-in-consciousness, a name for one type of space between image and representation, between mind and material. Realism measures not accuracy but attitude. For example, Cather finds absurd the effort to "reproduce on paper the actual city of Paris" (46). If one wants to see Paris, one should go there. A novel's correspondence to reality has very little to do with what the novel is about or the phenomena with which the cultural critic is concerned. As Fredric Jameson has said of *Lord Jim*, the "ostensible or manifest 'theme' of the novel is no more to be taken at face value than is the dreamer's immediate waking sense of what the dream was about" (217). I am less interested in how well Cather's narrative images fare under the scrutinizing light of tangible reality (the valuable task of the historicist) than I am in knowing how tangible reality moves within the space provided by a Catherian frame of reference. I call this the aesthetics of migration.

American culture, like Western culture in general, is packed full of references to houses: *The House of the Seven Gables, Little House on the Prairie, The House of Mirth*, the "big house," *House Beautiful, This Old House*, the doghouse, International House of Pancakes, and of course, the White House, to name a few random examples. In common usage the house is a metaphor for assessing general well-being, as in "a house divided against itself cannot stand." In *The Professor's House* Cather inserts a house metaphor from an Anglo-Saxon poem, one of Longfellow's translations. Professor St. Peter recalls the poem from a book his mother kept on her parlor table. The poem (titled "The Grave" by Longfellow) communicates the fate of the body by employing the image of the house. The speaker is Death:

> For thee a house was built
> Ere thou wast born;
> For thee a mold was made
> Ere thou of woman camest (248)

Recalling these lines from his childhood reading does not help St. Peter escape his funk; rather, the recollection seems to contribute to the lethargy that nearly kills him.

Traditional interpretations of house imagery, however, provide a misleading guide to this novel. First of all, Cather took poetic liberties with Longfellow's translation. The text of the line in question actually reads, "For thee a mold was *meant*," but Cather mutes the fatality of place by changing the line to "For thee a mold was *made.*" A thing made is a fiction; it can be undone or remade. A meant house, on the other hand, is subject to violation—or transgression—if one departs from what is intended or fated. Unlike a made thing, what is meant cannot be undone. It cannot be unmeant. A world of meant things is thus far different from a world of made things. Cather's rendition of the poem signals the modernist's concern for social construction, the evolution in human thought from essentialist considerations of human identity to the conceptualization of identity as the product of society and culture.

The analogy between a house and one's fate is made more complex by Cather's editorial touch, because a *made* house can be torn down or left behind. A professor who is inert, in other words, can move and still be himself in another house. In *The Professor's House* Cather negates the familiar sense that the house is the image of permanence and home, of productivity and integrity. Godfrey St. Peter possesses none of these qualities as he clings to his old house. Rather, his inability to move splits his family, disrupts his home, stalls his productivity, and confuses what is right and what is wrong so that he does not know who he is or what he should do. Professor St. Peter's physical inertia is the product of his momentary intellectual difficulties; Cather presents the two forms of immobility as simultaneous expressions of his languishing spirit.

Cather's St. Peter is a history professor, and the object of his thoughts in the novel is a boy whom he admired personally and whose work has transformed the local and international academic communities. Cather's novel focuses on what happens to the lives and the texts that professors take up for study. Tom Outland is the one who inspires; he is the focal point of the novel, the one who attracts scrutiny, admiration, and capitalization. People want to know him, to establish some claim to him or his work, to at least have something to do with him. The image he cast as a student, a lover, a scientist, an archeologist, a friend, a play-mate, a storyteller, and an inventor has generated a range of interest in him and opinions about his life. David Harrell points out that "Tom Outland's presence is so keenly felt that one can easily forget that he is not a character, but a memory." This signals a major theme of the novel, "how profoundly the dead can affect the living" (156). As Cather demonstrates, however, Outland has no control over the effect he will have on others after his death. He left an Indian blanket here, a piece of cliff dweller pottery there, a "turquoise set in dull silver" for the living to ponder and to explicate. He also left his diary, his writing, which the professor seeks to control editorially. In this sense, then, *The Professor's House* is a metanovel. The images it projects concern the interpretative control of textual materials.

"No image is either good or bad but interpretation makes it so," according to Richard Kearney. "We 'interpret' images . . . in the same manner as an actor 'interprets' a role (i.e., as a mode of relating to others)." Outland exists as a memory or an image throughout the novel, and his impression is exchanged and negotiated regularly in the text. He is an image to the reader (in "Tom Outland's Story") and an image to other characters in the first and third sections of the novel. St. Peter wishes to relate Outland to potential readers of his diary, to maintain the boy's legacy in accordance with his personal, intimate knowledge of Outland, his own memory. Kearney asks that we attend to "the interests which motivate the interpretation of images in a given context" and "to discriminate between a liberating and incarcerating use of images" (390). It is clear that St. Peter is motivated by love and by a sense of academic integrity. Nonetheless, the question to ask of St. Peter's inertia in *The Professor's House* is this: why does he find the interpretation of Outland's image such an obstacle, and why does Cather conflate that intellectual difficulty with St. Peter's refusal to move his workplace into the new house?

Images may certainly captivate us, and we may agree to or refuse to recognize or move among the images possessed by others. Rushdie spoke of stepping inside the frames of the world that we create. If minds make pictures, then images inevitably will contradict one another. If, as W. J. T. Mitchell writes, "knowledge is a social product, a matter of dialogue between different versions of the world, including different languages, ideologies, and modes of representation" (*Iconology* 38), then the continuous production of representational pictures is a result of social vitality. Cather casts St. Peter at a point in his life when he suffers "a diminution of ardour," a dimming of the imagination, a fading out. St. Peter fiercely desires that Outland mean to others just what he meant to him, that the contextual legacy created in the introduction to the diary be his own memory of the boy. Outland is gone, however; he is now only a memory occupying space in a number of minds, minds that knew him in radically divergent contexts. St. Peter is struggling with his sense that history ought to be linear, objective, and definitive — to the historian, there must be a singular, recoverable Tom Outland. Nevertheless, Catherian spatialized history will not allow it. In different places, with different people, Tom Outland possessed a variety of significance, of which the professor knew but one. St. Peter cannot write the introduction, and he cannot move into his new house. Cather's narrative implies an unmistakable correspondence between his new house and his new writing project. As the narrative unfolds Cather equates his inert condition with his eventual demise. If St. Peter is going to live, he will have to accept migration, both physical and intellectual.

A number of ambitious people are staking careers and livings on Tom Outland both as image and as authority: his text, his gas, the meaning of his life. Everyone concerned wants Tom to contribute to his or her own authenticity. For the classically educated Godfrey St. Peter, Outland's diary will have academic significance, and the life of the young man will represent the pure, noncommercial pursuit of knowledge to which Godfrey has devoted his own life. To Louis Marsellus, it is not the diary but the gas engine that must be produced; in the eyes of the technocrat Tom represents the boon of applied research. To Crane, Outland symbolizes a lifetime of being passed over, of unrewarded efforts. At stake for Crane is the entire issue of authorship and ownership of intellectual property. To Lillian, Tom's significance is largely an emblem of the fact that her husband's intellectual pursuits have always taken precedence over his familial and conjugal obligations. The situation in Tom Outland's surviving community is not unlike the "culture wars" described in recent polemics about the absence of a clear "moral authority" in the United States (Hunter 42). This problem is symptomatic of spatial consciousness, however, where competing moralities exist in mutual contradiction like time zones across continents.

Contending moral authorities in *The Professor's House* include St. Peter's intellectual elitism, the marriage of corporatism and consumerism embodied in the union of Marsellus and Rosamond, Langtry's utilitarianism, and Scott and Kathleen McGregor's middlebrow pride. None of these people can agree on what is right or wrong because they do not share a commitment to a common moral authority—they live, as it were, in different moral zones. St. Peter is committed to an intellectual ideal; Langtry, to meeting the needs of the largest numbers of people; Crane, the litigious, is committed to economic justice; Marsellus and Rosamond draw their values from the rewards of technical application; and the McGregors are committed to making the best of hard disappointment. In these characters Cather creates an American pluralism: the alienation of the intellectual in a democracy, the opportunism of public service, the function of the courts to assuage personal failure, the optimism of upward mobility, and the bitter nature of economic decline in a land of plenty. Among these constituencies Lillian St. Peter attempts to negotiate some sort of familial and collegial harmony, but her task is an impossible one. A culture war is inevitable in a place where moral contradiction is not simply tolerated but assumed as the basis of civic culture.

The Professor's House directly addresses the issue of moral authority within migratory consciousness. Susan Rosowski, placing Willa Cather definitively in the romantic tradition, finds this novel to be a watershed book in the development of Cather's romantic attitude of mind. "In redeeming St. Peter's original self by dreams, Cather shifted the terms of identity from individuality developed empirically—through experience —to that which lies beneath experience and which is protected from the vicissitudes of time" (*Voyage* 142). On these terms culture wars are recognizable as contests for claims to moral space. If human identity flows not from shared, verifiable experience but from highly individualized, very personal constructions of authority, even dreams, then common ground on vital issues will be thin indeed. Romanticism is good for the arts but not so good for the construction and maintenance of a traditional polity. In this sense Cather's novel addresses the fears of those who see the liberal virtues of pluralism, multiculturalism, and intellectual relativism as leading inevitably to moral and social chaos. The controversy surrounding Tom Outland provides a frame for analyzing the sense of moral vacuum among the heirs to romanticized political action.

William Monroe describes "several conflicting Tom Outland stories" in the novel, "each serving some strategic purpose for its author" (304). This conflict enters the professor's house regarding the proper way to think about Tom Outland. The Marselluses' decision to name their estate "Outland," Rosamond's wearing of jewelry that Tom brought from the Southwest, and any attempt by either her or Louis to give some of Tom's money to St. Peter (or to give anything to the McGregors) evoke crises in the family. Kathleen, Rosamond, and Lillian each have distinctive ideas about who Tom Outland was and what he means in their lives. As an image, then, Outland is in crisis. He left things undone, his intentions were unclear, and even those who knew him cannot agree on what he wanted. It is in the hands of the professors and the capitalist marketeers—even the lawyers are getting involved. The novel draws our attention to St. Peter, however, and what seems to be most at stake for Cather in this novel is his effort to come to terms with Outland.

There is no question that, as we say today, St. Peter has his own agenda. He has high standards for education and is certainly well read and accomplished. He is opinionated as well, however, and can be vindictive toward those who do not share his views. The title of his history project, *The Spanish Adventurers*, indicates where his sympathies lie in the great contest for North America. Although trained to suppress their biases, professors have them nonetheless, and these interests are what move intellectual history. *The Professor's House* casts the mechanism of intellectual history at the level of human drama. Cather's novel centers on the mind of this professor and looks closely at how he moves from a highly problematic, wholly incommunicable sense of Outland to a renewed sense of purpose and a readiness to get back to work.

The professor must make two migrations, one intellectual and the other literal. Intellectually he must finally come to terms with the death of a boy he loved, Tom Outland. He has used Outland for inspiration, and the books he wrote have won great prizes and have brought him success. Now he must find a place for Outland in his mind and contribute to the way that Outland will be remembered by others, by editing and writing an introduction to Outland's diary. Because his subject was known intimately by members of his family and professionally by his colleagues at the university, St. Peter cannot afford to be idiosyncratic. His version of Outland is bound to be scrutinized. Furthermore, his status as Oxford Prize winner makes his decision to edit Outland's diary all the more significant. At the same time, St. Peter must find a way to move his study from the old house to the new house. We never know whether St. Peter makes the transition to the new study, for he does not do so in the novel. This lack of movement, however, indicates something important about Cather's view of intellectual activity among migratory people.

Something in Outland's story has stopped St. Peter cold—something about the memory of the boy has left him listless and inert. He clearly sees Tom as an artist, someone who "had made something new in the world" and who had left "the rewards, the meaningless conventional gestures, . . . to others" (237). Tom left one of these conventional gestures to St. Peter, "to annotate the diary that Tom had kept on the mesa" (238). St. Peter works at his editorial project in a "desultory way," in fits and starts, often thinking more about himself than about Tom Outland. The thing that finally snaps him out of his funk is nothing external but "a temporary release from consciousness," a romantic turning inward, through which he realizes that "perhaps the mistake was merely in an attitude of mind" (258, 257). This is a used phrase for Cather; recall that "an attitude of mind on the part of the writer toward his material" is how Cather defined realism in her essay on poetics, published three years before *The Professor's House.* The problem for St. Peter is never "the real" Tom Outland but Godfrey St. Peter himself, his attitude of mind, or his consciousness. St. Peter needs not to get Outland historically correct but to move with the boy's "many-sided mind" in such a way as to serve some function to himself and to his readership. The historicist seeks linear consistency, but Cather makes it clear that Outland is not a historical but a spatial challenge to St. Peter. The professor is inert and he must move; his dilemma concerns what of Tom Outland he will pack up and take with him.

Cather saw art as both an escape and a regenerative force in human affairs. The usefulness of artists lies in their ability to "refresh and recharge the spirit of those who can read their language" (*On Writing* 20). To Cather, escape means not flight or avoidance but fruitful and necessary migration from the literal demands of living. Dominick LaCapra addresses literary escape by claiming that "the issue is the extent to which art serves the escapist function of imagining compensation for the defects of empirical reality and the extent to which it serves the contestatory function of questioning the empirical in a manner that has broader implications for the leading of life" (45). Cather collapsed the two, suggesting that such contestation can be done only through periodic escape, so that the weight of literal detail will not interfere with aesthetic judgment. In a 1936 letter to *Commonweal* she claimed that "the world has a habit of being in a bad way from time to time, and art has never contributed anything to help matters—except escape." To clarify, she added an example. "Anyone who looks over a collection of prehistoric Indian pottery dug up from old burial mounds knows at once that the potters experimented with form and colour to gratify something that had no concern with food and shelter" (*On Writing* 19). The pottery was necessary, but the form and color were purely escapist, perhaps attaching another significance to mundane water bearing. St. Peter's mind, represented in book 1 of *The Professor's House*, has got itself in a bad way, and the escape signaled by "Tom Outland's Story" is tied to its spiritual recharging but does not quite constitute it. The diary exists, the memory is clear in his mind, but these things exist like unformed, uncolored pots.

St. Peter does not move forward in his thinking about Outland. He comes to few intellectual conclusions about the boy, but we do not see him attempting to place Tom in any social, historical, or cultural context, as the editor of a diary might do. St. Peter comes to terms with Outland not by progressing in his thought but by abandoning forward-moving rationality altogether and moving within remembered spaces—recalling, emotionally, his childhood, going back to what Cather calls his "original ego." St. Peter, a man who is suffering a "diminution of ardour," uses "the ardour and excitement of the boy" (238) to find his own lost passion. Here Cather demonstrates again that St. Peter's opinion of Tom Outland has less to do with his memory of Tom than with St. Peter's sense of space.

In *The Professor's House* objective considerations of meaning or value do not determine the professor's judgments or conclusions. His training allows him only to explicate professionally what it is that he "accidentally" thinks or finds. The logic of the narrative casts the life of the intellectual within a spatial consciousness, journeying back and forth between the original ego and the present mind. If we come face to face with this original ego in the form of a fact or an idea, we agree with it; if it comes in the form of a student, we fall in love, as St. Peter fell in love with Tom Outland. With the death of Outland, however, St. Peter recast his original ego as a final destination, ominously signaling the end of his intellectual migrations. He began to see his memories as inherently and objectively tangible rather than as the sources of future imagination and projection.

St. Peter fell in love with Tom Outland and is trying to write the introduction to the dead boy's summer diary. "To mean anything," Cather writes of this introduction, "it must be prefaced by a sketch of Outland, and some account of his later life and achievements" (150). What will the professor write? St. Peter finds the task difficult, and no doubt it is. Tom Outland is emerging as a controversial figure, in and out of St. Peter's house. If Crane were to write the introduction, or if Langtry were to do it (or if Kathleen were given the chance), it would certainly come out differently. Cather gives us no one's introduction, leaving it finally to the reader to remember Outland. An objective sense of Outland is beside the point in this novel. "Tom Outland's Story," which forms book 2 of the novel, is not the diary; it is introduced as an oral account told in one sitting (155), but it is obviously too long and too formal to be a transcription. All it can be is the story as it has filtered into the mind of St. Peter, who is doing his best not to forget any of it.

St. Peter's effort to remember is critical, because through his memory he creates the text. "Tom Outland's Story" as it appears in *The Professor's House* is not *the* text, not Tom's writing, but the image conveyed to us through the mind of Professor St. Peter. Outland's diary has no essential or objective textual existence, although we are told that the diary does in fact exist on St. Peter's desk. If Cather had written "Tom Outland's Story" as a transcription of the diary (a literal duplication of the words read by St. Peter), then we would be faced with a completely different conception of cultural continuity. Had she presented the diary itself, the reader would confront the past as a burden, a force threatening to imprison the present with its determination. As Cather presents it, however, the original text is irrecoverable and perhaps even irrelevant. At best it occupies a vacuole, a space apart from the narrative itself. The certainty that would have been produced by a literal transcription of the diary is precisely the certainty that is left behind in a migratory culture. Migrants abandon valuable artifacts for lack of room; space is created within conscious memories for these valued sources. The first casualty of migration is a shared sense of certainty, which is replaced by a highly personalized sense of the past. St. Peter knows that when he moves, "something very precious" will be "relinquished," and he will be a changed man, less committed to the past, perhaps even apathetic (258).

Cather's text suggests that original meaning is largely absent in a culture of migration, an empty space into which rush the present needs of men and women in transit. Diaries, novels, and images from the past do not contain discrete meanings; rather, they project contexts for the creation of significance. What is important is not what the text was meant to say when it was written, or even whether it reflects its own time accurately, but the extent to which it provides a framework for comprehending contemporary phenomena and surviving in a new environment. Tom Outland is dead, and with him died his purposes, desires, and essence. What St. Peter searches for is the effect that Tom Outland may have against the great fact of his own imminent displacement.

St. Peter is attracted to Tom's story because it speaks directly to his own, and he uses his memory of Outland to regain a sense of himself. The parallels between "Tom Outland's Story" and Godfrey St. Peter's circumstances are intricate. The setting of Outland's tale inspires St. Peter because it takes place in the territory he has already researched. Rodney Blake's sale of the treasures on the Blue Mesa parallels the cheapening of the university in the hands of the state legislature. Tom's struggle to keep the Mesa from "vulgar curiosity" parallels the professor's struggle to maintain the integrity of the university in the face of the "new commercialism" (140). Blake, mistreated by Tom, is played in St. Peter's world by Professor Horace Langtry. St. Peter had vehemently and publicly opposed Langtry's lowering of academic standards, and as a result a feud erupted between the two rival historians. What happens to Outland not only parallels but contextualizes what happens to St. Peter, allowing St. Peter to comprehend his own predicament more clearly.

The disagreement between Outland and Blake is an important one. While Outland travels to Washington in a futile attempt to interest government officials in Native American remains, Blake is putting those remains to use by selling them to a German collector. Here his actions parallel those of Marsellus, who will also capitalize on Outland's discoveries. (Whereas Crane fails to do so; Cather ironically assigns him the scientific project of studying the phenomenon of space, or vacuoles.) The money that Blake raises by selling relics is put into a bank account to finance Outland's college education. In college Outland makes the scientific discoveries that gain him posthumous international recognition and meets St. Peter, who will eventually publish his diary. Outland carries to his grave regrets concerning his treatment of Blake, not about the fate of the relics. "Anyone who requites faith and friendship as I did, will have to pay for it" (229).

Outland's initial idea of preserving the remains as a kind of shrine parallels St. Peter's valuation of his memory over the demands of the present. Father Duchene, Outland's tutor, wants an archaeologist to excavate the site and "revive this civilization in a scholarly work." He tells Outland and Blake that he believes the site illuminates "some important points in the history of your country" (199). As events unfold the irony of this assessment is clarified. The remembered history of the country is not in cliff dweller remains but in Europe, and in all the places from which the ancestors of Outland, Blake, Duchene, St. Peter, and Marsellus migrated. In Washington the Smithsonian director wants to go to Paris, not Cliff City. What Outland discovers when he goes to Washington is that the cliff dweller remains have no significance in the present. Immigrants to the United States assume the history of previous migrants (or "settlers") as their own, not the history of the peoples they have supplanted. It is particularly telling that in college Outland's interests turn to science and technology rather than to archaeology. The pottery that he takes from the site he gives away as gifts and playthings.

Historical consciousness within a migratory culture is a tenuous phenomenon. One is perfectly free to move across group boundaries and assume a connection to a variety of mutually exclusive histories. Tom Outland's sympathies with the cliff dwellers and St. Peter's simpatico relation to Spanish explorers are only two items on a vast historical menu available within the spatial past of the American continent. Histories are like playthings to some, and they are gifts and valued possessions to others. The suspicion that objective history is not credible is quite strong among people who move within its varieties so freely. In this milieu the present is understood spatially, not as the result of historical forces, but as a compass point from which innumerable courses may be plotted.

This is the great fact of Cather's legacy. The past is no burden on the present; the burden comes from the future, where migrants must utilize what they have that is portable to make some journey in the world. St. Peter exists in a migratory culture where cliff dwellers serve as emblems for the idea that all those who cannot move must perish. Outland's strength was in believing that the Native American relics were not valuable in themselves, as essences. St. Peter's inertia, on the other hand, is due to an attitude of mind in which Outland's memory has to be preserved for its own sake—like the preservation of his study in the old house. What the professor receives finally from Outland is the great Catherian fact of migratory existence, a belief not so much in Judgment Day as in moving day. In Cather's worldview memories must always be measured against imminent migrations and ambitions. The future belongs to those whose suitcases are packed with keepsakes freely bartered for spatial autonomy.

While St. Peter is up in his study, close to death, something in his unconscious mind motivates him to rise and attempt to save himself from death by asphyxiation. He falls, and the noise his body makes alerts Augusta that he may be in trouble. She drags him out of the fumes to safety. What saves St. Peter's life? What provides him the resources to get his body and his mind through the crisis of spirit that pervades his consciousness in *The Professor's House?* Literally and physically, he is saved by the seamstress Augusta, the novel's representation of down-to-earth good sense and practicality. Spiritually, however, the matter is more complex.

Everything that truly matters to St. Peter, those things from which he draws inspiration and intellectual satisfaction, is absent from his immediate world in the novel. The young student that had he loved is dead; the "original, unmodified St. Peter" occupies the psychic space of memory; the introduction he must write to Outland's diary is an unwritten desire; the ambition and drive that produced *The Spanish Adventurers* exist in the past. The fact that these things are not present does not diminish them, however. On the contrary, their absence is among the novel's strongest cultural statements. What saves Godfrey St. Peter is his ability to draw on these resources to rejuvenate the diminution of ardor that afflicts him in the novel. In *The Professor's House* Cather asks whether the ideas and images that we have packed up to carry with us, our spiritual resources, possess the vitality to ensure our continued well-being within the context of continuous transit, of tremendous change and migration.

In the final paragraph of the novel Cather writes that St. Peter "had let something go—and it was gone; something very precious, that he could not consciously have relinquished, probably" (258). What he specifically lets go in this scene exists in a Catherian vacuole, and critics have attempted and will continue to attempt to identify the unnamed thing. Nonetheless, no matter what it is, the act or the process of relinquishing it is what is significant here. St. Peter's mind is able to forget (to let go) something that is no longer useful to him and to grasp something new, something the man now needs to survive. Cather's sense of memory includes remembering as well as discarding recollections: knowing what needs to be in mind and what has no place or use there.

An incident in "The Best Years," a story from Cather's posthumously published book *The Old Beauty and Others*, makes plain the idea of willful forgetting. The superintendent of schools, Miss Evangeline Knightly, is visiting Lesley Ferguesson's classroom: "Miss Knightly made a joking little talk to the children and told them about a very bright little girl in Scotland who knew nearly a whole play of Shakespeare's by heart, but who wrote in her diary: 'Nine times nine is the Devil'; which proved, she said, that there are two kinds of memory, and God is very good to anyone to whom he gives both kinds" (86–87). God has been very kind to Godfrey St. Peter, whose character demonstrates the indispensable conception of Cather's two kinds of memory.

One's past, and the history of the culture itself, teems with incidents and events that may be remembered or suppressed, that can be told or untold. The survival and vitality of the present generation depend on the uses to which these spiritual and ideological resources are put. Such is the word of Cather's Evangeline.

The cultural implications of Willa Cather's texts are myriad, and they are explored in the analyses that follow. Her novels provide a way of seeing American society and history as spatialized phenomena, countering many of the dominant myths that have sustained the culture in this century. Cather's America has no common past, only a set of conflicting stories and disparate origins. Her emphasis on transit—including the great fact of migration—reinforces the idea that the past must often be forgotten if one is to succeed in transferring self and value to a new environment. St. Peter, as we have seen, cannot move from one house to the other unless he sheds some precious intellectual belongings and assumes new ones. According to Grinberg and Grinberg, "the move from a village to a big city, from a city to the countryside, from the mountains to the plains, and even, for some people, the move from one house to another could . . . be called a migration in the psychological sense" (17). St. Peter's migration involves a move from one house to another and from one attitude of mind to another, both in the face of death and both as matters of physical and intellectual survival. Through his meditation on Outland the professor comes face to face with the great fact of migratory consciousness, in which the psychological stresses of moving day are identified as cultural frames of existence. Movement may certainly invite disaster; it entails forgetting and flirts with the dissolution of historic ties. Anxieties about losing touch with the past, with origins, and about the absence of traditional cultures constitute the signposts of U.S. migratory existence. The cliff dwellers ultimately were defeated by tribes that dwelt nowhere in particular, tribes that kept moving. These tribes were in turn conquered by migratory Americans who had traveled even further, with fewer ties to place, whose spatial conception of the future far outweighed their memories of the past.

2

The Brave Are Homeless:
Mobility and Vitality
in the United States

How can you keep on moving (unless you migrate too)?
They tell you to keep on moving,
But migrate you must not do.
The only reason I'm moving (the reason that I roam)
Is to move to a new location,
And find myself a home.
　　　—"The Migration Song," TRADITIONAL

O Pioneers!

The one thing that all Americans have in common is ancestors who, for any number of reasons, decided to detach themselves from one place and to move to another. "Displacement is the order of American history," according to Leonard Lutwack, "starting with migration from Europe, followed by the westward movement across the continent, and continuing with the flight from farms and towns to the cities and, presently, the removal of job-hunters from city to city" (180). The primary reason for migration to or within the United States is decline or dissatisfaction of some kind and the desire to reverse the decay or to try again. People who have succeeded and are satisfied with their situations generally do not move. Psychologists of migration have concluded that "those with high emotional potential, all the way from the wishful-thinkers through the activists and the revolutionaries to the refugees, [are those] who most readily take to the road" (Pierson 176). The United States was founded and has always been repopulated by ambitious malcontents, incurable optimists, and restless failures. No other culture is so attracted to the rhetoric of moving on and starting over, to images of reinvention, rebirth, and renewal.

To be an American is to accept the condition of the provisional home, or more succinctly, of homelessness. The United States receives its cultural vitality largely from the movements of its people. Great historical epochs are measured by shifts in population: the arrival of the Puritans, the importation of African slaves, the settling of the western territories, the removal of Native American populations (and the significant assignment of these peoples to reservations, or homes that are not permitted to move), the migration of southern blacks to northern cities, and the recent shift in population from the northeast to the southern rim. Demographic statistics show that no other "settled" people are so willing to move and actually do move so often. In fact, the right to move is protected by the United States Constitution, according to a Supreme Court decision: "The right to travel is part of the 'liberty' of which the citizen cannot be deprived without due process of law under the Fifth Amendment." In *Kent vs. Dulles* (1958) the Court continued to explain the origins of this right. "Freedom of movement across frontiers in either direction, and inside frontiers as well, was a part of our heritage. . . . Freedom of travel is, indeed, an important aspect of the citizen's 'liberty' " (quoted in Auerbach 325). Americans are protected by constitutional law first from unlawful seizure inside their homes and second from interference when they wish to transfer their homes from one place to another. The Fourteenth Amendment guarantees that legal rights are not lost in transit. Home is not a matter of permanence in the United States. Home in the United States is something of an abstraction, an ideology; it may be as well a future destination or a place left behind.

Willa Cather cast a large extent of her fiction over the idea of American homelessness. In what are known as the "pioneer novels" (*O Pioneers! My Ántonia*, and *A Lost Lady*), Cather provides a vision of America that rests quite firmly on the metaphysics of homelessness and human movement, both physical and intellectual. The intersection of historical preservation and future purpose—Cather's two kinds of memory, remembering and willful forgetting—is projected in *The Professor's House* and in a second set of novels. In *Lucy Gayheart, Shadows on the Rock*, and *Sapphira and the Slave Girl* Cather provides grounds for the comprehension of settled communities within an ideology of transit. A culture of migration and homelessness produces a peculiar sense of history, one that is not easily recognized separate from the assumption of continuing mobility. *The Song of the Lark, One of Ours*, and *Death Comes for the Archbishop* identify the way that ambitious migration leads logically and even inevitably to a U.S. empire. What distinguishes Cather from other twentieth-century American writers is her willingness to project the significance of the American empire within the culture itself, as a great fact of U.S. society.

A homeless people has few loyalties that are not subject to revision and reexamination. In her biography of Mary Baker Eddy, Cather speculates "whether there is anything in the world that can be quite so cruel as the service of an ideal" (324). The authorial commentary on Eddy's life consistently voices disapproval for those whose faith and beliefs stand in the way of intellectual curiosity. Abstract ideals and absolute loyalties are changeable phenomena (and highly suspicious possessions) in a culture of migration and transferal. As Cather's version of Eddy's life story demonstrates, however, superficial religiosity and profitable confidence games are common among a people that distrusts abstraction. Much of Cather's writing examines the borderline, or frontier, between the celebrated "open mind" and the vacuous thought associated with so many movers and shakers in U.S. culture. The profile of the pioneer that Cather draws, however, rests on a presupposition of continued mobility in both the material and intellectual dimensions of existence. What the frontier novels project are the roots and manifestations of American homelessness.

Regional affinities that depend on place are common to the United States—there are committed southerners and New Englanders and midwesterners—but national loyalty is completely movable, and one is not more or less of an American dependent on where one happens to live. On the contrary, an American's national identity increases with movement, for it becomes more difficult to claim a permanent regional membership or to identify in an absolute sense with a locality. The creation of the national newspaper, *U.S.A. Today*, testifies to the erosion of localized identity among a people in transit. In 1904 the German immigrant and Americanist Hugo Munsterberg identified a central aspect of this mobile nationality in *The Americans*, quoted at length for its remarkable continued relevance:

The American may be linked by personal ties to a particular plot of land, but his national patriotism is independent of the soil. It is also independent of the people. A nation which in every decade has assimilated millions of aliens, and whose historic past everywhere leads back to strange people, cannot with its racial variegation inspire a profound feeling of indissoluble unity. And yet that feeling is present here as it is perhaps in no other European country. American patriotism is directed neither to soil nor citizen, but to a system of ideas respecting society which is compacted by the desire for self-direction. And to be an American means to be a partisan of this system. Neither race nor tradition, nor yet the actual past binds him to his countryman, but rather the future which together they are building. It is a community of purpose, and it is more effective than any tradition, because it pervades the whole man. (5)

Munsterberg is right—so right that even to think of "American" as a nationality rooted in history is somewhat of a conundrum. One cannot trace history to find the original, ideal American because tracing back leads only to people who are not Americans at all. One can only project into the future for the original American, the American who exists in the best days of the nation, in the ideal conception. The source of American unity is in the future, not the past, which is why the study of history in America is always potentially divisive. The possible exception to this rule, however, is in the study of the American frontier. Frontier studies have traditionally served national unification, demonstrating American "character" or other more specific national tendencies. Nonetheless, frontier studies historically have been a matter more of the future than of the past.

By definition, all things are possible on the frontier. It is a place that exists primarily in relation to the future. Whether of New York State in the eighteenth century or of the Great Plains in the nineteenth century, frontier study allows the historical observer to enter a realm where history is erased and people are moving into potentiality. In the twentieth century frontier stories move across the globe and even into outer space, as the American ideology of what Munsterberg called self-direction becomes the culture's main export. For over a century myth producers in America—first in the media of magazine fiction and popular novels and later in film and television—have meditated on the exploration and settling of the frontier, on stories of lawmen and savage battle. The ideological function of the standard range of the mythology of the American West is explicated thoroughly in Richard Slotkin's historical trilogy about the American myth of the frontier. But another set of stories can be found on the same landscape, as Cather shows us.

In Cather's pioneer myth we are concerned with the psychological and historical erasure of the person who settles and with the emergence of the pioneer who roams, who cannot have a home because at the very core of his or her self-definition are mobility and homelessness.

Cather is not telling the story of the mysterious stranger, however, or the person who wanders out of hatred or for revenge. Cather's iconographic pioneer Alexandra Bergson, in *O Pioneers!* (1913), is a settler who establishes a home on the Nebraska plains, buys land, and becomes "rich, just from sitting still" and watching the land value appreciate over time (87). Despite her outward display of rootedness, however, Alexandra's single, recurring fantasy is "the illusion of being lifted up bodily and carried lightly by some one very strong." Her inner character is thus signaled by a desire to be mobile, to be light enough to be taken away in the arms of someone who is in motion. It is reductive—and much too literal—to see this solely as a sexual fantasy, although the sexual meaning is unmistakably present. "It was a man, certainly, who carried her," the passage continues, "but he was like no man she knew; he was much larger and stronger and swifter, and he carried her as easily as if she were a sheaf of wheat" (153). Deep in the heart of Cather's epic American settler is the belief and faith in "the mightiest of all lovers" (210), the one who lifted and carried the pioneer into the cultural paradox of homeless settlement. This lover may be a sexual phenomenon, but like all of human sexuality, it possesses cultural significance; it may signal the intersection of human nature and human history.

In *O Pioneers!* Cather defines the meaning of *pioneer* in America by addressing "the great fact [of] the land itself" (11). This great fact, like the lake in *The Professor's House*, reflects the minds that face it, and in many ways *O Pioneers!* is a study of the quality of mind that arises from the paradoxical conflation of homelessness and rootedness. Describing the meeting of the great fact and Alexandra's "great mind," Cather writes, "For the first time, perhaps, since that land emerged from the waters of the geologic ages, a human face was set toward it with love and yearning. . . . Then the Genius of the Divide, the great, free spirit which breathes across it, must have bent lower than it ever bent to a human will before" (50). This genius, this great free spirit, is equivalent to the mightiest of all lovers in Alexandra's fantasy of carriage, breathing across the continent toward historical change and animating her own epoch-making consciousness. The Genius of the Divide, in Cather's formulation, had yielded itself not to the nomadic homelessness of the plains Indian, or to the Christian mission of the Spaniard, or to the ambition of the Anglo-American hunter but only to the intellect that combines all these practices, to the mind that crosses borders easily, rooted in homelessness.

O Pioneers! plays out the intersection of rooted homelessness on many levels. Alexandra's father immigrated to America after his father had "died disgraced," an economic failure. Alexandra's grandfather was a speculator who lost not only all his own money but money entrusted to him by others. The son of this failure took his family to America and became a farmer. In his daughter, Alexandra, he recognizes his own father's strength of will. Alexandra will also become a speculator, investing her brothers' money profitably and succeeding where her grandfather did not by following "the Old-World belief that land, in itself, is desirable" (17). Whereas Alexandra is thus rooted in Old World ideas and practices, however, she is simultaneously adapting to the demands of New World conditions. What makes Alexandra a successful farmer is her willingness to do things that others are afraid to do, to develop "a new consciousness of the country" (54) based on its peculiar requirements.

Chapter 4 of "The Wild Land," the novel's initial section, juxtaposes two pivotal developments. The Linstrum family will move back to St. Louis, giving in to "the hard times that brought every one on the Divide to the brink of despair" (36). Alexandra tells Carl Linstrum that she will miss him not because he was of any physical help to her, which he was not, but because he was an intellectual help, because he understood her mind. Alexandra's brothers are tempted to move away as well, but her mother stoutly declares, "I don't want to move again" (45). All the talk about moving does not lead Alexandra to consider physical migration, however, but she does consider intellectual conversion: "maybe I am too set against making a change" (47). In chapter 5, the end of "The Wild Land" section, Alexandra visits some thriving farm areas and "learn[s] a great deal" from other farmers. She comes home revitalized and with both a renewed confidence in the land and a new idea: land speculation. Thus, as Carl's family moves physically toward a new place, taking their set ideas with them to try again, Alexandra stays put and moves on to new ideas. "Why are we better fixed than any of our neighbors?" Alexandra asks her brothers. "Because father had more brains. Our people were better people than these in the old country. We *ought* to do more than they do, and see further ahead" (52).

It is significant that Alexandra should invoke her forebears. Her new idea, speculation, is an old idea in her family. Speculation was the expression of her grandfather's intelligence and also the source of his downfall. The present is not a good time to recall this latter fact, however, and no one mentions it. Her grandfather's ruin through speculation is willfully forgotten by Alexandra, invoking the second of Cather's two kinds of memory. By making her success on precisely the same grounds where her grandfather failed, Alexandra exemplifies the condition of rooted homelessness. Her life story will become her grandfather's vindication: by succeeding in land speculation, she demonstrates that he was not unintelligent but unlucky, or perhaps simply that he was doing the right thing in the wrong place and at the wrong time. The Bergson family had to uproot and become homeless to show, eventually, that its roots were strong and its initial ideas valid.

By paralleling the necessity of physical mobility through migration with the need to remain intellectually mobile through the acceptance of new ideas, Cather refines the source and meaning of American accomplishments on the frontier. The Bergson family's failure in Europe is a key element in this equation, and Cather solves a central dilemma through her depiction of this family's evolution. If only failures and malcontents migrate, if Europe sent to the United States primarily those segments of the population that could not succeed, then how do we explain the rise of a prosperous middle class in twentieth-century America that traces its family history to European immigration? According to Cather, the act and process of migration proved that it was not the immigrant who had failed; rather, the original conditions had failed the immigrant. The willingness to migrate demonstrates a strength of spirit that could find no outlet in Europe but discovers ample prospects abroad. This is the source of Cather's frontier epic. What the frontier experience proves is that human beings are malleable and entirely movable, that they will fail miserably if they stay in the wrong place and refuse to move to the conditions or the ideas (the "soil") in which they can thrive.

It would be a mistake, though, to invoke the classic metaphor of the "transplanted" American immigrant—a metaphor at least as old as the eighteenth-century essayist Crèvecoeur. The metaphor may work among previous nationalisms, where populations, rooted in history, seem indelibly identified by their surroundings. In Cather's mind, however, immigrants uproot not to transplant themselves but to remain in and to transmit to future generations an ideology of spatial mobility fundamentally at odds with historical consciousness. Nationalism in the United States is a spatial phenomenon, and important components of this ideology are based in a consciousness perfectly willing to drop everything and go somewhere else or to cast aside one set of principles and take on another.

The story of migration is one among the "two or three human stories" that are repeated over and over again, as Carl tells Alexandra in the graveyard. Alexandra finishes the thought at the end of the novel, claiming that it is the living that write these stories, using "the best we have," or the blood of the dead, to write them. Alexandra has rewritten her grandfather's story, transforming the story of disgrace and decline into a paradigmatic romance, including marriage to her lifelong sweetheart, Carl. Alexandra will never emigrate; she says she will never move off the divide. Nonetheless, she will measure her success in part by her act of providing to Emil the resources necessary to emigrate. Emil, she thinks, is one "who had not been tied to the plow, and who had a personality apart from the soil. And that, she reflected, was what she had worked for" (158). The fact that Emil's story ends abruptly when he is murdered does not diminish Alexandra's success but underscores it. Emil's future was tied to migration, and he was killed, literally, because he stayed home too long.

When Carl tells Alexandra that he believes "that there are two or three human stories, and they go on repeating themselves," he has been thinking of migration. The image he uses to demonstrate his point about narrative ecology concerns "the larks in this country, that have been singing the same five notes over for thousands of years" (89). Much is made in *O Pioneers!* of migratory birds, their movements across the sky and their mournful, familiar voices (30–33). Indeed, migratory birds provide a naturalistic setting for the human birds of passage that populate all Cather's novels. Walter Nugent points out that the dominant American mythology of homesteading made it difficult for U.S. citizens to understand "labor-seeking migrants, many of them birds of passage, who arrived in large numbers during the 1870–1914 period" (161). American ambivalence for birds of passage is captured in the traditional folk song that claims that "they tell you to keep on moving / But migrate you must not do." As the conversation between Carl and Alexandra continues, they move toward the dialogue at the center of the novel, the dialogue between rootedness and homelessness, the migrant's dilemma. Carl is the homeless man; he says, "there are thousands of rolling stones like me. We are all alike; we have no ties, we know nobody, we own nothing." These wandering birds of passage, he says, "have no house, no place, no people of our own," and all they manage to do "is to pay our rent, the exorbitant rent" of the transient (91–92). Carl overstates his condition, but so does Alexandra as she counters with her statement of rootedness: "We pay a high rent too, though we pay differently. We grow hard and heavy here. We don't move lightly and easily as you do, and our minds get stiff" (92).

The Catherian "Great Divide," made emblematic by Carl and Alexandra, is that between homelessness and rootedness. Each envies the other, but neither can or will trade places with the other. Cather's answer, communicated in the conventional terms of romantic resolution, is for these two to conjoin and to accomplish the great American solution of rooted homelessness. In *My Ántonia* the complexities of this formula are demonstrated further with tremendous subtlety, as are the implications it holds for the idea of an American nationality. *A Lost Lady* raises the question of whether a people rooted in homelessness can possess a national history. As for *O Pioneers!* critics have seen its role in establishing the grounds on which a nationalistic "primary epic," or set of "public myths," can be formalized (Stouck, *Willa Cather's Imagination* 23) and have identified Alexandra as an "epic hero" or "patron goddess of a civilization" (Ryder 113). A critical consensus is articulated by Conrad Ostwalt, who finds that Cather's frontier is no Garden of Eden but "an alienating and harsh world" that had little to do with God's mission. Peopled by marginal and dislocated characters, the frontier is where the Catherian Americans "overcome their marginality by developing proper human relationships within a culturally and ethnically complex situation" (36). On the American frontier the historically marginal status of the homeless person is redefined on heroic terms so that the wandering man and woman reach an apotheosis. In Willa Cather's fiction the marginal becomes the center; the homeless wanderer arrives in the United States as an icon of settled, rocklike values.

The ideology of homelessness is worked out extensively in *O Pioneers!* As a cultural doctrine homelessness contains a complex set of interlocking ideas, including the need to root oneself so that the next generation can migrate and the compulsion to move on so that the next generation can establish roots. What Cather sees as a source of strength, however, other observers have identified as a major defect in

American culture. Out of houses "set about haphazard on the tough prairie sod," none of which "had any appearance of permanence" (3), comes, in Cather's imagination, a new consciousness that finds stability in spatial transience. The American philosopher John McDermott, on the other hand, defines homelessness as our "deepest contemporary ontological problem," with ramifications across consciousness. "The human abode becomes a jerry-built neighborhood in the vast reaches of cosmic unintelligibility. Our sky is a diaphanous roof to nowhere. 'Seize the time' is now joined by 'seize the place,' for neither is given to us. Human life is home-made" (69). The trait of unsettlement has made many American writers nervous, locating within it a national defect, a core imperfection. Indeed, the condition of wandering, in Western civilization, is not coveted. Sophocles, for example, reserved for Oedipus the curse of homelessness as penalty for his greatest transgression: "No man will ever be rooted from the earth as brutally as you" (252). No modern nation has ever rooted itself so deeply and overtly in movement as that of McDermott's jerry-built neighborhood or Cather's haphazard culture of impermanence.

Social critic Peter L. Berger, in *The Homeless Mind*, concurs with McDermott's observations, equating modernism with "a spreading condition of homelessness" (138). The symptoms of this condition are profound. Berger cites, for example, the loss of religious authority through pluralistic exposure to competing truths; a debilitating metaphysical and psychological nostalgia "for a condition of being at home" (82); a rise in moral and ethical relativism (because "what was considered right in one stage of the individual's social career becomes wrong in the next" [184]); and a general, devastating decline in a sense of purpose and direction to human life. According to Berger, "we no longer have beliefs that bestow meanings with certainty" on the human condition, and this, he says, produces a kind of cosmic homelessness. Reactions to this shared sense of universal displacement encompass a wide range of "demodernization quests" that seek "new ways of 'being at home' in society," including such media focal points as "global village," "tribalism," and "family" (214).

The presuppositions of both McDermott and Berger are thoroughly historicist. The spreading condition of homelessness has resulted in the disintegration of those values endemic to a firmly grasped historical consciousness: a sense of belonging to a specific place, a traditional morality, certainties rooted in authorities external to one's own experience. None of these values is readily available to a migratory conscious-ness. On the other hand, it is not entirely necessary to conceptualize human history in terms of what is discarded. Through Cather we can recognize the emergence of a homeless morality not simply in terms of the destruction of old ways but formulative of another stage in human development—perhaps even liberational. But this can be accomplished only once the passing of cultural phenomena (belief, behavior, tradi-tion) is identified not as unfortunate but as inevitable. A philosophical challenge facing the twenty-first century will be to reconceptualize the crisis of belief, now at least a century old, as an expression of the human, wandering condition.

There have been voices throughout the twentieth century, often marginal, that have echoed Cather's belief that the condition of the wanderer provides a more just model of existence, countering destruc-tive metaphors of human beings planted in particular places, possessing an absolute sense of belonging. Gabriel Marcel proposed the idea of cultural impermanence in 1951:

> Perhaps a stable order can only be established if man is acutely aware of his condition as a traveller, that is to say, if he perpetu-ally reminds himself that he is required to cut himself a dangerous path across the unsteady blocks of a universe which has collapsed and seems to be crumbling in every direction. This path leads to a world more firmly established in Being, a world whose changing and uncertain gleams are all that we can discern here below. Does not everything happen as though this ruined universe turned re-lentlessly upon whoever claimed that he could settle in it to the ex-tent of erecting a permanent dwelling there for himself? (153–54)

The belief in permanence serves destructive ends in the world; the quest for finality and absolute certainty has spread devastation and death to individuals and to entire civilizations. The idea that travel and migra-tion lead inevitably to a *destination*, or a "home," results in the identifica-tion of cosmic homelessness as a philosophical problem or a modernist anxiety rather than the liberating revelation of a fundamental condition of human life. After all, why should human beings feel as if the uni-verse, the continent, the nation, the region, or the city is their home? The idea of home itself may be no more than an expression of the delu-sion of permanence by which humans attempt to mitigate mortality.

We are passing through, and like Cather's pioneer town, we are "trying not to be blown away" (3) by circumstances or by the choices we make.

The condition of homelessness is the primary meaning, in Catherian terms, of the United States' frontier heritage. Most scholarly attention to this condition has focused on mobility, a condition of physical liberty and economic improvement. Long after Frederick Jackson Turner announced the closing of the frontier in 1893, the idea that opportunity exists in another place and that success comes through migration has persisted in America. Peter Morrison and Judith Wheeler call this "image of an 'elsewhere' with its idealized possibilities" an ideology that "inspirits the whole society and continues to define the American experience" (76). The legacy of the pioneer is a mode of consciousness, "a frontier of the mind—an abiding vision of some other *place* where the past can be discounted and the future shaped at will. The promise embodied in that legacy induces movement for a certain few, and their movement keeps the promise alive for all" (82). Life under these conditions becomes a perpetual odyssey from one place to another. The phenomenon has been called "restlessness" and "mobility" and "cosmic homelessness," but whatever the label, the activity itself expresses a profoundly altered sense of the relation between person and place. The curse on Oedipus becomes the migrant's ticket to ride.

The pervasiveness of mobility in the United States may be a commonplace observation among social observers, but the function of transit at the root of American consciousness is barely comprehended. If it were understood, culture wars concerning the disintegration of core values and the absence of shared morality would give way to serious discussion concerning the possibilities for social order among migratory individuals. Cather depicts the frontier metamorphosis of homelessness from temporary stage to established condition as a matter of life and death. The ducks that return to the same place each year only provide hunters in *O Pioneers!* with easy prey. There is nothing to be gained in Cather's imagination from staying in one place too long, past the moment when it is clearly time to move. The love story of Emil Bergson and Marie Shabata plays this out. Marie is married to Frank Shabata, and so the love she shares with Emil means that Emil must leave: "On my honor, Marie, if you will say you love me, I will go away" (173). Marie does, and Emil immediately begins "uprooting" (175). As he packs Alexandra tells him once again the story of his family's migration to America. Rather than migrate, however, "lazy" Emil remains in Hanover and moves toward death, taking Marie with him. Frank kills them both like sitting ducks. Cather narrates this story with her own brand of morbid humor. Emil has gone "softly down between the cherry trees" to make love to Marie, and Frank is "amazed" to come home to find "Emil's mare in his stable" (193, 194). In a frenzied response Frank fires three shots at the languishing lovers, aiming his .405 Winchester from a hiding place in the bushes. Frank, as Alexandra later realizes, is not a guilty man, for his actions are but the natural expression of outrage against those who will not go away.

Alexandra articulates the spatial consciousness that informs *O Pioneers!*: "The land belongs to the future," she claims, and here we might equate the land with the nation itself, a nation that has no existence apart from its future. "We come and go, but the land is always here. And the people who love it and understand it are the people who own it—for a little while" (229). If, as Cather declares at the beginning of the novel, "the great fact was the land itself" and if, as Alexandra asserts at the end of the novel, "the land belongs to the future," then the logic of *O Pioneers!* is that the great fact of pioneering and settlement in the United States is the future. A spatialized culture is thus defined more in terms of its prospects than its achievements, and it asserts a profound qualification to historical materialism. Munsterberg's observation is that Americans possess a community of purpose, not one of history or tradition. Cather plays out the logic of this assertion in the final chapters of the book, in which Alexandra decides to visit Frank in prison and to forgive him.

"Frank was the only one, Alexandra told herself, for whom anything could be done" (211). Emil and Marie are dead, situated irrevocably in the past, but Frank is alive, and because of this Alexandra has more in common with him than she has against him. As she leaves the prison, she thinks "how she and Frank had been wrecked by the same storm" (222) represented by the passionate love and deaths of her brother and Frank's wife. Alexandra is not interested in preserving the integrity of her brother's history or in vilifying forever his murder by Frank. She is concerned, rather, with the value of the story in her own time, in what she can *do* with it. The answer to that concern is that she can forgive Frank and elevate her own behavior above his and above that of the heedless lovers.

Cather's meaning here can too easily be confused with a simple, sentimental plot resolution, for it clearly draws on such traditional endings. Nonetheless, the final chapter strongly discourages this critical conclusion. If, as Carl declares, Marie and Emil died because they were "the best you had here," then the lovers who are left, Carl and Alexandra, are at most second-best. And throughout the final chapter of *O Pioneers!* there is an aura of consolation, of living with what is left after the best has been spent. The embrace, the romantic kiss, the loving commitment of Carl and Alexandra, and the decision to settle down (but also to do a little traveling) are, finally, a surrender. In the final paragraph of the text, when Alexandra and Carl go "into the house together, leaving the Divide behind them," they have conceded a temporal defeat (230).

The best move away or are killed in flights of passion. In Cather the brave are homeless. Those who live for some future gain, those who speculate, sacrifice, and settle either for selfish reasons or for the benefit of lovers and dependents—these are the ones left behind, the ones who, like Alexandra, "belong to the land." This, in the strongest terms, defines Willa Cather's sense of an American ideal. Cather's best American is restless, homeless, ambitious, with dubious loyalties to ideals or places of origin. It is Emil and Marie who are granted an apotheosis by the narrative, not the woman left weeping at the gravesite of the closest incarnation of the "mightiest of all lovers." Alexandra, called earth goddess and matriarch by many critics, is not a deity to inspire hubris in the eyes of wishful girls or ardent lovers.

In studying human migration historians have concentrated their stories on destination. The Franks and the Gauls are interesting because they settled and became France. The Visigoths hold interest once they settle in Spain. The conventions of narrative history make it difficult for us to imagine the history of a people that does not settle anywhere and "become" a civilization—such as the seagoing Vikings or, closer to Cather, the original, nomadic Navajos of the Great Plains. The history of America, we are told, begins in the imagination of Europeans, in Thomas More's *Utopia*, not in the wandering, uprooted culture of peoples without a written history. Human history follows people until they settle and then begins to tell their story. Until they do settle, however, a people has no history. This is the familiar narrative against which Willa Cather writes.

If we concentrate on those who settle—on Alexandra and Carl-the-husband—we miss the best we have in history. We miss Carl-the-traveler (whose wanderings possess no textual life), we miss the passion

of the lovers, and we miss the source of energy and vitality that animates the pioneer and the nation itself. Much of this vitality is deadly,
and Emil and Marie in *O Pioneers!* are only the beginning of the casualty list among Cather's most animated characters. Nonetheless, the
deaths themselves inform the living by providing inspiration to the
more lethargic. In Cather's vision settlement is antithetical to the fundamental life of U.S. culture. According to Cather we are travelers. At
the inauguration of President Clinton in January 1993, Maya Angelou restated this theme, addressing her American audience individually:
"Each of you, descendant of some passed on traveller." The inaugural poem was meant to express unity, and in it Americans are united
by their common homelessness. Angelou's inaugural poem stresses the
idea that America has always been a place through which peoples have
passed. In many ways the untold story of America is its own confrontation with homelessness.

My Ántonia

> Strong wind destroy our home
> Many dead, tonight it could be you
> Strong wind, strong wind
> Many dead, tonight it could be you
> And we are homeless, homeless
> Moonlight sleeping on a midnight lake.
> —PAUL SIMON AND JOSEPH SHABALALA,
>   "Homeless"

The thematic meaning of Willa Cather's pioneer novels would be no
more than nationalistic polemic if it were not for the acknowledgment,
usually quite explicit, of the political costs that migration incurs. The
culture's peculiar strengths may come from its restless population, but
so does the tremendous price exacted as a result of its historic mobility.
Among the sources of balance that form the aesthetic of *O Pioneers!* is
the notion that migration and settlement amount to a spatial dialectic,
each act containing the necessity of its opposing impulse. The nation
itself has only gradually come to recognize the global consequences of
its own foundation and expansion into an empire, through which the in-

dividualized sense of American liberty has resulted in a vast empire of world domination. Cather would eventually come to see such paradox as an American crucible, the endeavor that would come to define, on her terms, the American experience. The measure of Cather's crucible is taken throughout *My Ántonia*, Cather's great novel of crossing.

Crossing is a fundamental American rite of passage, crossing from one place or home to another and being prepared to answer the inevitable question: where do you come from? Passage itself, in other words, defines for Americans either psychically or actually what it means to be an American. The success stories told in small towns across the country are stories of sons and daughters who have left to make their fortunes elsewhere. *My Ántonia* opens twice, once in a brief introduction, where the narrator, Jim Burden, is "crossing Iowa" (1) on a train and thinking of Ántonia, and again in chapter 1, as Burden recalls his "interminable journey across the great midland plain of North America" (5). The man is always moving, in fact, from one place to another, from home to home and from region to region across America. Of course, Jim Burden would not initially think of himself as an immigrant, much less as a migrant—those people are the Shimerdas and the Lingards. But this is Cather's point. Despite what Jim thinks, he is essentially a migratory American, and it is not until his life crosses Ántonia's and those of the other first-generation European immigrants that he realizes the fact. Their historic immigrant crossing is the archetype of his own restlessness.

The apparent contradiction in something that Jim says to Lena Lingard expresses the incongruity that inspires the core of Burden's migratory consciousness. Jim and Lena are attracted to each other, and were they not so ambitious, they might have pursued their physical interests. Jim tells Lena, "I'll never settle down and grind if I stay here," and Lena accepts the paradox of the statement. The contradiction of "I cannot settle here if I stay here" is meaningful only in an American context of migratory consciousness. Jim does not need to explain. "You know that," he assures Lena (187), and she does know. She has just told him that she will never marry because her career will not survive someone who wants her "to stick at home all the time" (186).

Jim Burden is homeless. His parents die in Virginia when he is ten years old, and he is transported to his grandparent's homestead in Nebraska, to begin what will become a lifetime of movement. He is not and never will be homesick, however: "I don't think I was homesick. If we never arrived anywhere, it did not matter." He quickly internalizes the idea that his western journey will eventually articulate and project his entire future. Jim Burden's home will continue to recede into memory, and he will never possess a final destination, occupying instead only a succession of stopping places. As Cather will demonstrate in her novels of ambition and empire, this migration also allows a succession of renewed selves to emerge over the course of the journey. Jim senses this immediately: "Between that earth and that sky I felt erased" (8). He will come to think of Nebraska as home, of course, and feel very much a part of the landscape, but not until he has moved away from it will he articulate this feeling. At the very end of the novel, when he admits that he "felt at home again" (237) while visiting Ántonia, there is no suggestion that he intends to return permanently to this home. To Cather, home is situated within the places we leave; if it is not, home is the place to which we have reluctantly returned or in which we have got ourselves stuck. In every sense a Catherian home is understood relative to spatial movement.

For Jim Burden, then, home will always be in Nebraska, and Nebraska will always be elsewhere, a place in the past, a place he remembers and visits and writes about. (Virginia is simply where he was born.) When the novel opens the introduction presents him physically crossing Iowa. He is also at an intellectual crossroads. He has realized that the things and people who are lost to him forever mean the most to him. Romanticism comes easily to migrants, who must preserve things of tremendous value through conscious memory. These same experiences, memories, and people that Burden cannot possess are the qualities that have produced him; they have accounted for his prosperity and his success. Their loss to him produces the peculiar melancholy that characterizes his mind. This is the same quality of sadness that Jim remembers on the face of the immigrant Mr. Shimerda, the sadness that led both men to call their creations "My Ántonia." Each man's disenchantment affects his life profoundly, although Jim, unlike Shimerda, will learn to turn his sense of loss into productivity. His "disappointments have not changed him," according to the introduction; instead, they have formed his character. His sense of loss (his "romantic disposition") has been "one of the strongest elements in his success" (2).

Jim is not homesick in *My Ántonia*, for homesickness can be fatal, which is the story of Mr. Shimerda. On the other hand, Jim Burden is homeless. He is among the brave in the novel, along with Lena Lingard and the other "hired girls," and of course Ántonia herself. Ántonia, however, pays the highest price of all, save perhaps her father, and symbolizes the price that all Americans may have to pay for homelessness. She thus becomes the idea that is "a part of" Jim Burden's mind and a part of the minds of Cather's readers. The psychic crossroads that Jim Burden traverses throughout the novel is between making a home and continuing to move. What he finds is that, for Americans like himself, this crossroads is not a choice but a condition of being. Going home will always be a Catherian great idea, like the idea of Ántonia herself, but the great fact of American existence is to continue moving on to find a home.

Oscar Handlin, in his classic study of immigration, *The Uprooted*, develops the idea of the crossroad. As immigrants move toward a new home, "their sights are fixed backward rather than forward. From the crossroad, the man, alone or with his wife and children, turns to look upon the place of his birth. Once fixed, completely settled, he is now a wanderer" (34). Handlin's wanderer travels with a permanently affixed psychic rearview mirror, always moving ahead but always also looking behind. For the individual as wanderer, certain qualities not drawn on when he or she was settled become crucial and necessary. Handlin cites three primary traits of the migratory settler. First, "the power of adaptation" to foreign conditions (55) must be strong as one encounters new cultural codes both as a migrant and as host to migrants. Second, the recognition that "to live in the old ways [is] to court failure and hardship" (84) emerges foremost in the wanderer's mind. New codes of conduct require new methods; what is left behind is not only a place, therefore, but a social, ethical, and perhaps even moral situation as well. Finally, and most important, the migrant comes to associate flight with success and to fear that permanent settlement will only court the circumstances that compelled emigration in the first place.

Paradoxically, then, if wanderers are ever to settle, they must never believe that their settlement is immutable. To settle for good is to cultivate the conditions of failure that call for migration. Nonetheless, to migrate is to seek conditions favorable to settling down. The journey cannot end. All Willa Cather's great settlers (Ántonia Shimerda Cuzak, Alexandra Bergson, Godfrey St. Peter) carry within their minds the dream of flight or the memory of escape. Likewise, all her great travelers (Jim Burden, Carl Linstrum, Tom Outland) harbor fantasies of settlement and permanence. These characters, paired as they are, constitute emblems of the American crossroads. Willa Cather expresses in many ways the idea that journeys, desires, and acts of seeking are more valuable than destinations, consummations, and acts of finding. At the same time, because we are not dealing with a nomadic civilization, journeys cannot begin without destinations or ideals. "A shepherd people is not driving toward anything," Cather wrote in an essay on Thomas Mann. "With them . . . the end is nothing, the road is all. In fact, the road and the end are literally one" (*Not under Forty* 99). Acts of declaration, the achievement of something lasting through "the record of the plow" or adornments on pottery, are of eternal value and cannot exist apart from settled existences. The crossroads, as a resonant symbol, captures the tentative quality of American civilization, the ambivalence, restlessness, and contradictions that kindle the culture. In Handlin's conclusion the immigrant journey emerges from the crossroads of culture as a central American fact, even a Catherian great fact. At one point in every American's past there have been "strangers in the land; we cannot forget the experience of having all been rootless, adrift. . . . We will not deny our past as a people in motion and will find still a place in our lives for the values of flight" (273).

Fixity is antithetical to a nation that finds its strength in repeated beginnings; equally inassimilable are commitments to place, to tradition, or to absolute values. What all Americans share is not a sense of place but a sense of spatial passage—voluntary, compelled, or forced, but a crossing nonetheless—and a sense that flight or relocation is in itself of tremendous utility. If nothing else, move. This great fact has ideological consequences. The flight of persons from one place to another is enacted intellectually by the value placed on the corresponding shift in or displacement of established ideas. After all, it is not simply bodies that move from place to place but also worldviews, moral criteria, standards of judgment, and systems of belief. Americans who have lost touch with their roots are not those who have forgotten some moral, ethical, or religious base but those who have forgotten that the uprooting of these qualities was a prerequisite to the incarnation of an America state. The Declaration of Independence refers to "the course of human events" leading necessarily to the abolition of tradition and ties, not to the maintenance of bonds. Nothing, no policy, no idea, no president, will satisfy Americans for long, because anything that becomes settled becomes suspect. This includes people. The old, in America, will always be guilty of creating what is essentially wrong in society simply because they succeeded in creating something that threatens to endure.

Equally at odds with a migratory consciousness is the contemplation of *permanent* uprootedness. The ideology that arises from a shared sense of spatial passage finds in the possibility of ceaseless wandering a kind of social nightmare. Migratory consciousness demands a series of homes, and it exists within a spatialized dialectic between settling and uprooting. Each home becomes the starting place of migration; each migration begins the quest for home. It is not surprising, for example, to find the term *homeless population* possessing such social resonance as a peculiarly American term for indigence.

The homeless are those who are stuck, no less than the immobilized, on one side of the spatial dialectic of migratory consciousness. Sociologist Richard Ropers categorizes various types of homelessness and concludes that many Americans, perhaps the majority, face it at some point in their lives. The common causes of homelessness are conditions over which the vast majority of Americans skate tenuously: a change in employment status, a loss of family security, the exhaustion of health care resources (175–78). Economic catastrophe in America results not so much in dispossession, a historical phenomenon, but in homelessness, a spatial deprivation. With homelessness the rejuvenating process of crossing from home to home, of migrating from one environment to another, ceases. The great fact of crossing is thus debased and becomes a social death sentence.

The homeless man on the cross in *My Ántonia*, or rather, the man buried under the crossroads, is Ántonia's father, Mr. Shimerda. Although his body has uprooted and immigrated to Nebraska, his mind never left Bohemia. "I knew it was homesickness that had killed Mr. Shimerda," claims Jim (66), a homesickness that Jim Burden has already assured himself he does not (or will not) possess. The old man's discontent hits Jim hard, and the boy takes it personally. "People who don't like this country ought to stay at home," he says. Here Jim is thinking not historically but spatially. "We don't make them come here" (59), he concludes. Of course, no one made Jim's people come here either, although he may have felt about as much control over his conditions as did Shimerda in crossing. What Jim does not like about the choices made by Ántonia's father is that Mr. Shimerda attempted to maintain historical continuity in an environment of spatial, or migratory, consciousness. What Jim managed to erase on the passage to Nebraska, Ántonia's father will not delete from his mind. Mr. Shimerda, when he speaks, always talks of where he came from, explaining how things were better over there, how important he was, and he possesses a consequent "sadness" and "pity for things" in America. Jim Burden, when he grows up, will do something similar in his writing about Nebraska. The memories do not destroy him, however, but animate him throughout his life, contextualized as they will be within his spatial imagination.

Mr. Shimerda's spoken memories are not complete; that is, he does not tell exactly why he left Bohemia. He does not talk about the scandal he created by getting his mother's hired girl pregnant in the old country and then marrying her over the objections of his family (151). By marrying a woman from a lower class, Shimerda disgraced his family. His mother refused to allow his wife into her house, and Ántonia never visited her grandmother's house until the day of her funeral. This story, which Ántonia tells Jim, qualifies considerably Shimerda's sense of regret and sadness in America. It can only add to his importance for Jim Burden, however, as the emblem of the crossroads itself. "The old man's smile . . . was so full of sadness, of pity for things, that I never afterward forgot it" (29). Between Burden and Shimerda lies the crossing of romantic inspiration and Gothic madness, a spectrum of romanticism endemic to Cather. The experience that fires Burden's imagination and ambition for a lifetime consumes Shimerda in self-destructive anguish.

For the man who would not complete the psychic crossing, who would always regret his journey, Cather reserves the traditional suicide gravesite beneath a spot where "two roads would cross exactly" (73) on a corner of his land. The site, marked by a small wooden crucifix, becomes a local landmark. The road builders, however, would not construct the crossroads as surveyed but instead created "a little island" for the grave by slightly rerouting the intersecting roads, thus amending, or negating, the traditional curse on suicide. In Jim's mind, out of the entire landscape he calls home, this "was the spot most dear" (77). Homecoming drivers, he says, never fail to wish the sleeping man well beneath the cross. Buried there is the dark meaning of the American crucible, that the people who come here leave their original selves behind and carry with them the legacy of that loss, transmitting it to their children as psychic inheritance, creating second, third, and more "lost" generations.

Jim Burden's intense identification with Shimerda indicates his comprehension of himself as a traveler. The reverence with which the road builders and the local drivers treat the grave at the crossing also demonstrates that Shimerda's fate has psychological and ideological resonance for all Americans who understand their common origins in passage. To further underscore the point Cather later introduces a nativist tramp (114–15). This man goes to his death complaining about immigrants. "My God!" he exclaims, after learning of the latest wave of settlers, "so it's Norwegians now, is it? I thought this was Americy." The man claims that he is "tired of trampin'" moments before jumping headfirst into the threshing machine and killing himself. By setting himself in opposition to the immigrant population, setting "Americy" as an entity distinct from the people who come here, the tramp prepares for his demise. Then, to finish him off, Cather has him claim to be "tired of trampin,'" or in other words, to be dead as a traveler. He is the nativist version of Shimerda cut to pieces.

Jim Burden works hard to avoid the fate of Shimerda and the tramp and does not want to become immovable. He is away at college, studying under Cleric, when he comes to his own crossroads between loyalty to his Nebraska home and the promise of dialectical wandering and settling, the pursuit of professional status: "While I was in the very act of yearning toward the new forms that Cleric brought up before me, my mind plunged away from me, and I suddenly found myself thinking of the places and people of my own infinitesimal past. They stood out strengthened and simplified now, like the image of the plow against the sun. They were all I had for an answer to the new appeal" (168). Jim's resolution to this dilemma will not be Shimerda's. Origins will never overpower destinations for Jim Burden. Although the people and places that he leaves behind "accompanied me through all my new experiences," they never override those new experiences. In fact, they become valued more as vivid memories than as objective, lost realities: "They were so much alive in me that I scarcely stopped to wonder whether they were alive anywhere else, or how" (168). Cather thus explains the making of the American migratory type, the homeless individual who carries a vivid idea of a once and future home in his or her head. Survival depends at once on the maintenance of the idea and the perpetual deferment of its incarnation.

Hermione Lee calls *My Ántonia* a novel about a culture "at a transitional moment" in its development (148). Her reading is shared by Joseph Murphy, who suggests that "the immigrant challenge to the American order of things" (217) informs the book as a whole. This transitional moment is not one that passes away, however. The moment is not historical but spatial. It is a site to be revisited; it engages and vitalizes the population. As Jim acknowledges, the memory of transition becomes a source of inspiration for him. The immigrant challenge, then, is not something that passes but something that endures as the culture's sacred crossroads, like Shimerda's gravesite. Cather plays on the symbolic value of the image in the episode of Shimerda's suicide by having Ántonia's Catholic family crossing themselves repeatedly over the corpse. In other novels *(Death Comes to the Archbishop, Shadows on the Rock)* Cather will pursue the parallels between Catholicism and American imperial universality. Just as Christ's crucifixion is the transitional moment in Christian world history, incorporating the great fact of redemption into the world, the migrant's crossing is the spatial point of national identity in America, the incarnation of the homeless man and woman, the spirit of a rooted people.

Willa Cather is, according to Susan Rosowski, "the first to give immigrants heroic stature in serious American literature" *(Voyage* 45). What Cather creates is a poetics of migration as it is incorporated into the fabric of the culture. It is not the clash of languages, the quaint folkways and the bags of dried mushrooms, or even the accurate tracking of Bohemian, German, Czech, and Norwegian settlers that makes Cather so vital to knowing these poetics. Rather, it is the process of crossing cast in its historic and spatial significance, as physical fact and as intellectual legacy. Cather's migrations take place in space and time, and crossings both continental and intellectual work into her texts of transmission. Cather knew what many in the so-called lost generation would miss, that a sense of displacement or exile does not remove the writer from mass culture but, on the contrary, qualifies him or her for membership. The logic of a migratory culture reinvents the relationship between people and country, reinvents "nation," by rooting citizens in their movements across the landscape rather than in their establishment on it.

Crossing must not be confused with assimilation, which assumes the existence of a prior, fixed culture. Assimilation proceeds in the service of an ideal, which Cather found destructive. There has never been an America apart from the people who arrived here from somewhere else, renamed the land, fought others for its possession and definition, and continue to arrive and to make demands. The greatest division in America is between those who came here of their own accord and those who came here as slaves, between those whose volition delivered them and those who were stolen and then granted freedom as expediency. In both cases, however, assimilation is not the process by which the nation is created. The crossing, the passage itself, is the moving ground on which Americans share a heritage. To forget that all Americans have a history of transferring home from actuality to memory, of shifting from one set of allegiances to another, is to misconstrue the culture itself. Anthropologists in the 1950s and 1960s held that "the immigrant or person of immigrant derivation . . . is a prototypically American figure *not* because of any distinctiveness of cultural heritage but for exactly the opposite reason." The importance of the immigrant symbol was seen in "the 'character structure' produced by the *American* experience of change, mobility, and loss of contact with the past" (Gleason 169–70). It is now possible to fill in the perceived absence of cultural heritage with the great fact of migratory consciousness, an American heritage of cultural transference, the United States in transit. Postmodern conditions, such as the perception of fracture, dislocation, and decenteredness, might be identified specifically with the results of migratory experiences. The academy itself reflects the ideas of people whose lives have been shaped by migration, by their own sense of change, mobility, and loss. No doubt the theories produced by migratory intellectuals, especially the theories attendant to postmodernism, are rooted in the need to keep on moving. Difference (and *différance*), multiplicity, fragmentation—all these ideas flow logically and inevitably from the experience of migration and relocation.

Immigrant history has undergone a great migration of its own in American historiography. The earliest immigration historians, such as Marcus Lee Hansen, stressed the archetypal, individual experience of travel to America. Hansen's thesis, "what the son wishes to forget the grandson wishes to remember" (195), was delivered in 1937, on the eve of the great studies of American character that would dominate the fields of history and literary criticism in the 1940s and 1950s. Hansen's emphasis was on generational processes as they affected the construction of individual social attitudes within immigrant families. The generation of historians that followed Hansen, writing in the 1960s and 1970s, rejected his paradigm and created another. The new social history abandoned the individual as the focal point of analysis and turned to the historical analysis of individuals in groups: as classes, organizations, and institutions. As a result of a generation committed to this structural paradigm, a large gain was accomplished in factual information, statistics, differentiations among groups, and in exceptions to Hansen's thesis and to the work of his contemporaries. However, "the gain in concreteness did not yield greater coherence. An enormous fragmentation ensued," so that by the 1980s, "the need for a new synthesis could no longer be ignored" (Higham 12–13).

One problem with structural histories is that they produce "motionless history in which people are perceived as caught in a system or contained within a discontinuous moment." The shift in historical method has not changed the past itself, of course, but it has "altered profoundly the cast of American social, cultural, and intellectual history" (14). The way in which history is cast affects the intellectual climate of the present. The structural historian's sense of fragmentation and the stress on what Fred Matthews calls "the fixed, repetitive, limiting elements that contain experience" (167) have severely curtailed the usefulness of the great fact of immigration toward an understanding of American culture. If Hansen was not entirely correct about immigrant families, he may in fact be on target regarding historiography. According to Higham, the third generation of immigrant historians will (in the 1990s and after) want to remember Hansen's concern for synthesis.

The pioneer, or immigrant, novels of Willa Cather provide a frame within which we may begin to forge such a consolidation on literary grounds. Consideration of the functions of memory (both remembering and willfully forgetting the past), emphasis on the common experience of crossing (with its various manifestations), and the insistence on the synthetic nature of the past (which Cather takes up in *A Lost Lady*) provide the grounds on which a synthesis of American heritage might be forged based on a common migratory experience. As Cather establishes in *The Professor's House*, one can neither own the past nor finally control it. Like cliff dweller pottery, the past exists for the taking; it is for sale to the highest bidder or, in the telling, to the most engaging narrative, the most authoritative introduction. It is doubtlessly true that the particular experiences of Italian Catholics, Polish families, Jewish Zionists, German farmers, and Finnish socialists were and ought to be known as distinct historical phenomena. At the same time, however, the responsibility to differentiate must not override the challenge of locating larger patterns of significance. After all, there is a reason that these groups live in the United States, sometimes side by side, in relative peace even though they have killed one another in other places and at other times. In paralleling the fate of Jim Burden with that of Lena Lingard, and in contrasting both with that of Ántonia Shimerda, Cather issues a frame for just this synthesis. Ántonia is a part of Jim

Burden's mind, an integral part of the construction of his self-being. The connection between these two people is, in turn, a part of the definition of what coheres in the United States.

Surprisingly, few critics of *My Ántonia* want to identify with Jim Burden, the migratory man alien to his own home, the exile, the bird of passage who returns to the site of his erasure. Ántonia usually fares better in critical opinion that also manages to denigrate Jim's mobility. Ann Romines finds that "the novel's beauty grows from an exile's homesickness" for something he cannot possess. Centering her focus on Cather's depiction of the home place, Romines notes how Jim "cannot 'see' Ántonia and thus be an artist unless he exiles himself from domestic life" (149). David Stouck sees things similarly, pointing to how "the image of Jim restlessly traveling across the country is juxtaposed with the happiness and fixed security of Ántonia's Nebraska farm" (*Willa Cather's Imagination* 47). Nonetheless, I wonder how many critics—male and female alike—would choose to be Ántonia, the fecund woman on the prairie, "battered but not diminished," rather than to live Jim's life, the one who wrote about her so convincingly. One imagines them musing: "It is nice to think about Ántonia out there, and Jim likes to think about her, too. But I'll take the train, thank you." The dichotomy Cather presents between Jim Burden's "My Ántonia" manuscript and the visit to "Cuzak's Boys" once again enacts the crossroads between staying and going on. Despite Jim Burden's romantic frame of mind, among the last things Burden has to say in *My Ántonia* is that, like Ishmael, "I had escaped" (237).

If we set aside Jim's view of Ántonia and the clearly positive role his sense of her plays in his own development, another Ántonia emerges. She begins as the daughter of a rather unfortunate immigrant family, living in a sod house on the Nebraska plains. She manages to overcome a great deal of social and economic factors, learns English quickly, and joins a class of hired girls who work in the town of Black Hawk. Some of these girls do all right in life, especially Lena Lingard (whose story is the novel Theodore Dreiser would have written). But the one who fares the worst is Ántonia Shimerda, or "poor Ántonia," as she is known in the community. She falls victim to the irresponsible traveler—Jim's dark twin, perhaps—and returns pregnant and, in the local term, "disgraced." Ántonia rises to the occasion, although her heroic birthing scene is only the flip side of a pathetic self-immolation. She eventually marries and disappears. Cather's choice of title for the last section,

"Cuzak's Boys" (why not "Ántonia's Children?"), is indeed a kind of erasure for Ántonia. Her situation at the end is similar to her condition at the start: she is living in a sod house, speaking her old country language, and married to a man who (reminiscent of her mother) would rather not be living there. A writer other than Jim Burden might find a great deal of pathos and perhaps even tragic irony in Ántonia's story. Jim is kind. He must be, not for Ántonia's sake, but because he needs a certain kind of Ántonia for his own survival. And the novel is, finally, about *his* Ántonia. The two characters embody the spatial dialectic in Cather's America, each an affront to the other's way of life, each necessary to the other's psychic momentum and survival.

Ántonia and Jim share a sense of the road and the accidents of fortune that define passage. Specifically, they have very little in common; the things they hold valuable, even sacred, are completely at odds when they visit at the end of the novel. They are united by a common heritage of having made a crossing, however. They possess, from opposite perspectives and contrary fortunes, the fundamental, migratory consciousness on which their characters have arisen. The ability to endure a crossroads is, in the experience of the migratory citizen, of superior virtue to the tenacity of prior beliefs. Any migrant "calls into question settled values simply by his arrival and his presence" (Marty 395). What habitual, cultural migration questions is the very notion of settled values as an enviable quality of mind. Migrants will certainly have their values questioned by their host communities. Because of a history of crossings, transatlantic, transpacific, and transcontinental, Americans cannot legitimately entertain the idea of a culture that is not continually undergoing challenges to its settled values and to its essential definition. In Cather's vision, then, there is something distinctively American that emerges from the poetics of migration. It is not simply the immigrant who is given heroic status, however. Cather grants an apotheosis to the very idea that one must move spatially to cross over into the temporal future. In essence, this is Cather's piece of American mythology, a consciousness born of migration.

The ghost of Mr. Shimerda remains, his head blown off and bits of his brain sticking to the barn walls, and the crazy man Krajiek slamming an ax into the mutilated skull for good measure. Psychiatrists inform us that migration can induce any number of anxieties, even insanity. "Migration," according to one study, "constitutes a *catastrophic change* insofar as certain structures are exchanged for others and the changes entail periods of disorganization, pain, and frustration." These stimuli can result in "growth and development," but "sometimes the migratory experience ends in catastrophe" (Grinberg and Grinberg 70). The list of common personality disorders attendant to immigration resembles a popular profile of the American in the postmodern period of the late twentieth century. "The individual is confronted with the primary fears of losing established structures and of losing familiarity with pre-scribed rules of social behavior. In the wake of such fears a person experiences deep feelings of insecurity, increased isolation, loneliness, and a fundamentally weakened sense of belonging to an established social group" (59). What the Grinbergs do not recognize is that once such experiences become the common ground of cultural mythology, once consciousness is at home with migration, then changing struc-tures, periodic defamiliarization, and the disintegration of prescribed rules of social behavior emerge as social norms, existing instead as co-hesive elements, as cultural markers.

There is, nonetheless, a psychological balancing act necessary to suc-cessful migration and a frame of mind produced by repeated removes. The place of destination must be valued more than the place of ori-gin. Otherwise, why immigrate? On the other hand, the place of ori-gin cannot be simply dismissed as a wasteland, for the home somehow allowed, provided the means, and nurtured the character for successful emigration. To choose either the place of origin or the place of destina-tion as absolutely superior is to psychically damage the self. If origins are judged inferior, one must then confront the sense that the origi-nal self is somehow flawed by its association with that place. If origins are judged superior, however, then migration is a grave error. Cut off from familiarity, the newcomer comes to associate living in America with isolation, insecurity, and lack of connection to others. Migrants are thus at the crossroads, and if they are to continue to journey past the intersection of cultures, some decision must be made. Either one culture is preferred over the other—the choice itself may prove fatal— or both coexist in spatial relativity, with only the move itself being of unmitigated value.

A study of Japanese immigrants in California establishes a point about acculturation and crossroads. An individual "who lives in regular contact with more than one distinctly different culture must make some sense out of the contradictory habits and beliefs of human surround-ings or he will be confused in his thought and his behavior" (Kiefer

83). Confusion is overcome by holding each culture not as an absolute model but as a way of coping with distinctive predicaments. The person who knows "how to switch behavior according to context is a different sort of person from one who has never learned this skill" (90). What the person learns is a habit of mind crucial for anyone who possesses the culture Cather projects. Edward Shils calls it "a complicated ambivalence," wherein the migrant is free both "to break the primordial ties which bind him" to a country of origins and to maintain "the essential ties to 'the land which bore him'" (408). Psychological balance, complicated ambivalence, or the crossroads of conscious migration—all these terms capture an essentially Catherian depiction of American movement.

In *My Ántonia* Cather creates the "image of Ántonia," as one critic puts it, and describes the way that "this image acquires symbolic significance for Jim" (Terence Martin 95). Cather has paired two minds: one is the migrant who sees motion everywhere and feels the need to continue to move, to seek escape from settlement. He has made a career out of transcontinentalism. The other is seeking home, seeking shelter, returning to her language and her culture. No bird of passage, Ántonia is rooted, in the classical sense, to her family hearth (Tuan 153). Jim has paid a price for his success, including a loveless wife and a homeless existence, but his memory of Ántonia assuages his sense of loss and keeps him from feeling that he has never possessed home in fact or idea. For Jim has always known, from his initial trek from Virginia to Nebraska, that his home was always there, somewhere else.

Jim Burden is well suited to his migration, as indicated by his initial reactions to Nebraska. Moving west across the plains, Jim sees "so much motion" in the land that "the whole country seemed, somehow, to be running" (12). This eternal, panoramic movement has the immediate effect of erasing Jim's ties to his ancestral family: "I did not believe that my dead father and mother were watching me from up there; they would still be looking for me" in Virginia (8). Still feeling the forward chugging of the train, Jim finds an equilibrium on the prairie: "more than anything else I felt motion in the landscape." The motion on the ground is mirrored in the sky by the constant passage of hawks. "I kept looking up at the hawks that were doing what I might so easily do" (13). Jim Burden's move to Nebraska thus has three distinct effects on him: an immediate sense of severance from his established connections, the recognition that he has crossed over to a landscape characterized by continual motion, and the installation of a conscious need on his own part to be in flight. Later on he will make an association to which Cather will return in her fiction after World War I, namely, that this motion will lead to empire once "the great economic facts" of American agricultural production are realized. American productivity, Jim foresees, will "underlie all the activities of men, in peace or war" (88). For now, for *My Ántonia*, it underlies the poetics of migration within the culture of crossroads.

The drama of psychic migration is communicated in unforgettable terms by the remarkable story of Peter and Pavel, the Russian immigrants. "Of all the strange, uprooted people among the first settlers," Jim narrates, "these two men were the strangest and the most aloof" (24). Of all the disgraced immigrants who arrive in Cather's America to begin again, these two bear the heaviest guilt. They also challenge Cather's readers. The story of the two groomsmen who throw the bride to the wolves sends mixed signals to feminist analysis. Blanche Gelfant finds that in the novel "the real danger to man is woman, and his protection lies in avoiding or eliminating her." The Peter and Pavel story is thus "a grisly acting out of male aversion" ("Forgotten Reaping Hook" 115). This may be true, but the story means something different in the context of crossings or migrations. The two Russians do not thrive once they rid their sledge of the bride and groom. They are "run out of their village" and continue to run from town to town, and eventually to America, pursued by "the story of the wedding party." When Jim and Ántonia hear it, the event immediately enthralls them. It is their secret to possess and to guard, "to give us a painful and peculiar pleasure." Jim often puts himself to sleep by imagining himself in the story: "I often found myself in a sledge drawn by three horses, dashing through a country that looked something like Nebraska and something like Virginia" (40, 41). The question is whether Jim sees himself as one of the groomsmen or as the bride. Alternatively, and more likely given his centrality, he identifies thoroughly with the situation itself, seeing his own cultural framework captured in the predicament of the moving sledge.

Peter and Pavel survive their Ukrainian flight from death because they realize that "they must lighten" the sledge, throwing off their passengers. The situation as Cather depicts it is unthinkable. Those who would accuse Pavel and Peter of misogyny must say whether the two should have thrown themselves over. The story is less important to the narrative as a literal depiction and more vital as an allegory of the intellectual process of migration. The ones who sit in the sledge are killed—sacrificed for the sake of continued movement. The ones who do the sacrificing, who throw away the baggage—bodies, loyalties, allegiances—are the ones who survive. This must be what attracts Jim so personally to the story when he hears it as a boy. One way to read *My Ántonia* is as Jim's explanation of how he became the survivor, not the sacrifice, and also of how he will not forget who and what it was that he threw over.

To migrate successfully, the migrant must throw over something, the load must lighten. Judith Fryer identifies the "rhythms of the story of Pavel and Peter" as "the rhythms of the journey." These rhythms are echoed in "Ántonia and Jim's journey home in a rattling wagon, Jim's remembered journey home from Virginia, and his remembered Nebraska as he journeys by rail across the country" (284). Moreover, the Russian groomsmen's story is an emblematic narrative, a cautionary tale to all migratory citizens of the new country. Separation from absolutist values, such as a chivalric code of conduct that would keep the bride in the sledge at the cost of life to all, is a violent separation. The violence that Cather depicts in *My Ántonia* (the head of Shimerda, the bodies of the bride and groom) marks definitive crossroads in the lives of migrants. After Shimerda is dead and buried, his family begins to prosper. The neighbors help to build them a log house and they become "fairly equipped to begin their struggle with the soil" (78). Shimerda's suicide is equivalent to the Russian's sacrifice of the bride; in each case, the vessel is lightened to allow the passage to proceed, to complete the crossing. Both events profoundly affect Jim Burden, and his productive, inclusive comprehension of them ensures that he will also survive. Jim Burden always knows when to lighten the load, whether it be Lena Lingard at Lincoln or "Mrs. James Burden" in New York City. The man survives because he seems to know when he must move on in body and spirit. An attachment to home more powerful than a response to the demands of circumstance and accident is, to Cather, a fatality.

In the very last story that Cather completed, "The Best Years" (included in *The Old Beauty and Others*), the association between devotion to home and death is drawn clearly. Lesley Ferguesson is an ambitious, talented young schoolteacher who attracts the special interest of Miss Knightly, the county superintendent of public instruction, who is looking after her career. Lesley has a serious Catherian flaw, however:

she wants to return home. When Lesley visits home she sits "in the warm sun, with her feet on the good ground, even her mother away, she almost ceased to exist. The feeling of being at home was complete, absolute: it made her sleepy" (112). In effect, home erases conscious desire or ambition. Home, to Lesley, is a place where she "was safe from everything, . . . where she wanted to be, where she ought to be" (96). Cather kills off this character. In a distinctly anticlimactic act of heroism, Lesley Ferguesson protects her schoolchildren from a snowstorm and then contracts pneumonia and dies. So end the best years of her life and so ends a promising career. Lesley Ferguesson was too tied to home to survive in Cather's universe.

What *My Ántonia* suggests, as a novel that means (by its epic presumptions) to speak an American, cultural meaning, is not easy to accept. Cather suggests that one must keep moving or die. To return home is often fatal in Cather; it is, at best, a squandering of potential. Catherian travelers toss away what threatens to impede movement. Attempts to remain constant or true to a prior set of beliefs or commitments may drive one to suicide or some other form of personal catastrophe. To survive in Cather's American context is to possess the mutable skills of the traveler and to keep a clear distinction between the ideas that fire the imagination and the physical manifestation of those concepts. Ántonia, the "*my* Ántonia," as both her father and her mythographer call her, is a very pleasant idea to form a part of one's mind. We should join Jim Burden in his response to her rooted existence, which he says he has allowed to "influence my likes and dislikes, all my tastes, hundreds of times when I don't realize it." Ántonia, in return, cannot quite raise herself to the same intellectual plane, but her sense of Jim's meaning is clear: "Ain't it wonderful, Jim, how much people can mean to each other?" (206). Jim, for his part, "meant always to carry" the image of Ántonia's face with him, "at the very bottom of [his] memory" (207). The images we carry with us allow us to go about our business, even if that business contradicts the ideas represented by those images. In Cather's vision the images we carry, the images that define our sense of moral value and self-worth, often directly and quite productively contradict what we are and what we do.

Jim is a railroad man, a lawyer based in New York, a man who draws on his faith in and knowledge of the country for his great success. The railroad interests that Jim Burden represents and the interests of farmers across the nation's midsection are at odds in the era of his legal counsel. He himself is as far from being a farmer as is possible, a quality that Cuzak's boys detect in him immediately. Nevertheless, what fuels his imagination and his success as a corporation lawyer is his sense of having roots in Nebraska, his identification with Ántonia, the landscape, and such romantic agricultural images as the famous image of the plow at sunset. These images are compensatory; they exist in a dialectical relationship to Jim's actions, as do settling and migrating in Catherian consciousness. Jim no more wants to be a farmer (or to have farm interests precede railroad interests) than St. Peter, in *The Professor's House*, wants to be an archaeologist, a physicist, or a soldier. In *The Professor's House* St. Peter pursues the memory of Tom Outland with the same imaginative vigor with which Jim Burden pursues Ántonia. But he must stop at the crossroads of idea and actuality. If St. Peter pursues Outland to his narrative outcome, he pursues death—the body of Outland is left, finally, at the front in the Great War. Likewise, Jim Burden will return only so far to Ántonia, to the Ántonia who can "leave images in the mind that did not fade—that grew stronger with time" (226). The actual Ántonia, the prairie mother, dies the natural death of the hard-working farm woman, far from the historical movement of the railroad empire. Despite age and the births of many children, Ántonia still "fires the imagination," according to Jim. And that is just it: as Outland fueled St. Peter, Ántonia provides Jim what he needs to carry with him, in his head, as "legal counsel for one of the great Western railways."

The ideological implications of Cather's formulation of the crossroads, especially as it applies to the compensatory function of ideas, are profound. She does not suggest that ideas enable action. On the contrary, to Cather, ideas and ideal images compensate for the messiness of material circumstances or perhaps for their vacuity. On the other hand, to live solely for ideals is foolhardy, if not deadly. Social existence occurs at the crossroads of ideas and acts. The classic definition of ideology is that it serves as rationale, as organizational principle, and as consciousness for the execution of necessary actions. For example, the belief that Native Americans were savages enabled white settlers to kill them rather than to negotiate with them. Alternatively, the belief that the American continent was vacant enabled European powers to claim large landholdings without regard to the natural rights or historical claims of native populations.

Cather, on the other hand, portrays ideas as existing in part to compensate present activities by suggesting that actions emerge out of a dialectical crossing of imaginative, contradictory resources. In a culture of transferal and migration, a culture that "lightens" as it accumulates, acts and ideas will rarely coincide. The migratory consciousness produced by this culture will often be occupied by memories or intentions that complicate a simple correspondence between act and idea. Jim Burden, for example, sees himself as a member of a small-town Nebraska free-masonry, not as a member of the railroad elite or a minor player among his century's robber barons. What fuels Jim Burden's imagination is Ántonia and the countryside, not industrial expansion or economic in-corporation. This is true despite the fact that his railroad interests and the existence of Ántonia's primitivism are historically at cross-purposes. Nonetheless, Jim's imagination of Ántonia, his possession of her and his transformation of her into a national icon, enables the United States to continue to expand and incorporate while its proponents believe they are doing something else entirely. Jim Burden would be surprised to find himself called a businessman (as he would have been surprised to be called a migrant), and he would certainly reject the label of "corporate interest." The fact that he has written the manuscript of "My Ántonia" indicates that his imaginative life exists elsewhere, apart from what he does, as the badge of his homelessness.

A Lost Lady

> We gotta get out of this place,
> If it's the last thing we ever do.
> We gotta get out of this place:
> Girl there's a better life for me and you.
> —BARRY MANN AND CYNTHIA WEIL,
> "We Gotta Get out of This Place"

Sweet Water is a dying little town in *A Lost Lady* (1923). Not even the presence of the great Captain Daniel Forrester can reverse the eco-nomic decline besetting the failing town, a victim of the boom-and-bust cycles common to the late nineteenth-century American bonanza economy. As the town's resources erode, the people's responses to de-cline reveal their various abilities to survive. Those who manage to thrive are those who most readily break with old loyalties to place, time, and others. Mostly, they are the people who leave. Those who fail with the town are those who are unable to see that even the concept of loyalty may in fact be bound to contingencies, subject to revision. The ones who fail in *A Lost Lady* go down in the name of outmoded ways of thinking and doing business. How, then, ought one position oneself in relation to the past when, despite its glories, it has clearly led to decline?

The situation as it is presented in Cather's third pioneer novel is ripe for revisionist history. There is Captain Forrester's version of the past: heroic road builders, riding rough across plains and dreaming the railroads across the mountains. There is also Ivy Peters's view: "Good deal of bluff about those old-timers," he says (88). Finally, there is the view of those with a twentieth-century sensibility: the dispossession of Native American civilizations under the pressure of corporate capitalism and the U.S. Army and the continuation of boom-and-bust cycles that has led, in the 1990s, to a tremendous national debt. *A Lost Lady* suggests that until the past is organized into something that can be stamped with the brand of possessive assimilation, until we can do with the past what Jim Burden does with Ántonia, the plot will end with Niel Herbert stuck in Sweet Water, keeping his Uncle Pommeroy's books in order and ministering to dying men and fleeing women. Niel cannot leave until he has a sense of his country's past. *A Lost Lady* provides a way of framing our relation to the past in terms of emigration.

Salman Rushdie suggests that "the past is a country from which we have all emigrated, that its loss is a part of our common humanity" (*Imaginary Homelands* 12). Collapsing spatial and temporal homelessness does bring together a number of Cather's disparate characters. Niel Herbert, at the end of *A Lost Lady*, senses that he must leave Sweet Water and that his emigration will be from a mode of consciousness as well as from a place: "He was in a fever of impatience to be gone, and yet he felt that he was going away forever, and was making the final break with everything that had been dear to him in his boyhood. The people, the very country itself, were changing so fast that there would be nothing to come back to" (144). This condition of homelessness is felt in various ways by the emigrating Shimerdas; it is also experienced by Jim Burden en route to Nebraska, by Carl Linstrum, and by Godfrey St. Peter. The sense of crossing, of making a definitive break with the past, is Willa Cather's projection of the historical consciousness that holds the nation together.

A Lost Lady might have been an epic, a historical novel of a thousand pages, had Cather been a writer with the sensibilities of Tolstoy or Dickens. She could have poured into the vacuoles of this book the economic details of Captain Forrester's road-making generation, for example. His railroad project into the Black Hills alone might make a volume, filled with details about sacred grounds, broken treaties, and the boy general, George Armstrong Custer. The failure of the Herbert family is left undocumented, as are the specific circumstances that have produced the business ethics of Ivy Peters. Cather, however, does not concentrate on the massive weight of historical action in this novel; such is not the attitude of mind she has toward her material. She draws our attention away from what happened and toward the great fact of successive, unforeseeable events and the effect of this milieu on an essentially homeless people. It is clear that anyone of ambition and talent must either leave the town of Sweet Water (those who remain, such as Mrs. Beasley and Molly Tucker, are cast as subhuman "ants") or transform it into another kind of place, as Ivy Peters is doing. Those who cannot move are condemned to a steady, progressive decline: Captain Forrester in his garden, watching the progress of shadows across his sundial.

It is indisputable that Captain Forrester has completed a great movement in history, helping to build the railroad, establishing banks (although some are failing), and dealing with Native American encampments. Nevertheless, he cannot bring himself to move again, and so he must die, according to the brutal logic of Cather's narrative. Once the woodpecker at the beginning of the book is blinded—by accident or through maliciousness—she cannot see her way and will not live long. A boy (and later a man) like Ivy Peters welcomes the fading vision of the old or the wounded, but Niel Herbert agonizes over the eventual loss of his own home made emblematic by the failures of his elders. He will even place himself at risk in an attempt to forestall the inevitable deterioration of men like Daniel Forrester. Rosowski thus sees the novel as an extended study of "human adaptation to change" within a universe that is characterized by "a framework of mutability" ("Willa Cather's *A Lost Lady*" 52). Cather's presentation of eternal, unforgiving change as the great fact in *A Lost Lady* commands the condition of homelessness and relegates to the rooted the status of resignation and death.

The central crossroads in *A Lost Lady* is located between Captain Forrester, the "mountain" of present stability (and immobility) in decline, and Marian Forrester, the woman in motion who embodies homelessness and the principle of transferable loyalties. She fulfills her commitment to her husband but then moves on to another man and another continent. As was the case in *My Ántonia*, however, Cather finds in actual circumstances a limited significance. The story of the captain's past and the details of his activities are presented minimally, as are the particulars of Marian's background. Facts, however, have little significance apart from the way in which human beings invest them with meaning. For Cather, dramatic consequences flow not from events but from the record of those events on the mind of an active witness. In "Joseph and His Brothers," a critical essay on Thomas Mann, Cather explains her idea: "Had not Jacob been there to recognize and to foresee, to be destroyed by grief and raised up again, the story of Joseph would lose its highest value. Joseph is the brilliant actor in the scene, but Jacob is the mind which created the piece itself. His brooding spirit wraps the legend in a loftiness and grandeur which actual events can never, in themselves, possess" (*Not under Forty* 122). Marian and Daniel Forrester are the brilliant actors of *A Lost Lady*, but Niel Herbert is the mind that creates the piece itself. Similar to Jim Burden in his relation to Ántonia and to St. Peter in his relation to Outland, Niel Herbert needs a certain image of the captain and his wife to sustain his consciousness. Without it he will be stuck, both physically and intellectually, in the gray town of Sweet Water.

The image of the Forresters, however, is of people in crisis. The split between the captain and Marian, or the crossroads between dying with the past and emigrating away from it, introduces a rupture into Niel Herbert's mind. As he negotiates an attitude toward the past, he finds that the past will not keep still. He must integrate not simply the image of a lost lady but also the eventual passing of that image from its association with one era (embodied by the captain) to its association with a succession of subsequent eras (embodied by Ivy Peters and then Henry Collins). Because Marian Forrester "was not willing to immolate herself . . . and die with the pioneer period to which she belonged" (145), she takes on a significance that Niel is unable to assimilate with that of her counterpart, the captain. As such, Niel is without a clear sense of the past that has produced him. If Sweet Water is not worth dying in by the generation that founded it, then of what value is being from such a place? The captain confirms Niel's need to believe in the heroic significance of his origins, but the captain's wife is an affront to it.

Marian is among "the people, the very country itself," that "were changing so fast" that Niel cannot locate his own roots in the soil. The boy does a lot of wandering in the novel, going here and there, back and forth, with no sense of destination. At stake in the text is Cather's principle that one must be from somewhere, and that everyone is, in fact, from someplace either as an individual, a family, or a nation. As long as Niel stays in Sweet Water, he is not from anywhere and he is not going anywhere. To survive Niel must adapt, he must confront his homelessness and create an image of Marian Forrester ("never one like her, as she was in her best days" [147]) as a sustaining, compensatory idea. In doing this he will join the freemasonry to which Jim Burden belongs, the confederacy of migratory Americans to whom the past itself is homeland.

Sweet Water needs but does not get an Alexandra Bergson. Without such a heroic presence, the town and the surrounding farms are collapsing, crops are failing annually, and ranchers are moving back east, "disillusioned about the West." Furthermore, Burlington railroad barons have lost faith in Sweet Water and are unwilling to invest any more corporate money there. Sweet Water's failure is motivating ambitious people to move on, as decline does anywhere. Niel's father is a good example. Like Alexandra Bergson, Niel's father was a land speculator, making farm loans and investing in properties. Unlike Alexandra, however, he lost out and became "one of the first failures to be crowded to the wall" (24). Success makes no sense without the example of failure. In *O Pioneers!* Cather creates a place to which others would naturally want to immigrate in order to envision the future of the nation, symbolized by the joining of Alexandra and Carl. In *A Lost Lady*, on the other hand, Cather creates the conditions for *emigration* by establishing the idea of a place and a past from which one would naturally wish to emerge.

The story here could be fairly trite. A western town fails after a period of typical, bonanza-style American overexpansion. Throughout U.S. economic history boom-and-bust cycles have left ghost towns (or housing gluts) on the landscape. Sweet Water is nothing out of the ordinary. A former railroad mogul lives there, one who fell off a horse and injured himself. According to the individualist ethic to which he himself subscribes, the accident means that his career is through. He gets few visitors and no longer carries the clout that might have attracted additional investments to the town. Past business associates count him out and see no reason to interrupt their schedules to attend his funeral. His beautiful, younger wife is growing impatient with the decline of their fortunes (she begins to drink too much and indulge in sexual affairs); she leaves town soon after her husband's death. If, as New Historicist criticism claims, "history is best told as a story of power relations and struggle, a story that is contradictory, heterogeneous, fragmented" (Newton 166), then a number of stories could be told here. Among New Historicism's most important contributions is the useful reminder that the historical dimension is an imaginative one, dependent on the active participation of narrators and contexts. On display in the novel is Niel Herbert's view of things and the way that he assimilates the history of Sweet Water. In Niel Herbert's mind the potentially sordid tale of the fallen captain and his opportunist wife achieves mythic significance, a "loftiness and grandeur" never inherent in events themselves.

New Historicism, canon debates in literature, the continuous practice of writing revisionist history—these American academic commonplaces mitigate against naïve conceptions of the past as a fixed, stable, and ultimately knowable phenomenon. "Since we cannot wholly comprehend the world directly, it might be best to give up terms suggesting that we can," writes Gene Wise. "We *can* know our particular experiences of the world . . . even if we cannot know the world's entire reality." Given this observation, Wise advocates abandoning the meaningless distinctions of objectivity and using the term *experience* rather than *reality* when labeling perception. By the former term one conveys "not only some objective facts in the world (e.g., dates, names, places, artifacts, people, institutions, statistics), but also people's subjective sensations of same" (50). Neither the doings of Captain Forrester nor the survival of his wife, Marian, is central to the novel in the way that is Niel Herbert's intellectual experience of the couple.

Rosowski identifies the turn to subjective experience as "classically romantic" (*Voyage* 116), and Niel, Cather, and Gene Wise are all romantics. So too is the academic climate at the end of the twentieth century, with its frequent paeans to renewing, rebuilding, and restructuring notions of the real. The contemplation of subjectivity, however, is not sufficient as an epistemological end. Cather encourages an examination of those points at which subjectivities cross, the seeming oxymoron of intersubjective travel, the space, for example, in which Ántonia becomes a part of Jim Burden. If there were a "New Romanticism," it would declare that it is not subjectivity alone that defines the self but also those situations in which subjectivities cross. One cannot know oneself through one's subjectivity alone because knowing one's own mind is only a first step toward self-conception. Cather's fiction implies that the origins of subjectivity lie not in the singular self but in the intrusive subjectivity of others and in the way in which others have reflected and contributed to self-conception. All minds are thus linked to others in an endless braid, a continuum of experience. In this way Cather transcends the historical inconsistency between individual and community by denying the spatial integrity of either category of human existence.

In *O Pioneers!* and *My Ántonia* Cather began with her characters as children and ended with them as adults, moving from formative years to mature nostalgia and regret. But these novels are not simply fictional biographies. In *My Ántonia* Jim Burden records the great erasure of his personality and demonstrates (by virtue of his manuscript) his own efforts to reinscribe a migratory, or spatial, sense of himself. One thing he comes to realize is that the formation of "Jim Burden" is contingent not only on his own experiences but also on the intersections of his experiences with those of others. When he claims that Ántonia is a part of himself, he has asserted that he is not a self-made man but a self-gathering man, a traveler who carries a few things with him always and continues to accumulate and to discard. In *O Pioneers!* Alexandra and Carl intersect at pivotal moments in the narrative, like mass and energy in relativity theory, defining themselves in terms of the other. Cather's sense of the compensatory function of ideas emerges more clearly at the intersection of subjective existences. If the sense of self is tied intimately to the subjectivity of others, then self-conception is formed very much by what one is not, by what is left behind, and by what is not yet reached. Cather's conception of subjectivity is thus spatialized. Although the self is clearly a historical phenomenon—possessing a biography, in other words—it also possesses a spatial map on which one can chart its points of intersubjective existence.

Contemporary theories of human imagination endorse Cather's spatial projection of character formation. "After the disappearance of the self-sufficient imagination, another kind must now reappear . . . an imagination fully aware that meaning does not originate within the narrow chambers of its own subjectivity but emerges as a response to the other, as radical interdependence" (Kearney 387). Kearney provides another way to digest the compensatory function of intellectual life in Cather. Jim Burden defined himself and nurtured his own imaginative life in "radical interdependence" with Ántonia, as a response to his image of her as constant, heroic, and other. Throughout Cather's work the imagination blooms fully in dialectical relation to opposition; it is migratory; it moves creatively in response to the reactions of others. At the close of *My Ántonia* Jim sees past Cuzak's desire for urban life to the pairing of Ántonia and Cuzak. "Clearly, she was the impulse, and he the corrective," Jim says of Ántonia and Cuzak, finding some comfort in the observation (235).

In *A Lost Lady* Niel is faced with contending interlocutors, subjectivities in competition for influence on his development. When Niel was a child Marian and Daniel were synchronized, the world was whole, and Niel saw the Forrester house as the epitome of style and graciousness. Niel's character, his sense of himself, is completely tied to the unity of Marian and Daniel. When the town fails and his father moves to Denver, Niel attaches himself all the more to the Forresters. The image to which he attaches his consciousness is disintegrating, however, splitting along two distinct paths. Daniel Forrester does not change even as he fades, with a "defiant note" that Cather associates with "the voices of old Indians" (45). "You seem always the same to me, Mrs. Forrester," Niel observes while Marian is plotting a rendezvous with her lover, Frank Ellinger, and recalling the frailties of her husband (30–31). Niel remains oblivious—almost willfully so—to what is happening around him as he clings to the image of stability once secure in the Forresters.

Niel seeks the rocklike security of a mountain, something to cling to like a home, but in Cather's view there is no such place. Mountains, like their human analogues, collapse over time, and people must then migrate to new places or new ideas. The effort to counter this great fact is tantamount to endorsing an outmoded aristocratic ideal, something that tempts Niel when he thinks that Marian is "one of the people who ought always to have money" (68). Marian agrees with him, of course, which leads her to bed with Ivy Peters. Cather equates Niel's awakening need for human travel—intellectual, physical, and emotional—with his loss of sexual innocence. When he comes across Marian in bed with Frank Ellinger on that dewy morning, he is thoroughly initiated into violations of stability. He is also awakened to the Catherian world of compensatory experience. The scene ends with the following question, which for Cather is strictly rhetorical: "Beautiful women, whose beauty meant more than it said, was their brilliancy always fed by something coarse and concealed?" (72).

Niel is being battered around by Cather, who applies to his naïveté the sharp instruments of ideological vivisection. The beautiful idea that had been sustaining Niel, that of an unchanging Marian in the midst of decline and general failure, has ended. At the same time, in parallel narrative development, Daniel Forrester loses *his* fortune in a bank failure, reducing the couple to petty economies. Two years later, when he returns from school, Niel sees that the Forresters have split apart psychically. Marian complains to Niel that her husband is content to sit "hour after hour" with his sundial, watching "time visibly devoured." This image astonishes her and her sense of cyclical, renewable time. "We are all used to seeing clocks go round, but why does he want to see that shadow creep on that stone?" (94). With the collapse of the Forrester household Niel comes to a crossroads: the past is dying, its values proven temporal and made insufficient by the course of events. At the same time the future seems diminished, and its destination, charted by Ivy Peters, is uncertain. Of course, just before revisiting the Forresters, Niel encounters Ivy on the train and learns how he has "asserted his power" in Sweet Water, violating Niel's idea of propriety (89). Standing at the crossroads, Marian is leaning toward Ivy and the future.

Niel takes a year away from his formal education, devoting the time to the preservation of "the old things that had seemed so beautiful to him in his childhood" (121). Cather's narrative is rather severe with him on this point. Niel thinks that "the fear of losing a pleasant memory" is "another kind of cowardice" (130). He thinks this of someone else first, but this is merely the first step in thinking it about himself. The sentiment introduces an irony over his year-long vigil at the Forresters, an irony that eventually turns pathetic at Marian Forrester's dinner for the local youth. After the dinner Niel accepts the passage of time: "All those who had shared in fine undertakings and bright occasions were gone" to him (143). With this realization Niel is finally prepared to migrate, to leave Sweet Water and return to Boston. It is what he takes with him, though, that makes the novel's culmination.

Niel is finally able to move out of the dead town by synthesizing the dichotomous positions of Daniel and Marian Forrester. He rejects Marian as a mode of consciousness but by leaving nevertheless does precisely what she does. He rejects the captain's immobility while embracing his conception of life and of the value of a certain past. Hence, Niel enacts Marian's philosophy of movement ("that's what I'm struggling for," she told him, "to get out of this hole" [107]) while carrying with him Captain Forrester's view of a glorious, pioneer history. In fact, he is unable to emigrate until he possesses a sense of the past that is almost tangible enough to call home, something that he can own, something that Cather says "would always be his." Just as Jim Burden saw no deteriorated Ántonia but rather mother earth herself in Mrs. Cuzak's countenance, so too does necessity command experience in Niel's eyes. As he crosses the bridge from Marian's house "for the last time," he is ready to move on. In his memory, "it was the Captain who seemed the reality," sustaining Niel in his studies back east to become an architect. Presumably, Niel will draft plans for buildings, fueled by an internal life similar to that of the railroad lawyer Jim Burden. It is a kind of free-masonry, this migratory existence.

Niel Herbert will prosper, then, with a sustaining image of the past—heroic pioneers, the end of an era—as he makes his way in the present. His status as an architect has him performing a function of a secondary era in settling, that of building permanent structures. Assuming that he is not designing railroad cars, Niel will be involved in providing homes and workplaces for the sons and daughters of pioneers, sustained in the knowledge that he is building on greatness and serving something larger than himself. *A Lost Lady* thus neither eulogizes the past nor assaults it; it neither accepts modern culture nor denigrates it. Rather, it demonstrates the intersection of historical and spatial modes of consciousness. With closure comes movement, and all migrants carry with them a sense of an inviolable past. One may serve that past and be rendered immobile, perhaps even dead, or one may carry history into the next era, into the future itself, possessing and transforming the past into a sustaining, compensatory ideal that enables emigration away from it.

3

In the Context of Cather: The Spatial Future

I am truly a "lone traveler" and have never belonged to my country, my home, my friends, or even my immediate family, with my whole heart.

—ALBERT EINSTEIN, *Ideas and Opinions*

Sapphira and the Slave Girl

Albert Einstein introduced a sense of cosmic migration to the United States and became a national symbol of intellectual transit, even after his death. Einstein validates migratory culture: he is the epitome of the homeless man, the Horatio Alger of the cosmos. Einstein united time and space, collapsing concepts of duration and distance into a continuum of ongoing metamorphosis. American aesthetics of migration thus achieve scientific legitimacy after Einstein; movement into the future may be understood to take place on a stage of landscape and looking glass among a mobile people. Removed from migratory consciousness, a landscape threatens as a place of exile. Landscape thus disintegrates into scenery, its metamorphic implications eclipsed, if it is disentangled from a sense of spatial temporality. Albert Einstein, by his own testimony, recognized his essential homelessness after settling in America. The man who had unlocked secrets of the universe thus came to know that his place in the cosmos was tenuous, secured either by what lay beyond his time or by where he had yet to travel. Einstein was readily captured as an icon by the American media because his life already existed as cultural capital. Einstein is the cosmic immigrant.

The empire of migration that has emerged in the United States has firmly inscribed itself on the consciousness of its people. The nation cannot easily recognize itself in where it has been, in its past, but instead locates its historic mission in the clarity of future direction. The present is better understood as a jumping-off place. The twin mythologies of the nation's founding—migration and declaration—implicate history in a logic whereby spatial transference supersedes historical necessity. Catherian history is charted by compass point, constructed with the materials of migrations and journeys. "Cather has a geographic *imagination*" (Winters 5), and her aesthetics foreground the tension between spatial and historical patterns of mind, a tension resolved through migration. The context that her novels create provides a corrective for what is often mistaken as a distinctly American historical amnesia. The culture of the United States is not simply ahistorical, however, although its history is largely unrecognizable absent an articulated, spatialized future. Memory itself in Cather is always marked by a migration into what looms ahead, not back to what has gone by. The past cannot be a burden to this culture; only the future can weigh heavily on a community of purpose.

Sapphira and the Slave Girl (1940) is a meditation on the confluence of time and space and on the way in which the future looms ominously over past and present events. It is also Cather's meditation on the significance of the tremendous undertaking of forced African migration to America. The narrator projects her imagination back in time to incidents leading to the flight of the slave girl, Nancy, from her home in Back Creek, Virginia. Movement in time for Cather is thus mirrored by movement in space for Nancy. Recovery, or "reconstitution of the lost past," has been likened to geographical colonization in modern historiography (Kemp 158). Cather's novel demonstrates this imaginative linkage. Nancy takes flight to Canada and twenty-five years later returns in triumph to Virginia, dressed in a fur-lined coat and speaking English in a noticeably dignified and nonsouthern manner. Cather had left Virginia as a child, and in creating the novel she also returns, in professional triumph, to write what would be her final novel on the map of her geographical origins. The movement of the narrative, however, is not into the past but toward the future. The boldly written name, "Willa Cather," on the final page of the novel is no nostalgic return to Virginia origins but the child's anticipation of Nebraska, the Southwest, Quebec, and Avignon. The signature serves as a reminder: this is a migratory author. The novel is written, so to speak, with the suitcases packed.

Sapphira and the Slave Girl focuses on a moment when the cultural sights of many Americans were set on the contingencies of future events. The twice-inscribed date of 1856 on the novel's opening page gives to the banal breakfast-table conversation concerning the fate of the slave girl, Nancy, an ominous content that it would not possess had Cather left the date ambiguous. Through this technique the novel projects a sense of the unfolding of the future within the prosaic events of everyday life. By placing the marker, "*The Breakfast Table, 1856,*" before the first words of chapter 1, Cather has the discussion over before it has begun; the events and the setting take on the atmosphere of a foregone conclusion. The reader knows it to be 1861 that looms over the breakfast dishes more ominously than 1856. It seems to follow that the narrative thereby endorses a fatalistic view of history, a sense of necessity behind all things. At the end of the book the narrator "appears" to say that she knows the story that she has just recounted to be true, for she had witnessed the end of this story herself when, as a child, she saw Nancy return. But what is true, to Cather, in this tale? Through flight Nancy escapes history, escapes the inescapable reality of Sapphira's absolute control over her. The text's date, 1856, establishes the necessity of events, a narrative aura of unstoppable, unavoidable fate. Nancy's escape, however, counters fatalism with all the force of a Cather directive: nothing on earth is more powerful than human mobility in body and in mind, not even events that overwhelm and sharply define our choices.

Sapphira and the Slave Girl returns to a point in American history at which events are generally considered to have been unavoidable (historians do not agree on the causes of the American Civil War, but they seem to agree that a conflict was inevitable) and within that context constructs the grounds on which human freedom was still entirely possible. The novel thus moves against historical determinism, against the idea of the past as an intellectual burden. Published in 1940, on the eve of World War II, the novel is a profoundly challenging statement to its readers. There is no question, moreover, that the novel is directed to readers—on more than one occasion the narrative is interrupted and the reader is addressed directly: "Even today, if you should be motoring through Winchester . . ." (275). The challenge lies in the child's voice in the epilogue saying "I saw this, and it has never left me." There is in human mobility, as long as it is maintained, a spatial movement away from historical necessity, away from fatalism. The novel thus provides a model of the peculiar historical consciousness possessed by a migratory culture, a history that cannot be written or told without a geographic sense of future purpose. American history is no more a portrait of inescapable fact than is the cultural conception of home; it is not time or space but movement itself that determines fate, migrations and memories, crossings and returns, escape routes and mobilities of imagination. The definitive history of the United States exists in its future, not in its past.

When considered as a whole, then, the narrative of *Sapphira and the Slave Girl* concerns itself with the author's construction, in 1940, of a spatialized past. The narrator repeatedly makes it clear that she is traveling back to say something in the present, something that motorists might otherwise miss in their high-speed journeys across the surface of the present. The novel contains a variety of formulaic plot devices, none of which becomes central, such as antebellum plantation fiction, southern literary stereotypes, and myths and truisms in American history. Each of these formulas, as Merrill Skaggs points out, is "deliberately disappointed" rather than carried through (172). According to Richard Giannone, the novel contains as well "a cycle of expatriation narratives" in which characters must "make alien ground into a home, a condition of reconciliation" ("Willa Cather" 31). Every narrative device and plot formula within the novel serves the larger purpose of the text, to project a framework for comprehending American historical identity as a geographical construction, the product of movements in time and space and of intellectual transfiguration. The narrator's presence in the epilogue casts the novel as a revelatory tale; the narrator makes it clear that the story is important to her because it contains something essential in its plot and resolution, something carried into the future world of motorists.

If "the act of fictionalizing is a crossing of boundaries," allowing "the imaginary to take on an essential quality of the real" (Iser 3), questions arise concerning the boundaries that Cather transgresses in this novel. What does *Sapphira and the Slave Girl* tell those motorists to whom its narrative is directed so blatantly? What does motoring have to do with historical consciousness? Nancy's flight—the product of conspiratorial efforts and secret, unspoken complicities—has become, in the twentieth century, a fact of existence. Motoring is a national phenomenon. Today moving vans transport homes from one state to another; automobiles equipped with telephones serve as accelerated workplaces. In the early years of the cold war, when history seemed to have come to a stalemate, Americans began to build an interstate highway system. If we cannot close historical gaps, surely we can overcome those of physical distance. The history of the United States is, in one sense, the history of travel made easier, as if the entire purpose of American civilization were to make escape more convenient, to make flight a repeatable experience. If we collapse time and space into Einstein's continuum, we can see that the American quarrel with history is a quarrel with distance as well. Constraints on time, according to Yi-Fu Tuan, are nearly always constraints on movement or distance (130). The need to go somewhere always implies the need to be there at a definite time—destinations imply deadlines. Boundaries of neither time nor space will deter the journey of the American motorist—nor will they deter "Willa Cather" in *Sapphira and the Slave Girl*, the motorized American novelist.

Nancy is the incarnation of the assertion that "movement means life" in American folklore (Pierson 83). *Sapphira and the Slave Girl* is wrought with movement. Henry and Sapphira Colbert have moved into an area of Virginia in which they are considered "immigrants" (23). The novel's plot is instigated by Sapphira's intention to move the slave girl Nancy off her property. Nancy's escape from slavery is orchestrated by Rachel Blake, a woman whose own move away from home was thwarted when her husband and child died. There are numerous inset stories (e.g., Caspar Flight, Tansy Dave, and Tap) about migration, escape, and poignant immobility. The novel's conclusion is made out of the runaway slave's triumphant return. And in the epilogue we learn that the entire tale is an authorial recollection, an intellectual movement back to childhood memories. Throughout the novel, then, *movement means life:* Cather's characters move to survive, either by moving physically to a place where they can live or by remembering what they need to face their present circumstances and to migrate into the future.

The clearest indication of the narrator's presentist motivation in telling the tale comes at a moment in the narrative when the future-oriented perspective of the novel is clearly revealed. The passage comes just after Rachel has learned from Nancy why Sapphira invited Martin Colbert to visit. It is the moment when Rachel confronts her mother's potential for evil ("she had never known . . . anything quite so ugly as this"), and Rachel resolves to "meet the present occasion" (169). Nancy is afraid to go outside alone because Martin Colbert will be waiting for her, so Rachel decides to accompany her into the woods: "The road followed the ravine, climbing all the way, until at the 'Double S' it swung out in four great loops round hills of solid rock; rock which the destroying armament of modern road-building has not yet succeeded in blasting away. The four loops are now denuded and ugly, but motorists, however unwillingly, must swing round them if they go on that road at all" (170–71). Motorists from the present who travel this road—the road that Rachel is traveling as she resolves to defend Nancy against her mother's plotting—must confront the same solid rock that Rachel and Nancy confront. Even modern road building cannot transcend this rock. The past has a tendency to become palpable and to stand between present and future. Readers who follow the narrative path of *Sapphira and the Slave Girl* must also confront certain solidities. History moves by acts of consent. Only when Rachel sees Nancy's future as Nancy sees it is consensual action possible. On the Double S road together, Nancy and Rachel are beginning the process of writing Nancy's future.

Without a vision of the future, in other words, historically significant action is impossible and events appear inevitable. The future is fated only to those who cannot envision it as something beyond the reach of the past. Cather spatializes historical consciousness (imagining it as an American road) to demonstrate that it is essentially reconstructible. Henry Colbert, for instance, can see no road leading out of the 1856 predicament of slavery. The road over which Rachel and Nancy will travel begins here, at the Double S rock, and does not end until Nancy's story is completed at the close of the novel. Significantly, the action that Rachel consents to is a direct violation of traditional loyalties owed to home and family. At the end of the novel, in the epilogue, the narrator appears as a child who has been set by her mother in a vantage point where she "could watch the turnpike" for Nancy's return. The return, however, marks the triumph of historical action that turned daughter against mother and the present against the past in the name of physical survival. *Sapphira and the Slave Girl* projects the terms on which the community of purpose, a community grounded in historical upheaval, is understood in American culture.

Werner Sollers has distinguished between two competing foundations of community ties in the United States, those of descent ("by blood or nature") and those based on consent ("of law or marriage"). "Descent language emphasizes our positions as heirs, our hereditary qualities, liabilities, and entitlements; consent language stresses our abilities as mature free agents and 'architects of our fates' to choose our spouses, our destinies, and our political systems" (6). Sollers refers to the "persistent conflict between consent and descent in America," a historical contradiction integral to the concept of U.S. citizenship: "the symbolic construction of American kinship has helped weld Americans of diverse origins into one people" (15). American political culture is made possible only by muting the exclusive language of descent within the realm of the personal ("where *my* people came from") and by raising consent relations to ideological status ("we the people"). In the United States the official definition of "the people" is consensual and not a matter of blood or nature. Nonetheless (or perhaps as a result), the meaning of *American* has historically been a matter of some debate. In fact, it is safest to say that any definition of the term is always provisional, and it has been challenged recently by those who consider it to be a linguistic fiction and call for a more politically accurate term, such as *United Statesian* (based upon the Spanish term, *estadosunidense*). Sacvan Bercovitch, for example, understands America as "a rhetorical battleground, a symbol that has been made to stand for diverse and sometimes mutually conflicting outlooks" (*Rites of Assent* 355).

Consent language extends into meditations on American history and into the use to which writers such as Willa Cather put the past. Out of what Bercovitch calls the "manifold contradictions" in American history, myths of consent and the groundwork of an unquestionably hegemonic ideology have emerged. This has been possible only because as a culture Americans do not believe in history as a matter of descent but rather hold to a spatial sense of history in which there is always room for competing (or contradictory) senses of the past. History occupies the dimension not of blood or nature in the United States but of geography—and of the kinds of partisan, territorial rhetoric that surround geographic disputes. Richard Slotkin prefers the ahistorical term *myth* to describe what Americans know of their past. "The primary function of any mythological system is to provide a people with meaningful emotional and intellectual links to its own past," according to Slotkin. "Myth is the language in which a society remembers its history" (*Gunfighter Nation* 638, 655). In the American imagination the objective past might then be conceptualized as the space within which subjective myth is formulated. The concept of an objective telling of the past is as vacant today as the American continent was to European adventurers and settlers in the colonial era. Historical relativism appeals directly to American ideals of pluralism, and multihistoricism was a part of the American scene long before the invention of multiculturalism. What Americans know as history is, in practice, a rhetorical battleground, a struggle for authoritative space. Out of these presuppositions, then, Slotkin can argue that "historical memory will have to be revised, not to invent an imaginary role for supposedly marginal minorities, but to register the fact that our history in the West and the East was shaped from the beginning by the meeting, conversation, and mutual adaptation of different cultures" (655). Confrontations in space result in progressive movements in time.

Calls for the revision of American history come in times when the dominant sense of that past has been exhausted in the face of an altered sense of the future. It is always an idea of future movement that determines the American past. For example, some of the most vehement challenges to historical consciousness have emerged from New Age writing in the last few decades. Calvin Luther Martin, for example, calling for "a massive structural change" in consciousness, cites "history's hammerlock on our imagination" as the single most serious impediment to social progress. "Historical consciousness itself has become perhaps our greatest enemy to true progress, the greatest obstacle to imagining ourselves and recalibrating our affairs in line with the new environmental consciousness" (120). Similarly, debates at the end of the twentieth century over multiculturalism, pluralism, and language restrictions have sent historians back to the evidence to provide precedents for present geographical predicaments. A lack of a clear sense of the future, however, has led most historians to visions of gridlock in the past. Because ambitions set in the future determine American conceptions of the past, the absence of a consensual national mission obscures the culture's historical perspective.

"One could say that the West has lost the future," is Salman Rushdie's claim, "and without the future, the one validating concept of its political systems is removed" (*Imaginary Homelands* 388). One consequence is to locate dissensus in the past as a way of naturalizing the present absence of an articulated future. Literary historian Sam Girgus sees the American literary tradition "as a dialog between a narrative of consensus and dissensus and desire" in which "the depth of the hunger for the safety of selfhood and community" is articulated. "American literature . . . tends to structure division and fragmentation" (9, 5). Under the influence of dissensus and fragmentation, even the secure literary theories of the past appear to some as ideological constructs. For example, William Ellis has argued that the theory of the American romance emerged in the cold war and "served an ideological need for emotional safety" while expressing "a triumphant and melancholy patriotism" (161). The powerful idea of American exceptionalism, moreover, reflected even further the confidence of an era with a clear mission and purpose. One result was the founding of American studies as a discipline to explain the exceptional qualities of the nation. The collapse of the mission, however, has left the United States without a past. The lack of consent regarding the future has left Americanists feeling a bit self-conscious.

Sapphira and the Slave Girl addresses an era of self-conscious transit by projecting, in a number of ways, the relationship between memory and direction. The sudden presence of an authorial "I" in the novel's epilogue casts a shadow of hyper-self-awareness over the events depicted. Throughout the novel, however, it is clear that the narrator is remembering and relating events from the past. The references to present-day motorists and the description of the depicted historical period as "the old times" (170) are arresting signposts, working to stave off readings of the novel as a naïve act of historical fiction. Cather is not, then, simply telling a story set in history but rather articulating a self-conscious, historical reconstruction, a willed return to the past, a movement back in time to narrate a tale of flight into the future.

In the novel's final section, "Nancy's Return," the slave girl Nancy revisits the plantation from which she ran away twenty-five years before. The narrator makes it clear that the reunion of Nancy and her mother, Till, was of cosmic significance: "There was something Scriptural in that meeting, like the pictures in our old Bible" (283). The phenomenal nature of Nancy's return, however, is not in the sentimental reunion of mother and daughter but in the transformation of Nancy's identity. As a result of her flight from slavery, Nancy has become another person. Her language and her pronunciation are no longer that of a Back Creek native; she dresses differently and even moves in contradiction to the way in which the narrator's mother and father had always described her (284). In addition, Nancy has married a man "half Scotch and half Indian" and has thus produced children of ambiguous descent. Before she left Back Creek Nancy was a "lissome," frightened, largely passive woman unable by inner resource or social convention to protect herself from unwelcome masculine advances. When she returns she is stately, in control of herself; she symbolizes to the narrator movement's centrality to the creation of destiny. Mobility and the decisions that attend movement are the novel's focus. The very last words in the novel observe that all the troubles of Sapphira's life were brought

about because Sapphira made an ill-directed, final move. The narrator
recalls that Till often said that Sapphira "oughtn't never to a' come out
here . . . where nobody was anybody much" (294–95).

The narrator tells a story by moving back into the past, into "the old
times," to present the tale of Sapphira and Nancy. Sapphira and Nancy
move in opposite directions, but both migrate in response to threats
of humiliation. Sapphira marries a social inferior and moves to escape
social embarrassment. She relocates in an area where her slaves are not
welcome and makes little effort to adapt to local conditions. Rather,
she tries to transplant the Dodderidge lifestyle into a hostile environment, but the only results are a general reputation of having "broken
away from her rightful station" (28). Sapphira engages in the historical range of master tactics, from extreme cruelty and ruthlessness to
acts of genuine kindness and tenderness, enacting the contradictions of
the slave system. Nancy is saved from physical humiliation by running
away from a scene of probable disaster to a setting in which her destiny
is reborn. The plot is set along the tracks of the underground railroad,
including the archetypal role of Pennsylvania Quakers and the symbolic crossing of the Ohio River out of slave territory. The womb of
the runaway mulatto slave then produces transnational offspring, becoming the very image of the melting pot.

Cather centers her narrative on a complex web of sexual power politics. Sapphira is jealous over the groundless suspicion that her husband
is sexually involved with her slave. The husband, however innocent of
the charge, is nonetheless physically aroused by the girl. Sapphira then
engages in a rather astounding plot: she attempts to have Nancy raped
and imports her nephew to accomplish the act. Only the intervention
of another woman saves Nancy, although Sapphira remains unaccused
of any cruelty. Ann Romines says that Cather "scrutinizes women as
they plot their lives" in this novel (191). Cather, as usual, holds women
to a much higher standard than she does her male characters. Martin
Colbert is presented as a rake, but in Cather's view he is of an entire
genre of males who can always be enlisted for seduction or rape if the
need arises. Henry Colbert is, at least, a confused man. He gets no
help from his Bible concerning slavery, and his loins do not help matters where Nancy is concerned. The evil he possesses is banal; he tries
just to do his job as miller. Cather's fullest attention is, as the title indicates, on Sapphira and the female slave. Sapphira is a powerful woman.
She married Colbert, her social inferior, and so easily controls him. She

withholds sex from Till by marrying her to an impotent slave, thereby ensuring that her personal servant will have no competing obligations. Sapphira is among the most evil women in American literature. In creating her Cather bestows on the female character what she rarely possesses in American literary culture: power and responsibility.

Sapphira is matched not only by the slave girl Nancy, however, but also by the slave matriarch Jezebel. Sapphira's character, which is paired with Jezebel and with Nancy, stands thus in the space between Jezebel's forced passage from Africa and Nancy's escape into emancipation. The migratory consciousness of Africans is thus produced in confrontation with the American institution of slavery, and that consciousness in turn further refines a unified, cultural mentality. Cather is, as always, coldly assessing in her conception of Jezebel and of the slave trade. One could argue that Jezebel's position in Back Creek is an improvement over the conditions she would have faced among the "fierce cannibal people" (91) of her village in Africa. The movement of bodies from Africa to America, even under the conditions of forced passage, is a great migration nonetheless.

Sapphira's sexual cruelty, then, is foreshadowed by events in Jezebel's middle passage. The account of Jezebel's migration contains its own elements of sexuality and sexual criminality, beginning with the "mutilated bodies" left behind in her village in the intertribal slave wars in Africa. The description of the slave ship, *Albert Horn*, is historically accurate, and details are selected to emphasize both the horror and the prurience of the middle passage. When Jezebel bites the thumb of one of the slavers, her life is spared only because she is judged anatomically "remarkable" by the captain of the ship as she stands naked and chained before him. After Jezebel's death the plot turns on some of the sexual facts of the American slave system, as if this account has been bequeathed by her spirit. On the night of the funeral Sapphira witnesses the personal nature of the affection between her husband and Nancy (103) and experiences her worst case of sexual paranoia. "The thought of being befooled, hoodwinked in any way, was unendurable to her" (106). According to Toni Morrison, the black slaves around her embody Sapphira's "fantasies of sexual ravish and intimacy with her husband, and, not inconsiderably, her sole source of love" (27). Sapphira's social and sexual construction, in other words, depends on the existence of Jezebel's history and Nancy's presence.

Sex is a survival instinct, and the function of sexuality in *Sapphira and the Slave Girl* is tied closely to the will of mistress and slave each to endure the other. Sapphira moves toward an expression of her sexual potency through the manipulation of Martin Colbert, and Nancy moves into an appreciation of the danger in which this places her body. As the plot develops, Sapphira's power depends on Nancy's vulnerability. This is a matter of personal integrity to Nancy, who tells Rachel that "I'd druther drown myself before he got at me than after!" (217). In other words, it is the state of vulnerability itself that is unendurable. Sapphira's use of her sexual power against Nancy aligns her husband and daughter against her, and they conspire to remove Nancy from the atmosphere of threat. The price of Nancy's survival, however, is a high one. Nancy suffers "homesickness and dread" (237), and the text defines her forced removal from home as "the bitterest of all drugs" (239). At Back Creek the price is equally high. Sapphira's letter to Rachel (245) ends the ties between them, and the estrangement indirectly contributes to the death of Rachel's child Betty.

Cather's emphasis on survival throughout *Sapphira and the Slave Girl* underscores the text as a present-day remembrance, a tale of having returned. The scene in which Rachel's ailing daughter Mary, out of pure instinct, sneaks downstairs to give her body what it needs is emblematic of the text's presentist concerns. It is only the living who matter. Even the deaths of others, as Sapphira tells her husband, enhance the lives of those who survive. She consoles Henry in the loss of their granddaughter by telling him that because of Betty's death, "Mary will get *so much more* out of life" (266; Cather's emphasis). Sapphira herself has survived over the bodies of others, maintaining what Henry sees as "that composure which he had sometimes called heartlessness, but which now seemed to him strength. As long as she was conscious, she would be mistress of the situation and of herself" (268).

Henry Colbert is the conscience of the text, pondering the rightness and wrongness of the slave system in his room at the mill, unable to see his way, morally inert. After the death of Jezebel, Colbert reaches an impasse in his thinking about slavery because he cannot envision existence otherwise. To Willa Cather, the only human failure that truly matters is that of the imagination, the inability to project a future. Slavery presents to Henry Colbert the kind of impossible situation that racism represents today. It is obviously wrong, but putting an end to it is both simple and impossible. "We must rest, he told himself, on our confidence in His design. Design was clear enough in the stars, the seasons, in the woods and fields. But in human affairs—? Perhaps our bewilderment came from a fault in our perceptions; we could never see what was behind the next turn of the road" (111). Not even modern highway-building armament can blast away certain roadblocks, or faults in perception, that must be either confronted or circumvented. Human failure lies not in a miscarriage of the past or a misdeed in the present but in the incapacity to project intellectual and physical migrations into the future. In a community of purpose the solution to political and social dilemmas lies ahead, not in tradition or descent, but in the mapping of future relations. Colbert realizes that the evil he confronts is not in slavery itself (it began, after all, as a legal business with historical and biblical precedents) but in not perceiving when the institution had become anachronistic. Cather presents Colbert's dilemma in familiar terms of a crossroad. He must either make the crossing or fail the future.

The terms of cultural survival outlined in *Sapphira and the Slave Girl* amount to a kind of Catherian contract between past and future, a negotiated settlement in the present. Neither past nor future can be conceived independently of each other in a world that defines itself in the terms of migration and change. These temporal relations, however, are only a portion of an essential Catherian cosmology. Many of the principal characters in the main drama of *Sapphira and the Slave Girl* (e.g., Sapphira and Henry) are dead in the epilogue. Rachel Blake, the woman who helped Nancy to escape from slavery, is alive, as is Nancy's mother, Till. If Nancy represents migration, Till is her opposite, believing that serving Sapphira's family is her "natural place in the world" (219) and accepting Sapphira's power completely. It is the dialectic between flight and settlement, between migration and place, that forms the second portion of the Catherian cultural contract. In Cather's America the projected future determines the remembered past as definitively as migration defines settlement. Without migration, settlement is unknowable; without a sense of place, there would be no purpose, no direction, to migration.

Once again, the crossing itself unites these Catherian oppositions. Migratory consciousness relinquishes the past as place and as narrative identity and transfers a sense of self into unknown space. Confined to her mother's control, the child-narrator is particularly sensitive to enforced spatial limitations (279). Nancy, in her eyes, is the female slave who abandoned her "natural place" and confronted the Catherian truth that human beings, in the slave vernacular, "belong nowheres" (237). This is a painful lesson for Nancy, but it is the historical significance of the American institution of slavery understood as a geographic phenomenon. Not even the late twentieth-century term *African American* can assign the ethnic roots of black Americans to a specific location. African American, understood as an ethnicity, must trace its origins to the middle passage itself.

The little girl in the epilogue watches the road to witness Nancy's return; Willa Cather watches, or narrates, the tale to project the centrality of its meaning on to the present. Like Rachel's daughter Mary, human beings will do what they must to survive. Mary sneaks downstairs to eat forbidden soup, transgressing the boundaries of medical thought of her time and place to save herself from death. Nancy does the same thing, transgressing the bounds of legal institutions to protect her body. These are Catherian stories of transmission, of movement and metamorphosis. The villain in the novel is a woman who not only migrated to the wrong place but who can no longer move of her own volition, perhaps symbolizing historical inertia, anachronism, an intellectual roadblock. Her husband is equally static, imprisoned by useless structures of thought. A culture will come upon these arresting conditions, and its vitality will be tested through its capacity for redirection.

Willa Cather's novels take on an enhanced relevance at cultural crossroads, when certain truths of past eras no longer satisfy the capacity and the necessity of human beings to believe in what they are doing in the present. Letting go of belief places a culture in the impossible situation of considering history to be fraudulent, of turning past orthodoxy into present heresy. Maintaining tradition for its own sake places the mind in an equal predicament, turning the future into doomsday, turning creation into assault. *Sapphira and the Slave Girl* contains within its narrative of historical momentum the memory not of ideals or lost perfection but of transformation. It is a narrative of how one gets from one place to another, in space, in time, and in terms of intellectual bearing. It is a novel of transmission: the slave girl becomes the mature woman of freely acquired obligations; the little girl who witnesses becomes the author, her memory projected across time and space. At cultural crossroads narratives of choices made, of actions taken in the absence of clearly marked passageways, and of the geography over which the past is renegotiated reaffirm the historic phenomenon of migratory consciousness in America. Such tremendously fixed and solid rock is not easily blasted away; the road itself is often denuded and ugly, but in Cather's image, "motorists, however unwillingly, must swing around them if they go on that road at all" (171). That solid rock will always be there, of course—what alters is the effect of the rock on the great fact of human passage.

Shadows on the Rock

> The martyrdoms of a thousand years have proved what men and women can do and endure under the tyranny of an idea.
>
> —WILLA CATHER, *The Life of Mary Baker G. Eddy*

At the end of *Shadows on the Rock* (1931) Monseigneur de Saint-Vallier returns to Quebec after a thirteen-year absence and visits Euclide Auclair. Auclair might not have recognized the man and is "shocked at the change" in his countenance (270). As the two men discuss affairs, the bishop laments certain European political developments and voices his envy of Auclair's frontier existence, far from the political turmoil of their native France. "The changes in the nations are all those of the old growing older," according to Saint-Vallier. "You have done well to remain here where nothing changes" (277). The bishop then asks about Cécile, Auclair's "little daughter," and is told that she has married the frontier scout, Pierre Charron, and that Auclair now provides a home between voyages for the sailor Jacques Gaux, Cécile's childhood friend and the son of a local prostitute.

Great changes have occurred in Quebec in the generation charted by Cather. The French immigrants have become Canadians, class divisions have loosened, and the wilderness has been incorporated into the culture. The Canadian-born and those who emigrated quite young, like Cécile, have severed emotional ties to France. For these travelers the center of existence has shifted from Europe to America, and the saints, miracles, and devotions of Catholic France have been transmitted to a new setting. Cécile and Pierre have four sons, whom Auclair calls "the Canadians of the future," and Auclair himself is resigned to Canada's future, no longer counting his fortunes with those of France. Nonetheless, Auclair feels himself "fortunate to spend his old age here where nothing changed," far from the political divisions of Europe (280). Paradoxically, it is Auclair's sense of stability and order that strengthens his ability to endure the tremendous changes he has witnessed.

The relationship between what people believe and their ability to survive time and changing circumstances forms the narrative continuum of *Shadows on the Rock*. The price of survival is simply stated: the culture must change if it is to persist, but it can persist only if it constructs some notion of permanence. At the same time, embedded within a migratory culture is a hostility for permanence that results in an existence eternally on the brink of the unknown. This novel of migration and settlement focuses on intellectual transformations, specifically, the mutable quality of communal memories and the recurrence of the miraculous, or the irreducible dimension of existence. The title, in this sense, refers to the passage of ideas over matter, the projection of particular forms of recurring structural phenomena endemic to human survival. Cather's rock is the rock of stability, immutability, the values without which a civilization will not survive. Cather's shadows, images of passage, migration, and movement, are the shades of meaning cast by those in momentary possession of the rock, the closest that human life can get to something that will not change. The novel thus narrates a web of interlocking processes both spatial and temporal. Ideas change in passage from one place to another and alter over time; beliefs change as well when brought in contact with other cultures and subjected to experience. What the novel projects into the present is a sense of imminence. One puts the text aside to wonder what mode of thought lies beyond the present shadow of belief, what mind will look back on our convictions with a sense of bewilderment and distance.

Cather wrote often of the human attraction for the symbol, and at times for the fact, of the rock. The cliff dwellers of *The Professor's House*, Thea Kronberg's trip to Panther Canyon in *Song of the Lark*, the Navajo sacred grounds in *Death Comes for the Archbishop*—each of these evokes a civilization that has identified itself closely with the rock and has perished. A society that associates survival with nontransferable property, one that must live in a certain place or die in the attempt, is doomed by Catherian standards. Cather's emphasis, therefore, is not simply on the rock but on the shadows that traverse it, the human beings who identify with permanence but who do not, in their own essence, possess that quality. The notion of "shadows on the rock" in this sense captures the interplay of change on permanence, of travel and settlement across both time and space. Cécile has emigrated from France and is moving away from a France-centered world; she is identified with the first-generation Canadians, along with Pierre Charron, and is moving in time away from her father's French consciousness. Change and stability relate to each other as phenomena in the way that temporal and spatial qualities interact—as the continuum that contextualizes human existence. Catherian space (the rock) is measured by mobility and change; Catherian time (the shadows) is measured by the durations of movement that span continents and oceans. Both time and space are subject to the constancy of change, and only through tremendous effort is an illusion of stability achieved. Intellectual order is vigilantly maintained so that the inevitable alterations in human predicaments may be endured.

In the first scene in the novel a supply ship, *La Bonne Espérance*, is sailing away from Quebec in October 1697, leaving the French colony "to face the stern realities of life" for the next nine months (3). There will be no communication with the world outside Quebec until July. "There might be new wars, floods, conflagrations, epidemics, but the colonists would never know of them until next summer" (4). When the ships are gone, making the long voyage to France, time slows down, and the narrative turns to an exploration of the culture on the Kebec Rock—the stories told, the relation to the wilderness, the mysteries sustained by the Christian believers. When the ships return in July, time accelerates: the war is at a standstill, the wheat harvest was good, the vintage is among the best, the apothecary has new medicines, the kitchen has new spices, and Cécile has become a young lady, as attested by the kinds of gifts sent to her by her French aunts. Tremendous changes are realized instantaneously and close space makes up for lost time once the ships arrive.

The arrival of the ships also accentuates the generational space between Cécile and her father. Auclair awaits the word that will allow him to return to France with Count Frontenac; Cécile dreads abandoning the home she has made in Canada. For Auclair, the true rock—permanence and authority—will always be in the Old World, under the agency of the count. But Cécile has remade the rock out of indigenous materials. She will eventually recognize it in Pierre Charron: "he had authority, and a power which came from knowledge of the country and its people; from knowledge, and from a kind of passion" (268). The distance traveled between father and daughter, between France and Canada, is an epochal one in time, space, and consciousness. The price of survival for Cécile and the other colonists is the recognition that cultural authority will shift in response to the exigencies of the country and its people. Cécile's womb, producing four sons, "the Canadians of the future," is (like Nancy's) the melting pot itself, participating in "a tradition which ranges from Medea's magic caldron of rejuvenation to the figure of the Statue of Liberty" (Sollers 78).

Cather's narrative is concerned with the resources available to a people that will ensure its survival. Late in his life Count Frontenac contemplates his death in Quebec, when "his spirit would go before God to be judged."

> He believed this, because he had been taught it in childhood, and because he knew there was something in himself and in other men that this world did not explain. Even the Indians had to make a story to account for something in their lives that did not come out of their appetites; conceptions of courage, duty, honour. The Indians had these, in their own fashion. These ideas came from some unknown source, and they were not the least part of life. (247)

The Catholic faith in *Shadows on the Rock* is strong enough to withstand the overwhelming sense of abandonment the settlers experience at Quebec. The colony's ability to endure "this severance from the world" (4) depends on the power of its culture's ideas, the way in which the culture defines the nonmaterial essence of human life. If the definition of nonmateriality is strong enough, the human mind in possession of the idea will be capable of withstanding material deprivation, even abandonment, and will be able to make a home anywhere in the world. Mind and circumstance must be aligned for survival, but home for Cather is always a relationship to a place, not a place itself. At his death Count Frontenac glimpses the relative nature of all belief, where the function of a religious system is to meet the structural demands of transcendent reality.

The pluralist implications of the ideological projection made in *Shadows on the Rock* are clear. The tolerance for diversity is contingent not on the perpetuation of ethnic and racial distinctions but on the recognition that all cultures must somehow cast the mysterious dimension of human existence into patterns of language and traditional behavior. Toleration can be constructed only on structural grounds, where the common struggle to make sense of the unknown is what defines spirituality—what Cather calls desire. This is the essence of Count

Frontenac's previously quoted realization. The world was not what he had thought it to be as a young man. He has been abandoned by his superiors, he has faced other cultural styles of being, and he has even made friends with "absolute unbelievers" (247). Through it all he has been struck not by what people believe but by the quality of these beliefs, by the way that the mind defines its relation to place. As cultural anthropologist Philip Gleason has argued, diversity is not equivalent to what is popularly known as "cultural pluralism," or the "indefinite perpetuation of immigrant cultures." The confusion on this issue has led to such convolutions as praise for diversity but scorn for divisiveness, where "divisiveness was somehow bad, even though pluralism was good" (166–67). Only Count Frontenac's view can save this situation from impossibility (it is "extreme and unrealistic," according to Gleason): the recognition that all religions, ethnicities, and identities are "shadows on the rock."

Cather's emphasis on provisional structures of survival in *Shadows on the Rock* fictionalizes what sociologists call cultural modularities. Modular structures include "open-ended" relationships (such as that between the colonists and the Holy Family), the "dismantling" of hierarchies, and provisional conceptions of authority (Blair 129). Modular social and political structures affect the construction of character as well. The open-ended personality, the migratory individual, defines Cather's sense of the spirit at home in this world, a sense that is not contingent on place but that interacts with both time and space. Father Hector does not understand why Auclair wants to return to France and says that he will never go back. "Listen, my friend," he explains, articulating Cécile's point of view as well as his own, the ascendant view in the novel, "No man can give himself heart and soul to one thing while in the back of his mind he cherishes a desire, a secret hope, for something very different." When one migrates one must be "giving of oneself altogether and finally. Since I made that sacrifice, I have been twice the man I was before" (149). Father Hector then tells the story of Noel Chabanal, the nonmigrating migrant, for whom Canada "was one long humiliation." He could not learn the language, did not love his converts, the Native Americans, and would not eat their food. As a consequence, and worst of all, Chabanal suffered "an almost continual sense of the withdrawal of God." God withdrew from Chabanal, and he was "constantly beset by temptation in the form of homesickness. He longed to leave the mission. . . . Everything that he had lost was awaiting him in France" (152). God's withdrawal from Chabanal is the result of not a Catholic but a

Catherian heresy. One's self, and one's identity, is rooted where one has arrived, not where one had originated.

Rock and shadow, permanence and mutation, story and amendment; Cather's continuum engages the narrator from the departure of the ships through Auclair's final sense of security in exile. Culture is "the product of interaction between past and present," in Lawrence Levine's conception. "Its toughness and resiliency are determined not by a culture's ability to withstand change, which indeed may be a sign of stagnation not life, but by its ability to react creatively and responsibly to the realities of a new situation" (5). Omitted from Levine's formulation is the spatial dimension that is inherent in the emergence of any new situation. Culture is equally the product of interaction between here and there; it is not a fixed place but a migratory process. *Shadows on the Rock* records a historical transmission of consciousness. Cather's focus is on migratory intellectuals, a lost generation: a "philosopher apothecary," bishops and mothers superior, and a precocious young girl. "It is enough here to remember that civilization is still in transit; as we move about we are all carriers in greater or less degree" (Dixon Fox 36). Human intelligence often outdistances the institutions it has created to administer its ideas. The discourse of the twentieth century has made a truism of the observation that nothing is permanent but change; nonetheless, it maintains social institutions and legal structures that privilege stability and permanence and tend to discourage innovation. Cather's fictional universe is wrought with examples of deadly stasis. On the other hand, pure movement and change for their own sake are equally fatal. The refusal to create order in the knowledge that all order is transitory results in the pathetic lives of Cather's tramps and beggars, those without any sense of stability by which to recognize and measure movement. Cather's aesthetics reflect a vision of the continuum of stasis and metamorphosis. It is not true that nothing changes, nor is it true that change is all there is or that nothing endures.

The elders in the Auclair family, on emigrating to Quebec, are intent on preserving its cultural traditions. Cécile's mother brings with her all "her household goods, without which she could not imagine life at all." These include carpets, furniture, wall decorations, curtains, and linens: "As long as she lived, she tried to make the new life as much as possible like the old" (23). Cultural transplantation is vital to Madame Auclair, and she fears that the seeds will not take root in her daughter, that "something so precious, so intangible," as a "feeling about life" would be lost in transit "across the wastes of obliterating, brutal ocean." Madame Auclair has had a vision of permanence. "She wanted to believe that when she herself was lying in this rude Canadian earth, life would go on almost unchanged in this room with its dear (and, to her, beautiful) objects" (25). Madame Auclair's belief in established practices is complemented by her husband's rejection of New World realities. He refuses to consider "savage" medicinal procedures (such as those for the treatment of sprains), despite the fact that these methods work. He dismisses them on racial grounds. Auclair believes, for example, "that the savages were much less sensitive to pain than Europeans" (35). Auclair's life in Canada is marked by his attempt to resist the assimilation of native practices. The terror he experienced in France before emigrating subsides in Quebec but never actually dissipates. "He could not imagine facing any kind of life but the one he had always lived" (33). His daughter, however, is not so limited in her imaginative resources.

At the core of American historical mythology is the sense of generational change. From the young revolutionaries in 1776 through the passing of the torch to the Kennedy generation in 1961, Americans have been attracted to a sense that history is a supersessive phenomenon, in which successive waves of revolution, however banal, define the historical process (Kemp 177). The youth culture discovered by the mass media in the middle of the twentieth century and exploited for profit ever since has institutionalized a generational conception of cultural upheaval wherein the young are expected to challenge, confront, and occasionally defy the old revolution. Political implications are important in this mythology, for revolutionary shifts in focus can be of a homely sort if they are understood as rites of passage. Werner Sollers sees as well a construction of national identity within the American language of generational continuity. "Apparently talking about lineage, they are actually inventing not only a sense of communal descendants—the coming generation so much worried about—but also a metaphoric ancestry in order to authenticate their own identity" (234). Lacking traditional national ties of blood and ethnicity, Americans construct ancestry out of arbitrary temporal divisions called generations. Cather projects these generational structures of historical change in *Shadows on the Rock*, setting their effects in the Canadian wilderness.

The heroine of the novel is young Cécile, foremost among the emerging generation of Canadians. After characterizing Madame Auclair's devotion to cultural preservation and Euclide Auclair's stand against native medicinal practices, Cather relates one of Cécile's favorite stories. The legend of Sister Catherine and Marie is told by Mother Juschereau. Marie was an unregenerate sinner in Bayeux who lived a "shameful life," lost to all mortal attempts to save her soul. She was physically diseased and exiled from the community, and she eventually died alone and was buried anonymously. Sister Catherine prayed for all the dead, but she never prayed for Marie, "believing, as did everyone else, that she was for ever lost" (37). Twelve years after Marie's body was thrown into a ditch, Sister Catherine emigrated to Canada. There, in the wilderness outpost, "a soul from purgatory appeared to her, all pale and suffering," and admonished her for her negligence. It was Marie. Just before death, the sinful woman had appealed to the Virgin Mary and was saved. Now, she tells Sister Catherine in Canada, "only a few masses are required to deliver me from purgatory." Of course Catherine has the masses performed, and Marie is delivered to paradise (38–39).

Cécile identifies closely with this legend. Mother Juschereau is about to explain the story when the girl stops her: "*N'expliquez pas, chère Mère, je vous en supplie!*" (Don't explain, dear Mother, I beg you). Apparently Cécile has never allowed Mother Juschereau to interpret this story for her and so has never had to endure the orthodox explanation about the necessity of faith. Mother Juschereau suspects the meaning that Cécile takes from the legend to be a departure from orthodoxy. Although "she knew that her words fell into an eager mind," the "admiration and rapture she found in the girl's face . . . was not the rapture of self-abnegation. It was something very different,—almost like the glow of worldly pleasure" (40). The twelve-year-old Cécile is probably taken with the image of the sinner, Marie, who despite the disfavor of her elders is loved by a power higher than the living. It is a story with a damaging subtext of adult negligence, and Cécile may well be drawn to the worldly pleasure of undermining the authority of the generation in power. The story provides Cécile with a context, an authorization to make her own way, knowing that she will be able eventually either to demand compliance or outlive the authorities.

The culture of French Canada is preserved and maintained by these "stories of the rock," as Cather calls them, "the shades of the early martyrs and great missionaries . . . the miracles that had happened there . . . the dreams that had been dreamed." These stories, in Cécile's consciousness, "overshadowed the living" (95) and gave to the frontier outpost a sense of continuity that assuaged fears of abandonment.

But the meaning of the stories can never be fixed; what they project as contexts into the present are determined by the use to which the living generation will put them within the community of purpose. Nonetheless, we all live within the contexts created by what we believe, read, and tell. The minds of those on the rock are subject to fears and sorrows, "memories of families once together and now scattered," fears that "hung over the rock of Kebec . . . like the dark fogs from the river." Against human nihilism stands "the Holy Family, the saints and martyrs, the glorious company of the Apostles, the heavenly host" (96–97). The believer carries in mind what is needed to survive; "the world of the mind (which for each of us is the only world)" sustains the movement of culture. "When an adventurer carries his gods with him into a remote and savage country, the colony he founds will, from the beginning, have graces, traditions, riches of the mind and spirit" (98).

On the other hand, Cécile is not so sure about all this. "Cécile liked to think they had things of their own in Canada" (101). To her, the stories of martyrs in her *Lives of the Saints* were not as impressive as were the lives of local missionaries and martyrs tortured by Iroquois and enduring the Canadian wilderness. Cécile's point of view is made emblematic by the addition of Jacques's toy beaver to the Christmas crèche. She will eventually marry Pierre Charron, the novel's Natty Bumppo figure, the man who knows Indians and who can live in the woods, survive on dog meat, and master other indigenous practices. The passage made by Cécile indicates that the religiosity of her father's generation is passing, that the reliance on miraculous interventions will fade as the community gains control over the environment. "I do not belong to the old time," she tells her father in response to one of his nostalgic reveries for France. "I have got to live on into a new time" (261) and in a new place.

Cécile will make the passage into the new time, however, on the strength of the mythology of the old. Her marriage to Pierre Charron marks her movement away from the centrality of the Old World religion of her father's generation. Charron refers to the religion of his own youth and his love for Jeanne Le Ber as "those early memories; one can not get another set; one has but those" (181). The memories are Charron's intellectual resources, and it is as memories that they function in his survival. This is the man to whom Cécile is married at the end of the novel, although Cather moves the marriage outside the narrative. The novel does not project what Cécile becomes. More than anything else, *Shadows on the Rock* charts the span of a cultural style as it sustains life and then passes by, yielding to another. The value of the novel today lies in its provision of a way in which to think about the passage of a mode of consciousness through space and time. Cather is interested, as always, in the utility of thought processes, in the relationship between what people believe and the particular activities for which those beliefs compensate. The transmission of the saints and martyrs to the New World mitigated against the fear and terror of the Canadian wilderness. Nonetheless, those saints and martyrs are soon (within a generation) supplanted by local heroes whose lives follow the structures of received stories transformed by native circumstances.

Jeanne Le Ber, the Quebec recluse, is among the colony's most fruitful resources. The story of her devotions and her self-sacrifice "was told and re-told with loving exaggeration," as a kind of antidote to "tales of Indian massacres and lost hunters" that terrorize the colonists (136–37). Cécile tells Jacques of the angels' visit to Le Ber; the story of her faith sustains the entire colony through the long winter months. Cather describes the function of such legends in language she has used to describe all human activity informed by desire:

> The people have loved miracles for so many hundred years, not as proof or evidence, but because they are the actual flowering of desire. In them the vague worship and devotion of the simplehearted assumes a form. From being a shapeless longing, it becomes a beautiful image; a dumb rapture becomes a melody that can be remembered and repeated; and the experience of a moment, which might have been a lost ecstacy, is made an actual possession and can be bequeathed to another. (137)

Social critics today refer to myths and ideologies to delineate the actual possession that one constructs from the longings, images, and ecstasies of the culture. Pierre Charron is rejected by Jeanne Le Ber, and in response he rejects the rock for the wilderness. He lives among the Native Americans, is admired and trusted by them. His marriage to Cécile then completes the logic of the narrative. Jeanne Le Ber's devotion marks the strength necessary to endure the initial migration into the wilderness. In essence, nonetheless, Le Ber's faith is a rejection of place; it believes not in passage but in holistic transferal. After all, she is not really "in" Canada at all but among "the Holy Family, the saints and martyrs." To Charron, she becomes a childhood memory, likened to the idea of one's original home, not something to return to but not something to forget, either. The marriage of Cécile and Charron signals the end of the Canadian medieval. Cather's novel is not of saints and martyrs; rather, it is of the power of belief that sustained events of such magnitude.

Critics have grappled with the otherworldly concerns of the novel and have come up with a number of ways to characterize its focus on the miraculous. "The text embodies the process by which fictions narrated in a society compose its history," according to Deborah Carlin. "If the narrative of *Shadows on the Rock* translates fiction into history, then the text as metanarrative reinscribes history as fiction" (66). Carlin accurately collapses history, fiction, and (I suspect) religious legend into the single framework of narrative. The novel presents, then, "a sense of historical narrative as an ever-changing, distorting, altering tradition of telling. . . . It is a text about perpetual transformations in narrative" (87–88). Contemporary consciousness will recognize that narrative itself possesses the miraculous dimension of existence. Accordingly, narrative functions as the means by which the mysteriously transformative power of storytelling is communicated. To Merrill Skaggs, it is the continuity of a community "that is itself a kind of miracle," and the text is thus "Cather's story of communal miracle" (148). The unfolding of events, in a Tolstoyan sense, is evidence of the miraculous.

History, then, is the miraculous dimension of modern existence. It is universally believed in as a force, and the culture honors and consecrates the power of its memory, often institutionally. The continuity of a community is miraculous—but so is its passing. Where did it go? Lewis Simpson describes the "omnipresent subject matter of modern letters" as "man's idea of himself as a creature of his own conception of history, and his resistance to this idea" (238). The American writer most often associated with the burden and weight of history is William Faulkner. In Faulkner the past can overwhelm the present, its monumental legacy diminishing the significance of the living. In Cather's productions, however, the opposite is true. The experience of the migrant—immigrant or traveler—renders the past invisible, dreamlike. The sheer momentousness of the present, the work of cultural transaction, and the weight of future responsibilities turn the past into a fantasy, a series of tableaux. One's connection to the past, in Cather's migratory culture, is mysterious, as mysterious as the stories of the rock that sustain Quebec. There have been cultures that did not believe in history, epochs without a sense of history (such as the medieval period), and an appreciation of such eras cannot help but qualify our own belief in history as a great fact of human existence. Anthony Kemp reminds us that "history is not the past, any more than theology is God; history is made of language and nothing else" (46). Our culture's sense of history is nothing more — and nothing less, on Catherian terms — than our own shadows on the rock.

Antoine Frichette makes his way through the wilderness, nearly starves, and is nursed by Auclair. "A man sits here by the warm fire," he says, and his past suffering fades away. The sensations of the present override memory until "all that happened out there in the woods seems like a dream" (145). To Cather, those who cannot focus so clearly on the present suffer as if from a psychic malignity. Frichette's sense of the present is stronger than his memories of what he endured, despite the fact that his injuries threaten to make him "no good anymore" as a hunter. His physical limitations are not matched by intellectual trauma. On the other hand, stasis threatens those for whom the past intrudes on the present. These are Cather's tragic figures, objects of pathos and regret. Blinker, for example, is an "unserviceable" man, an outcast with no trade, no connection to the living save the charity he receives from Auclair. He is plagued by the work he did in the king's prison at Rouen, haunted by the "faces of people he had put to torture," especially that of an innocent woman who was hanged on the strength of a false confession that he elicited from her through torture. Similar to Peter and Pavel in *My Ántonia*, Blinker emigrated to the New World thinking that he could escape his memories, but it did not work. "They are inside me," he says. "I carry them with me" (161). Cather's language is nearly identical to that used to describe the spiritual emigration of the Ursulines: "they carried all" (97). What the Ursulines carry, however, are not memories but unfinished stories, "the glorious company of the Apostles, the heavenly host." Blinker, in contrast, brings closure with him, a history that cannot be changed. Auclair describes Blinker to Cécile as "one of the unfortunate of this world" and compares him to Dido in the *Aeneid* (163).

Neither time nor distance relieves Blinker from the past's mysterious effect on his state of mind. Neither time nor distance lessens the faith of the Ursulines, who carry with them an entire universe, "lovingly arranged and ordered" (97). Neither Blinker nor the Ursulines have traveled very far, despite the distance and duration of their exile from France. This is true as well of Auclair, who scarcely moves intellectually over the course of the novel. The rock to which these individuals cling is their sense of spatial permanence; for Blinker it is eternal ostracism,

for the Ursulines it is the well-ordered universe, and for Auclair it is
France. In the next generation, that of Pierre and Cécile Charron, the
stories of the rock will become legends of the early settlers, missionaries, shopkeepers, and traders who built Quebec. And Cécile's sons will
believe beyond a doubt in what was accomplished to give them life.
When they stop believing, the rock will disappear.

In *Shadows on the Rock* Willa Cather contextualizes the relativist
nature of human systems of belief, including the historical creed. The
colonists at Quebec were sustained by a Catholicism that is now archaic. The wilderness landscape was conquered and possessed by a belief in native savagery that is now rejected, or at least qualified. To read
the novel one must accept an intellectual passage into a mode of consciousness now closed to human experience. That ideology, a form of
medieval Catholicism, may be imagined, but only as an kind of thought-
experiment. Closed systems of belief, totalizing worldviews, confidence
enough to enforce intellectual compliance—these are discredited structures of thought in the contemporary world. What we now believe, as a
culture, is closer to a sense that people possess the capability of believing almost anything. The level of existential freedom taken for granted
in the late twentieth century is hardly benign for vast portions of the
population. These days, people "snap" from too much relativism and
are drawn to the security (or the rock) of what are often called cults
or fanatic groups. The extensive media coverage given state confrontations with these organizations indicates that the idea of such total
devotion to a single cosmic explanation intrigues Americans on a profound level. The well-ordered cosmos, the congenial universe in which
there is sin and punishment, hope and repentance, is no longer the public universe. It is acceptable to believe in such a cosmos, of course, but
it is also perfectly acceptable not to.

A culture does not travel such a great distance in moving from a
vision of pluralistic tolerance, to relativism, and finally to public skep-
ticism toward any absolute. Movement, to Cather, means movement
away. One does not go back. As a culture, this means that convictions
will serve only for a while before people move on. A migratory culture cannot believe in anything for very long, because it believes above
all else in the mutability of belief. It may also come to suspect the immutability of its own past, particularly if the past stands in the way
of future migrations. Those who cling to beliefs despite movements
in time and space must answer to charges of intransigence and fanati-

cism — or worse, of having made the wrong move. Religious conviction, in America, is a private affair once one progresses past some generic acknowledgment of God and a faith in something. *Shadows on the Rock* makes clear a culture's inability to survive without some sense of the sacred. It also makes clear that it is the function of belief, not the ideas themselves, that is rocklike, structural; the forms of the sacred pass over human experience like shadows.

Pierre Charron takes Cécile to stay with the Harnois family, and she is repulsed by the slovenly habits of this clan. Dirty linen, unwashed floors, soiled bodies — Cécile can barely survive in the atmosphere of neglect. It is not the conditions themselves that disgust Cécile but the human failure represented by the accepted level of filth. At the end of the episode the narrator concludes: "One made a climate within a climate; one made the days . . . one made life" (198). This realization comes to Cécile in the company of Pierre Charron and at the end of the section that bears his name. It is, in the logic of the narrative, the perspective of generations who consider themselves citizens of a New World. "One made life"; one was not given it by God or provided a destiny under the watch of divine providence. This conviction moves Cécile away from the Christian cosmology of the Ursulines, away from the ambitious faith of Jeanne Le Ber, and into the relativist existentialism of Pierre Charron. "I've known the time when dog meat cooked in a dirty pot seemed delicious," he tells Cécile to dramatize his point about survival in the wilderness. The experience of emigration and colonization has convinced Cécile that life is a constructed phenomenon and that she, like all her fellows, is responsible for the quality of life produced.

Cécile's belief indicates a turn in the culture's attention away from the past, away from European Catholicism, toward the future of infinite possibility in the Canadian wilderness. If one makes life, then what is made can never possess the ideological force of what is yet to be made. Desire is the constant animus in Cather's fiction, including the passion to move, to create. Freedom is demonstrated by the act of construction, not in a devotion to what is accomplished or revealed. Anything established — a faith, a belief, an account of the miraculous — threatens to curtail the very freedom it once represented should it hold validity for too long. The terms on which migratory consciousness envisions its own survival are transient.

By projecting a past in *Shadows on the Rock* that is so removed from the present, so foreign in the mode of thought re-created there, Cather accentuates the distance traveled between the origins of Quebec and modern consciousness. The novel also projects a sense of the human condition in which all structures of thought are transient, impermanent, migratory. If we are unable to envision ourselves among the Quebec colonists, the recognition only emphasizes our own sense of exile from the history represented there. Furthermore, the novel implicitly suggests that our own vantage point is next in line for future mystery: the world of miracles has passed away, and so too will the world of historical consciousness. Already the cultural condition of the American is to feel separated from the past, to look on the past as the storehouse of dead ideas, failed experiments, and naïve gestures toward improvement. As the U.S. national debt accumulates, hostility for the past (the inevitable position of the debtor) may become a national condition. Cather's novel provides a way of seeing contemporary frustration with historical consciousness as the indication of another passing shadow. Perhaps survival in the twenty-first century will depend, as it did in seventeenth-century Quebec, on our making the past into a world apart, something from which no debt can emerge that will impinge on the future. Cather claims that miracles cease when longing erodes; history may also lose its power over the present when desire overtakes memory. A migratory culture has within its structures of thought the means by which to move beyond history, to make the crossing into the next dimension of human consciousness.

Lucy Gayheart

Something in the way she moves
Attracts me like no other lover.
Something in the way she moves me.
—GEORGE HARRISON, "Something"

In the U.S. middle-class social order the imagination is vital to the maintenance of such notions as home, family relations, and community. An essentially migratory consciousness recognizes these values as abstractions. As people migrate the signposts of individual identity become less the matter of unconscious assumption and more the subject

of imaginative construction. What was given to the person in a traditionally rooted society must be sought after and maintained through
intellectual vigilance in a migratory culture. People who move to survive must carry in their minds essential definitions of the self and the
sacred as they continually travel away from familiar supports. Americans, by historical experience, are passengers, a nation in-between cultural affinities, a people under construction whose ultimate characteristics exist primarily in the future. To a community of purpose these
migrations into the imaginary are expressions of faith. Americans believe in the future because only there does the nation exist as a single,
harmonious whole; only in a projected "elsewhere" can historical and
spatial demands be reconciled. No such condition can be found in the
United States' past.

Cather's critics have always recognized her attempt to buttress the
imagined space occupied by notions of America with spiritual conceptions of national identity. According to Conrad Ostwalt, Cather was
writing at "an important crossroads for America—a time when Americans began to think of their land in secular terms rather than sacred
categories—a time when Americans lost and regained a meaningful
world" (31). Cather's novels, however, do not project new meanings or
new contexts by which to understand the significance of the American
landscape itself. Rather, they recast the relationship between human
beings and their environment so that what is sacred is not the land alone
but human migration across landscapes and frontiers.

Richard Giannone identifies pilgrimage as "the underlying movement in Cather's book-by-book exploration of the human quest for
wholeness" ("Willa Cather" 32). John J. Murphy builds on Giannone's
argument, charting Cather's "pilgrimages toward the integration of
personal and communal visions" and the casting of "a desire for an integrating spiritual context" in her novels ("Cather's New World" 33). A
sense of Catherian spirituality is located in the author's critical statements as well as in her fiction, and Cather's equation of art and religion is a familiar one among Cather scholars. God's laws, according to
a statement written by Cather in 1894, "are the laws of beauty, and all
the natural forces work together to produce it. . . . God's nature is just
a great artistic creation, and the zones and climes are only moods of
a Divine Artist" (*The World and the Parish* 1:117). Nonetheless, to take
the art and religion connection at its literal meaning is to risk an overly
simplistic understanding of the Catherian pilgrimage and to diminish
Cather's relevance to a secular culture.

The artist's imagination and what Colin Falck calls "our spiritual awareness" (xii) are the forces that mythologize phenomena, attaching meaning and transcendent significance to them. If we translate Cather's equation of art and religion into contemporary terms (for contemporary critics feel more than a little uneasy talking about divinely inspired creation), the equation points to ideology. After all, Cather is talking not about morality ("In nature God does not teach morals," she asserts in the previously quoted statement) but about the ideas and social equations that move human life. It is clear from her fiction, furthermore, that when Cather writes of pilgrimages and journeys, she is not employing figurative devices but means to evoke literal migrations and to explore the implications of American mobility. A critical emphasis on the Catherian idea of pilgrimage risks confusing migratory culture with traditional societies of stasis in which a journey is taken as an extraordinary expression of faith. To Cather, pilgrimage is a contemporary condition of being, part of the price of survival. No one makes a pilgrimage today, although some will attempt the extraordinary act of staying put.

At the end of the twentieth century the critical study of human motivation and expression on literary terms takes place not on moral or spiritual grounds but largely within the sociological and political vocabulary of ideology. Definitions of ambition, empire, migration, and rootedness are ideological issues, and critical arguments resort to textual analysis and empirical references, not divine authorization. Falck's idea of the "business of soul-making" (xii) is only one of numerous attempts in the late twentieth century to reinscribe the conception of spirituality (more often referred to as "the imagination" or "creativity") into literary discourse. A public declaration of human spirituality was something with which Cather's era was more comfortable than is our own. Nonetheless, the terms on which discussions of ideology and mythology proceed today often resemble quite closely the assertions about faith and spirit made by Cather's generation. Take W. J. T. Mitchell's assertion, for example, in *The Politics of Interpretation:* "Ideology need not be just a shameful secret; it can also be the body of values affirmed by a community" (4). In a religious era one has one's spirituality; in a politicized era one's body of values is a reasonable, ideological substitute. But, Cather would add, the rock is still there.

In a culture of migration the challenge to artists and critics is to formulate and articulate the realm of the sacred within the context of packed suitcases toted by birds of passage. Critical discourse has as its cultural charge the negotiation of the terms of intellectual survival, hanging its arguments on the aesthetic guideposts of the era. Willa Cather projects a frame of reference that can lead us away from dead-end theories of literal correspondence. If people migrate to survive, then migration becomes, in Cather's terminology, a great fact. As a great fact migration is the stuff of which life itself is constructed, the mirror by which we know ourselves and our destinies—like the land, the railroad, and the empire. In her three novels of human endurance, *Sapphira and the Slave Girl*, *Shadows on the Rock*, and *Lucy Gayheart*, Cather projects the terms of future survival within a migratory culture. These terms involve abandoning conceptions of existence grounded in securely rooted places and times—in literalism—in favor of a conception of the human condition grounded in continual uprooting and dislocations, in flight, and in the imagination of the future.

Lucy Gayheart (1936) cannot be read literally, for to do so obliterates its meaning. The first two sentences warn the reader against a simple correspondence between the plot and the meaning of the book: "In Haverford on the Platte the townspeople still talk of Lucy Gayheart. They do not talk of her a great deal, to be sure; life goes on and we live in the present" (3). So begins Willa Cather's great survival novel. *Lucy Gayheart* is a testament to the most supreme power possessed by the migratory, to take from the dead the grounds on which the future will be constructed, even if the construction is done over the dead bodies themselves. The townspeople still discuss poor dead Lucy, but they have concerns more pressing than eulogizing drowned adolescents. Employing the book's imagery, one might put it thus: the reader may easily skate across the surface of the novel and read it as a romantic tragedy, the story of a star-crossed young woman and her (possibly) bisexual lover, where everyone who seems to matter plunges to death, grabbed from underneath by lovers and other forces. On this level Cather makes a good teary story of it, the tale of Lucy Gayheart, "a bird being shot down when it rises in its morning flight toward the sun" (207). The townspeople imagine the dead girl "like a bird flying home"; she provides the town with a compensatory image, serving as a cautionary tale about the one that did not get away—a bird of stoppage.

Cather's startling sarcasm in the novel's opening passage sets the reader on guard, however, suggesting that the narrator holds another level of meaning in store. Lucy does not learn a great deal in her brief life, and her character is handled roughly by the narrator. She is "not ambitious" (34); rather, she is "mercurial, vacillating" (18), and she craves safety (117). On the whole, these are signal deficiencies in a Cather hero. Moreover, she returns home, reversing the direction in which Cather most often casts her characters' fortunes. Lucy is not talented and self-directed like Thea Kronberg, although she is smarter than Claude Wheeler and more self-consciously intelligent. When she comes on her own personal crossroads, however, at the death of Clément Sebastian, she hightails it home. According to the formula of ambition and migration, Lucy is a model failure. Nonetheless, the novel is more than the trashing of a weak young woman.

Before she goes under the ice, Lucy does reawaken to one great fact, which is demonstrated to her by the singer Clément Sebastian. The truth is that of the function of the imagination, a truth that Lucy can scarcely digest before its pull grips her from underneath and kills her. The same force that animates Alexandra Bergson, that Thea Kronberg seeks and finds at Panther Canyon, the vitality that compels so many in Cather's narrative projections, exists for Lucy as a kind of "tragic force" (31). It is as if the truth is too much for her. She cannot keep it foremost in mind in the face of the literal. In any case, the realization does not do Lucy much good; she dies never profiting from the revelation. She awakens too late to benefit. Despite its title, however, the novel is not about Lucy Gayheart in the sense that her consciousness or development is what ultimately matters. The narrative is more concerned with what the town of Haverford will do with Lucy's survival into the future as an idea or an image. Lucy projects a frame, or a context, through which the living might see their own situation more clearly. In *Lucy Gayheart* the title figure is not so much a fictional character as a cultural resource. In a migratory culture, Cather suggests, the dead (and their texts) become imaginary resources to be mined by the living to secure their future survival.

Cather remythologizes the spiritual dimension of American existence through the story of a young woman whose death inspires the townspeople to recall her in terms of moving images. In particular Lucy's biography transforms the life of a distinctly mundane and linear-minded businessman. Critics who have read the novel as a literal tale of love-struck adolescence and feminine weakness have missed even what Lucy manages to learn. "Until she began to play for Sebastian," Cather explains, "she had never known that words had any value aside from their direct meaning" (95). This realization temporarily changes the way in which Lucy sees the world and how the narrator treats her. Once

Lucy begins to see beyond literalism, Cather treats her more sympathetically, as if to say that now this woman deserves to be taken more seriously. Her newly acquired vision spoils her ability to tolerate Harry Gordon and ultimately leads her to despair and death. But if Lucy sees into the value of words aside from their direct meaning, readers of *Lucy Gayheart* are challenged to see into the meaning of the novel aside from *its* direct, or literal, signification. The novel's stress is not on poor Lucy's demise, in other words, but on the meaning of Lucy's life and death in the town, in Harry's Gordon's life, and ultimately, in the minds of readers.

David Stouck claims that *Lucy Gayheart* is Cather's "most complex novel philosophically" and that it contains "some of the author's most profound reflection on art and human relationships—above all, on the human condition as defined by mortality" (*Willa Cather's Imagination* 214). Stouck centers his analysis on images of Lucy Gayheart in motion, skating, running, expressing the essence of her vitality through movement. "The image of all living things unwittingly caught up in a dance of death informs the novel throughout" (219). Other critics have seen less to commend in Lucy's motion. Merrill Skaggs finds in Lucy's characteristic "rush of movement" a "movement that goes nowhere." Skaggs finds the character highly problematic for her "need to serve" and for her "lack of ambition" and thus locates the "primary moral" of the story in the negative example that Lucy provides: "the crucial importance of a woman's self-consciously and energetically choosing the direction of her own life" (156, 157). Deborah Carlin sums up critical difficulties with the novel by pointing out "the contradictory elements within Lucy's character," such as her concurrent desire for both individual autonomy and Clément Sebastian, for the freedom of a liberated woman and the shield of "a safe, masculine presence." These qualities "render her confusing to read, and they make it difficult to render her decidedly 'untraditional' development" (124). Both Carlin and Skaggs conclude that *Lucy Gayheart* ends up being as much about Harry Gordon as about the titular character.

Susan Rosowski, finally, sees the book as "a novel of slippages," "a text that contradicts its own laws." Rosowski cites the book's dominant image of "clinging briefly over an abyss" to conclude that "the yawning abyss of indeterminacy" lies just beyond the character of Lucy herself, "a character so insubstantial that we ask, finally, where she is in her own story" ("Writing against Silences" 72). This is precisely the question that the narrative asks in the opening and closing chapters of the text: where is Lucy? The cultural implications of the text begin where Lucy Gayheart disappears, where her character goes down into the black water, and with the confusion rendered by Cather's creation of the dense girl, the "dance with death" indicated by young Lucy's footprints in the sidewalk. We come to the edge of a Catherian abyss indeed, the abyss at which *Lucy Gayheart* becomes indispensable for understanding Cather's migratory aesthetics.

Most people, most of the time, live their lives in the here and now, skating across the surface of what is often referred to as reality, living life "in the present." Harry Gordon and Lucy Gayheart are excellent at this sort of thing, and all of Haverford's residents recognize their right to skate together. Harry's main contribution to the town, the installation of streetlamps, is emblematic of his commitment to clear, unimpeded surface vision. But Lucy senses that there might be more to life. After the skating party at the beginning of the book, Harry and Lucy ride home in his sleigh. Warmed and made drowsy by Harry's scotch whiskey, Lucy experiences the release of "another kind of life and feeling which did not belong here. It overpowered her" (11). Lucy's sense is that material existence may not be the limit of human life on earth, that there may be a spiritual dimension yet unrecognized by her. Cather is not constructing a romantic tale of awakening, however, and quickly qualifies Lucy's experience. "That joy of saluting what is far above one was an eternal thing, not merely something that had happened to her ignorance and her foolish heart." The glimpse of an alternative to skating parties is not liberating but burdensome, "too bright and too sharp" for Lucy, making her feel not larger and more alive but "small and lost" (12). A literal reading of this scene would find in it a rather cruel depiction of a mind just bright enough to recognize its own limitations. Lucy has nothing by which to measure this flash of recognition and so is frightened by it.

At this point it is useful to recall that Cather is writing fiction, that Lucy Gayheart exists only as a narrated image. To read the novel, or any novel for that matter, one must be able to suspend literal understanding to some extent. If this were not the case, the very first sentence ("In Haverford on the Platte the townspeople still talk of Lucy Gayheart") would make no sense because there is no town called Haverford on the Platte. Differences in critical comprehension occur regarding the point at which literal reading is invoked. No one will fault Cather

for creating a town called Haverford and placing it in Nebraska. There
is not even room for interpretation here; *Haverford* is meaningless, just
a name, and only an excessively literal reader would confuse the place
with the actual town in Pennsylvania. (Of course, this does not prevent
biographical criticism from assuming that it is a mask for Red Cloud.)
But what of Lucy Gayheart? In book 1, chapter 1, the character Lucy is
already dead. When her name is uttered, however, a physical presence
is evoked: "They still see her as a slight figure always in motion . . .
like a bird flying home." The chapter then proceeds to offer a series of
images of Lucy, in the winter, in the summer, walking, running, "they
always knew her by the way she moved" (4). Before Cather presents the
character Lucy, she provides an account of her name's evocative quality
in her community. Lucy is granted spiritual existence, or mythic significance, prior to acquiring a narrative presence. Before she becomes
a character in the novel, in other words, she exists as a legend, a communal memory. The narrator says that Lucy was missed when she left
Haverford. Her persistent image, then, serves a function, compensating for her absence, fulfilling some need possessed by the living. The
novel is constructed as the account of the process by which Lucy Gayheart is mythologized—in other words, the way in which she achieves
her distinctive, spiritual significance. *Lucy Gayheart* projects a situation
of cultural evocation; we might call her St. Lucy, patron saint of the
migratory dimension, the compensatory image.

Lucy made an impression on the Haverford townspeople, and she
continues to exist in that impression. "There was something in her
nature that was like her movements," and her nature is characterized
as "gaiety and grace." "Life seemed to lie very near the surface in her,"
and she was "talented, but too careless and light-hearted to take herself
very seriously" (4, 5). Nonetheless, her life is taken seriously enough to
be invoked by confidential glances ("Yes, you, too, remember?") and by
the narrator of *Lucy Gayheart*, who seems alternately hostile and sympathetic toward the girl. Lucy's attitude regarding herself and her life
is not as important to the novel as is the attitude that others held about
her, that impression's function on the living. Thus Cather introduces
the titular character to the reader as an image, an idea, a memory, an
impression made on her observers that persists, even though "life goes
on and we live in the present." Lucy Gayheart is the personification of
motion, of the quality of human movement so vital to Cather's understanding of social and cultural existence.

Literal depictions and historical artifacts of Lucy do not comfort the townspeople at all. "Photographs of Lucy meant nothing to her old friends," and the significance of her life cannot be captured by material means. At the end of the novel Harry Gordon wants to preserve her footprints in cement because of the "suggestion of quick motion" that the image possesses. He associates the prints with "the herald Mercury" bearing a message and a story for the living (227). What can the message be? In the novel Cather again and again warns against excessive literalism, stressing the centrality of the elusive meaning possessed by the imaginative act. The narrative teeters on an abyss, and we are tempted to read it through the fearful eyes of Harry Gordon's employee Milton Chase, the bank cashier: "It had made him feel older; made life seem terribly short and not very—not very important" (230). And life is not very important if all we can see is the death of some misguided American teenager. The message borne by the herald Mercury, however, the message captured in the cement markings, is that life extends far beyond material death and that the marks left behind—footprints, scratches in the landscape—are bought and paid for in the currency of cultural survival. Lucy is among Haverford's spiritual, mythic resources.

The novel might be considered in the same way that Lucy encourages Harry to view works of French impressionist art: "some are meant to represent objects, and others are meant to express a kind of feeling merely, and then accuracy doesn't matter." Harry Gordon cannot see this when the two meet in Chicago; he insists on accuracy. Regarding the liberties taken with the human body in the impressionist painting before them, Harry protests that "anatomy is a fact" and that "facts are at the bottom of everything" (101). Cather's novel as a whole suggests otherwise. Lucy Gayheart is presented as an idea and an image before she is presented as a character; in fact, Cather's initial description of her resembles that of an impressionist painting. Her walk is "like an expression of irrepressible light-heartedness"; in her eyes is "something direct and unhesitating and joyous"; on her mouth "every shadow of feeling made a change" (4, 5). Lucy Gayheart is depicted not as a fleshly character in the opening chapter but as a series of impressions meant to "express a kind of feeling merely," before assuming the function of a character in the novel.

As an impressionist novel *Lucy Gayheart* amounts to considerably more than a bleak tale of a short and unimportant life. If accuracy or the standard linear measurements of plot and theme are set aside, then the novel assumes another life. The novel is not about Lucy Gayheart but about the canonization of Lucy Gayheart, the processes and circumstances by which she came to represent something important to the community of Haverford, an image evoked by the snowfall or the summer heat. What does Lucy Gayheart mean? In her short life she was awakened to the knowledge that the world amounts to much more than the activities engaged in by Harry Gordon, those of buying and selling, loaning and collecting. Lucy awakened to the subtler levels of aesthetic realities and emotional authenticities and then plunged to her death: "She was young, she was strong, she would show them they couldn't crush her. She would get away from these people who were cruel and stupid" (198). And she does. Nevertheless, this is not what she means to those who survive her. Lucy is not a reproach to the town or to Harry but something of far greater significance to their material existence.

The twentieth century has confirmed Willa Cather's fears that Americans were becoming increasingly materialistic. The reliance on facts, statistical reason, and logical expressions pummels from cultural legitimacy the authority of the imagination as a source of knowledge. It may be inevitable, however, that a migratory people will attempt to create a solidity of facts to compensate for its real experience of impermanence and alteration. "The ultimate truths are never seen through reason," Cather wrote in 1894, "but through the imagination" (*Kingdom* 143). Even this sentiment has become a "fact," and anyone can say it without having the first intention of following it through. One can even take lessons in creative thinking. (It is under the spell of empirical truth that Cather's biographical critics can portray her art as primarily autobiographical.) Cather may have equated literature with religion because she saw in imaginative writing an emphasis on nonrational and associational ways of knowing.

Bernice Slote explains that for Willa Cather "the substance of a thing was in the spirit, and the spirit was in the experience" created by the fiction. "Facts that remained facts were like buckets of rattling marbles; to be art, they must be part of a body that could move and touch you, could stand with a personal presence. Art, it remained, was the experience" (in Cather, *Kingdom* 50). Slote may as well be describing the status of Lucy Gayheart in the opening chapter of the novel, her personal presence persisting in the town long after her physicality had expired, the substance of her life existing in her spirit. What Cather does, then, in the rest of the novel is to explain to the reader how

Lucy Gayheart passed from mere physicality to spiritual significance. The novel is about the transaction by which one woman's experience can produce a communal memory, as well as a personal one in the case of Harry Gordon. Because the novel as a whole narrates both the life of Lucy Gayheart and the process of her apotheosis, it must be read, finally, as the means by which material reality is transubstantiated into spiritual wealth. To use language more suited to the late twentieth century, *Lucy Gayheart* is a study in the making of cultural significance, the nonmaterial basis of secular existence, the body of values affirmed by a community. Lucy is among Cather's great migratory Americans: she emigrates into the imagination of those who survive her.

When Lucy travels from Haverford to Chicago Cather makes it clear that her journey is not simply physical. The "incalculable distance" that she covers stretches between two neo-Augustinian cities, the "city of feeling" and "the city of fact" (24). In the city of feeling Lucy transcends the popular, superficial definitions on which she has been raised and begins to learn the deeper meanings of experience closed off to most by common necessities. "A new conception of art? It came closer than that. A new kind of personality? But it was much more. It was a discovery about life, a revelation of love as a tragic force, not a melting mood, of passion that drowns like black water" (31). The conception of love as merely a melting mood is the idea held by Lucy the skater, the notion common to the dime-store romances and popular media within the city of fact. A melting mood is wholly absorbable into the empirical city, allowing three days off for a funeral or a week away after marriage. The revelation of love as a tragic force, however, as a force that transforms, overwhelms, and destroys the living, is the conception reserved for the city of feeling. Here Lucy confronts the romantic insistence that human passions are not absorbable, that they are in fact fatal to material realities.

The aesthetic existence of one drowned Lucy Gayheart may provide psychic resources to an entire town, an entire culture, where the city of fact is in ascension. "Some peoples' lives are affected by what happens to their person or their property; but for others fate is what happens to their feelings and their thoughts—that and nothing more" (32). In the city of feeling the power struggle between fact and emotion is reversed. When she leaves home, Lucy lives by her passions and desires for the first time in her life. "If only one could lose one's life and one's body and be nothing but one's desire," Lucy muses, "if the rest could melt away" (102). This kind of emotional purity, of undiluted spirituality, is what Lucy means to the town after her death. Her image continues to move across the community's consciousness as the emblem of release from the empirical city's material limitations.

Lucy's removal from the world of fact and necessity is dramatized in the scene where Harry Gordon proposes to her. To convince him that no means no, Lucy "lies" to Harry concerning her relationship with Clément Sebastian. He asks her how far the relation has gone, and she responds, "How far? All the way; all the way! There's no going back. Can't you understand *anything?*" (111). Cather explains that Lucy "had tried to tell him the truth about a feeling; but a feeling meant nothing to him, he had to be clubbed by a situation." What Lucy tells Harry is in fact a lie, but within the city of feeling it is truthful. Lucy had gone all the way in her emotions, and she could never go back to being the girl in Harry Gordon's sleigh who could not comprehend another existence. Lucy's lie effectively kills any feeling that Harry has for Lucy, kills him emotionally. When the two confront each other at the end of Lucy's life, when Lucy appeals to Harry for help in the snowstorm, it is Harry's turn to lie, claiming to have no time to stop and give her a ride. His lie effectively kills her—not spiritually (she dies returning to "light and freedom") but physically, dead in the city of fact.

The survival of Lucy's spirit is made evident by its effect on Harry Gordon's life. Through the example of his transformation Cather explains the compensatory function of Lucy's image in the town as a whole. Lucy had suffered for lying to him, but his treatment of her and his refusal to allow her even to explain herself leaves him "tired and beaten" (209). He withdraws from his marriage, goes off to war, and returns a changed man. "Years ago he used to fight against reflection," Cather narrates. "But now he sometimes felt a melancholy pleasure in looking back over his life" (214). Lucy's death catapults Harry out of his limited existence and affords him a glimpse into the city of feeling. "The world in which he had been cruel to her no longer existed" (220); Lucy ceases to be a painful reproach to him and becomes "the best thing he had to remember" (223). More than that, Lucy comes to represent the substance of his belief in another dimension of living. She is the source of his own sense of fulfillment, a quality that transcends his business dealings and at times makes his banking decisions seem "shocking" to his cashier, Milton Chase. "In the course of the years queer things

had happened which Milton could never explain; things which were out
of order, which ought not to occur in business" (212).

Cather defines the function of Lucy's image in Harry's conscious
existence: "He is not a man haunted by remorse; all that he went
through with long ago. He enjoys his prosperity and his good health.
Lucy Gayheart is no longer a despairing little creature standing in the
icy wind and lifting beseeching eyes to him. She is no longer near, beside his sleigh. She has receded to the far horizon line, along with all
the fine things of youth, which do not change" (224). Lucy has become
the rock in Harry's psychic existence, a quality that passes in the city of
fact but is eternal in the city of feeling. She is to Harry what Clément
Sebastian termed "youth, love, hope—all the things that pass" (69).
To the town as a whole, Lucy is movement, "a slight figure always in
motion" (3); to Harry, her footprints possess "some baffling suggestion
of quick motion," the symbol of human passions, "swiftness, mischief,
and lightness" (227). Moreover, as Cather establishes in her novels of
migration and movement, of ambition and empire, these are the qualities of the American rock, valued above all else by the migratory culture
at large. After Lucy's death her deficiencies do not matter; they are not
useful and so they are forgotten.

Lucy tries to do something that no Cather character can do, something that even Cather herself found impossible—she tried to go back.
In Cather's mind, according to Edith Lewis's memoir, "one does not go
back" to origins (43). As Lucy's neighbor observes on Lucy's return,
"It used to be as if she were hurrying toward something delightful. . . .
Now it was as if she were running away from something" (146). This reversal is culturally fatal, and having made the decision to return home,
Lucy begins her journey to death. Godfrey St. Peter had made a similar regression in *The Professor's House*, nearly dying in his pursuit of his
younger self. Back in Haverford Lucy is constantly confronted by the
demands of the city of fact: her family debt, her sister's sacrifices, her
physical status as a local curiosity. When she finally realizes her mistake, she experiences "a purpose forming" in her mind and wishes to
"take some plunge or departure" (182). At this point her own limitations resurface, however, and the best that Lucy Gayheart can envision
for herself is to imitate Clément Sebastian. "She must go back into the
world and get all she could of everything that had made him what he
was" (184). She even imagines renting his studio and assuming his place

in the world. But to pursue Clément is to pursue death, and Cather has Lucy "plunge" rather than depart or ascend.

If Lucy were more like Thea Kronberg, she would be more acceptable as a kind of martyr to female ambition, but Cather is not concerned in *Lucy Gayheart* with a tale so conventionally romantic. The fact that Lucy is so limited, so obviously disappointing in her own thoughts and in her own life, only emphasizes the point Cather projects in the text. The novel's significance lies in the use to which Harry Gordon and the town as a whole put Lucy's memory. Lucy is an imaginative frame of local reference. Compensation is taken by the living, by those who negotiate the terms of cultural survival. That Lucy herself did not embody in fact what she eventually becomes in spirit only underscores the novel's concern with her mythogenesis. Ántonia Shimerda Cuzak, recall, was not quite what Jim Burden saw in *My Ántonia*. It is the gap between fact and feeling, the incalculable distance traveled by the mind in pursuit of spiritual meaning, that *Lucy Gayheart* examines. The living take what they must have to survive, just as the young take from their elders. It never enters Lucy's mind, for example, to repay her sister for Pauline's sacrifices. On the contrary, Lucy "never seemed to think about money," even though the family farm has suffered for its support of Lucy's education. "She refused to be poor in spirit" (172). Lucy conceives of no debt to the past, no sense of historical determinism that may delimit her desires. She is seen by others as pure movement. When she dies Lucy becomes a natural resource in the spiritual life of Haverford.

In Chicago, among the musicians and music teachers, Lucy is recognized as a someone with limited talent and ambition (134). In fact, those very limitations make her suitable as a substitute accompanist. Lucy's vision is far from encompassing. Cather makes it clear that Lucy's perception of Clément Sebastian is only partial, that she comprehends only a portion of the world in which she has immersed herself. Cather continually suggests that there is much more to Sebastian than the reader gets from Lucy's view of him. Lucy sees him emerge from the cathedral, convinced "that he had been there with a purpose that had to do with the needs of his soul" but without a clue as to what constituted or satisfied those needs (136). Neither does Lucy realize what she provides Sebastian, why he hired her instead of a professional accompanist. Rather than characterize Lucy as ambitious, Cather makes a point to cast her as without a will of her own: "she herself was a twig or a leaf swept along on the current" (75). In the narrative of Lucy's life in Chicago, Cather makes it impossible to read anything less than disappointment out of the character. By all standards Lucy Gayheart is a limited young woman, not the stuff into which inspiration is embodied. Nonetheless, the need of the living for images of irrepressible light-heartedness, for gaiety and grace, is not qualified by fact or by the limitations of empirical reality. Lucy Gayheart has little to do with what those who survive her remember about her.

The characterization of Clément Sebastian serves to underscore the purpose that Lucy will eventually serve in Haverford after her death. Sebastian mourns the death of his own youth, the emptiness he feels as he drifts away from the city of feeling under the demands of scheduling and professional travel. Cather assigns to his consciousness an American migrant's lament:

> Life had so turned out that now, when he was nearing fifty, he was without a country, without a home, without a family, and very nearly without friends. Surely a man couldn't congratulate himself upon a career which had led to such results. He had missed the deepest of all companionships, a relation with the earth itself, with a countryside and a people. That relationship, he knew, cannot be gone after and found; it must be long and deliberate, unconscious. It must, indeed, be a way of living. Well, he had missed it. (78)

Sebastian's situation speaks here to the condition of all Americans who migrate, whose relation with the earth is often limited to transitory landscapes. His attraction to Lucy is in part due to his perception of her as "struggling to get a foothold in a slippery world" (80), struggling to survive above all else. He is drawn to "the rush of feeling in her warm young voice" (85), to precisely the same qualities of motion and vitality that will eventually inform the memories of Lucy possessed by Haverford and Harry Gordon.

The price of survival that Sebastian's profession extracts from him is, not incidentally, the price of cultural survival in the United States. A severance from home and family and the lack of connection to any particular place or people arouse sympathy for the musician. The sympathetic treatment of this man is accomplished against the odds of a standard plot situation that would otherwise cast him as the villain. Sebastian Clément, after all, fits the profile of a man who takes advantage of his position of power to seduce a protégée, a course of action usually deplored in contemporary society, although it persists as the subject of fantasy in formulaic romantic fiction. Cather, however, manages to shift the reader's sense of disappointment away from Sebastian and onto Lucy for sublimating her aesthetic desires and for putting herself in a position where "He could sweep her existence blank with one word" (88).

Cather enforces Lucy's diminution by portraying her as living vicariously through Clément. When she is separated from him and does not hear from him, she believes that "the important thing" is that "all was going well with Sebastian" (114). In Chicago for the first time, Lucy senses a new freedom: "for the first time in her life she could come and go like a boy" (26). Cather makes it clear, however, that Lucy is not liberated by this freedom but ultimately anguished because "there was nothing sure or safe in this life she was leading" (117). Furthermore, her self-doubts produce in her the fear that one cannot, "after all, live above your level." If you try to do so, Lucy believes, you drop "down, down, into flatness" (118). One conclusion to draw here is that Lucy Gayheart dies because she attempts to have more than she can withstand, that her desires far exceed her capabilities and her emotional resources.

Lucy Gayheart thus occupies a middle ground between the wildly unattainable fantasies of success represented by such rags to riches stories as those of Horatio Alger and Thea Kronberg and the insistence on material limitations represented by adherents to the city of fact. The young tart Fairy Blair, with her short skirt and her "fresh little mouth" (14), represents the culturally feminine version of such limited ambition. Lucy Gayheart is the embodiment of a specifically Catherian mythology, involving the negotiations between ambition and self-fulfillment, a kind of commuter life between the city of fact and the city of feeling. Her apotheosis in the town emerges out of the facility with which her memory, after her death, addresses the specific anxieties that arise from paying the price of cultural survival in Haverford, U.S.A. Somehow, Lucy speaks directly and confidentially to the needs of the living.

Lewis Simpson has explored the relationship between imaginative literature and the demands of modern consciousness. "The portrayal by the novelist of the struggle for consciousness against its own imperative to internalize history—and thus to acknowledge its loss of divine authorization and its utter dependence on itself—affords an index to the novelty of modern existence" (269). According to Simpson, the rise of the novel in the nineteenth and twentieth centuries has "completed the transfer of man, world, and God into mind" (275). In *Lucy Gayheart* Cather charts a similar transaction. The significance of Lucy Gayheart's life does not lie within God's judgment of her; it does not even rely on the rather harsh judgment of the narrator toward her intellectual limitations. The final arbiter of Lucy's life is in the minds of her survivors, in the use to which her memory is put. Harry Gordon wants to preserve Lucy's sidewalk footprints not because he wishes to honor her existence but because he wishes to authorize his own internalization of her. "Was there really some baffling suggestion of quick motion in those impressions, Gordon often wondered, or was it merely because he had seen them made, that to him they always had a look of swiftness, mischief, and lightness?" (227). The narrative emphasis is on his latter assumption, the principle of impressionist art itself. Harry Gordon may not have understood this aesthetic method at the art museum in Chicago, but he does finally learn his lesson. Authorization lies in the impression made on the witness, and "accuracy doesn't matter."

The glimpse into the city of feeling experienced fleetingly by Lucy Gayheart becomes the substance of her image as it persists in the minds of Harry Gordon and of others who remember her. The plight of Clément Sebastian, the migratory man, is the predicament of all who attempt to see in Lucy an authorization for their own homeless existence. In the absence of divine authorization, the price of survival is the creation of images and the quest for impressions that endorse the desires and situations of the living. The value of the image lies not in the image intrinsically, in other words, but in the projection it casts across the minds of its witnesses. It is the function of the image (or the text) in the present that determines genuine meaning. Original signification is irrecoverable, or if it is discoverable, it comes with the price of its own inevitable anachronism. Lucy herself was not the woman that Harry Gordon recalls, and neither was she the image possessed by the town of Haverford. But this is of no consequence. In a Catherian worldview it is the shadow cast, not the rock itself, that possesses functional meaning. Transferals of bodies, meanings, and cultures characterize the intellectual situation of the social order. This is a world of cultural transaction.

If Lucy's actual experiences were uncovered for Haverford in the name of accuracy, if her limitations could be explained along with her romantic delusions, her suicidal love for Clément Sebastian, what would be accomplished? The town would be surprised to learn that, in her heart, Lucy may have had more in common with Chicago's tramp population than with its successful artists. In the city Lucy "thought she had never before seen so many sad and discouraged people. Tramps, wet as horses, stood in the empty doorways for shelter" (62). The homeless hold for Lucy the same fascination they hold for all migrants. When she senses that she will not become a part of Sebastian's life, that there is in fact no place for her in that world, the city tramps "seemed like companions, and she felt a kind of humble affection for them" (63). When Lucy returns home her neighbors know that she has somehow encountered failure. Nonetheless, her importance to the town lies not in her inadequacy but in the attempt she makes to transcend those limits. Lucy serves a function in the present. The image that she casts across Harry Gordon's mind compensates for the mundane nature of his daily tasks and provides a context for the construction of his own integrity. Her brief escape and tragic death remind the townspeople as a whole that their own settlement is merely a contingency.

Cather insists on the primacy of mind over material, of the imaginative over the factual, as the means of cultural subsistence. A cultural spirit based on material resources will inevitably fail to survive. Lucy's own spiritual survival was dependent on the life of Clément Sebastian and so drowned along with his body. If we listen today to the endless literal projections, we will hear that we will run out of food, the water will be poisoned, the sun will burn out, the ozone will blast away, and a new disease will kill us all. The odds have always been against human life and will continue to mount if we rely exclusively on literal observation and material resources for survival. Had Harry Gordon depended on Lucy Gayheart's physical existence, he would never be able to draw sustenance from the footprints she left behind. The price of cultural survival is paid out of its spiritual resources. If those resources are limited or confined to destructive tales of limitation and violence, the culture may not be able to subsidize the demands of the living. *Lucy Gayheart* suggests that Lucy's significance is not in her death but in her flight, in the refusal to allow material circumstances to dictate the imagination, the stand against accuracy as a reproach to creation.

Cather's fiction ultimately is drawn to the capacity of a culture and a people to meet the price of survival. Through *Lucy Gayheart*, a novel in many ways fashioned to disorient, Willa Cather emphasizes that it is the witness who creates the significance, the shadow that authenticates the rock. As an epistemological principle, the primacy of the witness and the privileged position of the survivor is indispensable to an understanding of Willa Cather's literary project. It is this quality that defines her novels as being among the resources of American culture, projecting in monumental terms the community of purpose, the common future of a civilization in transit. What distinguishes Cather's work further, however, is her lifelong meditation on the links between the culture of migration and the world empire that it eventually produced. Cather projects a clear vision of the nation's global capacity, connecting the truism of individualized American ambition with the more controversial fact of empire.

4

Ambition, Empire, and the Great Fact of America

Think Globally / Act Locally
—BUMPER STICKER

Even the Chinese philosopher [Confucius] was wise enough
to regard the individual as the basis of the empire.
—HENRY DAVID THOREAU, *Civil Disobedience*

The Song of the Lark

Very early in *The Song of the Lark* (1915) Cather makes connections between her main characters' ambitions and the nation's movement toward empire. When Thea Kronberg and her friends take a Sunday expedition to the sand hills, a place of "constant tantalization" to Thea (40), the first significant suggestion of the novel's imperial theme occurs. The trekkers are resting, each "busy with his own thoughts" (46), and the narrative turns its attention to Thea's mind. She was "recalling a great adventure of her own" that she undertook earlier, when she accompanied her father on a "reunion of old frontiersmen" in Wyoming. They visited the pathways of migratory pioneer wagon trains. Thea recalls being moved to tears when she saw the dozens of trails,

> deep furrows, cut in the earth by heavy wagon-wheels, and now grown over with dry, whitish grass. The furrows ran side by side; when one trail had been worn too deep, the next party had abandoned it and made a new trail to the right or left. They were, indeed, only old wagon-ruts, running east and west, and grown over with grass. But as Thea ran about among the white stones, her skirts blowing this way and that, the wind brought to her eyes tears that might have come, anyway. (47–48)

The furrows are evidence of human ambition, of repeated efforts to make new trails across an unyielding landscape, and they touch Thea as a kind of validation for her own aspirations. The trails form images of restated, unflagging persistence toward an unknown destination, emblems of an "unusual power of work" (153), a capacity Thea also possesses. The narrative then establishes a configuration of resonant images that weaves this individual style into a larger pattern of empire.

While Thea meditates on the wagon trail, eagles fly over the sky above her, the symbols of empire. Meanwhile, the old man who serves as the Kronbergs' guide on this summer expedition explains to Thea that he was in Brownsville, Nebraska, when the first telegraph message to cross the Missouri River was received. Here Cather inserts into *The Song of the Lark* the mythic American first message: "Westward the course of Empire takes its way." The guide's story has a profound effect on Thea, and she recalls it "when she sighted down the wagon-tracks toward the blue mountains. She told herself she would never, never forget it" (48). She never does, and in the novel Cather makes universal Thea Kronberg's desires and aspirations by linking them in time through the recurring symbol of the indigenous eagle. Eagles appear among the ruins of ancient people, overhead in the sky above the trails of the pioneers, keeping watch over the Americanization of the continent by the Moonstonian middle class.

It may be that the one obligation possessed exclusively by a country's literary artists is to render the story of the nation into poetic form. Willa Cather wrote her novels between 1913 and 1947, precisely the years in which the position of the United States as a world power solidified. Her life spans the close of the western continental frontier and the opening of the global imperial frontier, from the settling of the American continent to the height of what has been called the American Century. Of all her great contemporaries, however—including Faulkner and Hemingway—Cather alone confronted the poetic potential of a transnational, American empire in the process of formation. Although William Faulkner projected a global, indeed cosmic, scope in *A Fable*, the emphasis of his work overall is on relations within a fixed and established American state. And while Ernest Hemingway sought to link continents in his fiction, portraying the fate of Americans in Europe socially and at war, a conception of the nation itself as a developing force was not foremost in his narrative purposes. Willa Cather, however, went about a serious project of writing that depicts a burgeoning

American presence on the face of the earth as a historical force of spiritual dimensions.

Critics have discussed *Death Comes for the Archbishop* as historical fiction and have recognized that it transcends that literary genre. Readers have also considered *One of Ours* as a critique of militarism and global ambition but sense that its meaning, too, is limited by that categorization. These two novels transform the American empire into epic material. By this I do not mean that Cather is an apologist or a propagandist; she was too thoroughly a modernist to settle for or even engage herself in celebratory paean. Instead, Cather came to see the emergence of an American empire as another great fact, an inescapable part of life, as rocklike and immovable as the weather in *My Ántonia* or the land in *O Pioneers!* The essential benevolence of this empire, or the potential evil it possessed, was beside the great fact of its presence; it was, simply, a force to reckon with in art. *Death Comes to the Archbishop* parallels the expansion of the nineteenth-century American empire with the spread of Christianity in premedieval Europe. The implied narrative correspondence suggests that the strength of an empire depends on its people's possessing an idea and that this aspect of humanity provides an unstoppable motivation for mobility. In Cather's vision empire requires motion, expansion, and restlessness; empire depends on a population convinced that it holds something that must travel. *One of Ours* focuses on an individual American man and demonstrates how the logic of empire—or its ideology—informs private decisions and makes sense of private dilemmas. What distinguished Cather in these novels is that she takes empire as a political fact and depicts life within the context created by that historical contingency. The scope of her literary vision is consistently global in its projection of a spatialized conception of history.

Americans do not talk about their empire; it is not the topic of dinner conversation in the way that imagined Victorian social intercourse contained comments about the state of the British flag abroad. Professional critics are not any more inclined to bring up the uncomfortable fact of the American cultural (and military) dominance underscoring the vitality of any literary canon that is produced in the United States. But this neglect of empire cannot continue. Amy Kaplan has noted "the absence of empire from the study of American culture" in the introduction to a volume of critical essays intended to address that absence (Kaplan 11). Canon debates, for example, are tied inextricably to empire. Regardless of what the critics decide is canonical, and even if the idea of canon is discarded entirely, underlying all debates over specific literary value is the assumption that it truly matters to the rest of the world what texts are produced and read by Americans. If it did not matter, there would be no debate. It is only because the whole world is watching that Americanist critics are empowered in the first place. Much of the explicitly political discussion surrounding American litera-ture arises from typically isolationist motives: the fate of those within our own borders, of people who are not among the privileged class of the white, male, healthy, and employed. Once again, however, it is only the position of empire that makes the plight of the underclass relevant to literary discussion. If the United States were not an imperial power, it would not matter as much who was in charge of the mediocrity.

Despite the presence of empire, then, empire is not discussed. It is nevertheless a force, demonstrated, for example, in certain academic programs. It is considered an academic honor to be selected for a Fulbright Grant, an essentially imperial program. Fulbright lecturers in American studies bring U.S. texts abroad and teach young non-Americans the names, plots, and situations of American literature. The program is highly formalized, a system of selective reward in the United States and a source of subsidized labor in a world market of professorial scarcity. In a foreign classroom the literature professor is an imperial agent. The professor's words, chosen texts, and arguments are com-pletely secondary to the great fact of presence. Like Bishop Latour, the professor has come in possession of an idea; what the idea is does not matter, for the natives will probably misunderstand it anyway. Nonethe-less, the natives will be struck, and probably converted, simply because the idea is strong enough to bring its agent this far from home. That, finally, is empire in the Catherian sense. Any idea that will carry people far from home, that will induce them even to relocate, to migrate, to settle, and then to share the idea with others (or impose it on them), possesses the quality of imperial force. Once the idea was Christianity. Now the idea is America.

The particulars of the imperial idea are not crucial. They may be contradictory, but they must by necessity be encompassing. The prolif-eration of stories about Christ in the fourth century contributed to the intellectual and spiritual migration of the new religious force. Cather's attention was all over the continent in her effort to conceive and project the various forms of the American idea: the Southwest, the Midwest, the Northeast, the South, and Canada. Literary criticism today, as an imperial force, is also "all over the place" in projecting the vitality of the empire's voice: the traditional canon, women's studies, African American studies, race and ethnicity, and Chicano/a, Latino/a, gay, lesbian, and queer studies. These endless divisions appear as fragmentation but are actually the force of the universalist, transhuman impulse of Americanism. The epoch of historic crossing from points abroad into the United States has passed. The debates over canon and inclusion that take place today, however, do so in an intellectual Ellis Island, where the great migrations of ideas and texts pass through and are stamped, validated, and often renamed (Hispanic? Chicana? Latino?) in the process. Even so, these parochial battles are meaningless beside the great fact that the battlefield is *here*, in the United States. It is within these borders that the future of the world is being negotiated.

To comprehend the workings of the American empire within the daily tasks of its citizens, connections between local activities and global relations are drawn. The popular bumper sticker, "Think Globally / Act Locally," is a Green party statement meant to foster ethically responsible environmental behavior. Nonetheless, it is more sensibly understood as an acknowledgment of imperial status. Only in the United States do local decisions have global implications; only here is a global context relevant to local decision making. The links between local ambition and global empire are seldom made so explicit. It is as if these links are portions of plain good sense. The connections assumed by common knowledge are all too often the equations least articulated and examined.

The Song of the Lark describes a young woman's ambition and ascent to great success. It has attracted interest among feminist critics for its depiction of the development of an independent, artful female voice, for its statement of literary independence from "Moonstone" (Red Cloud) by Cather herself, and for its serious treatment of feminine achievement. It is all these things, of course, but the novel also has a persistent imperial undercurrent that unites its elements into an even grander, epic statement. Tom Quirk, acknowledging the novel's status as an American success story, points out that Cather "sought . . . to connect the resources and achievements of her artist to the life of the republic" (143). By paralleling Thea Kronberg's individual ascent with national aspiration, by grounding her consciousness thoroughly in "the spirit of human courage" that "seemed to live up there with the eagles," Cather's text suggests that this story be regarded as an epic of imperial design. In *The Song of the Lark*, that is, Willa Cather demonstrates the essential links between homelessness, migration, historical passage, provisional loyalties, and the development of a new world imperial force. At the end of the novel, moreover, Cather projects, with arresting accuracy, the sense of loss that accompanies world dominance. The portrait of Thea in the last section of the novel can provide a frame for reading the national angst over the American century itself.

In the second section of Cather's novel, entitled "The Song of the Lark," Thea comes to possess a sense of herself and of her commitment to achievement. In chapter 8 of this section Cather makes plain the logic that begins with the ethos of individualism and culminates in the will to create an imperial force in the world. Cather chooses the high-speed, relatively uncomfortable Denver Express train as the setting for the scene, with an enduring Thea juxtaposed to an anonymous, sickly girl, emphasizing the ideology of individualist success and failure. Thea has compassion for this girl, but she also possesses a revulsion for her, "the natural contempt of strength for weakness" (190). Thea, then, in motion on the fast-moving train, is placed in a microcosmic, social Darwinian setting as her thoughts turn to the prospects of her own success. She envisions herself fulfilling her own particular destiny, "as if she had an appointment to meet the rest of herself sometime, somewhere. It was moving to meet her and she was moving to meet it." This meeting was as sure as the "hole in the earth" that awaited the sick girl behind her (189). Thea compares the hole in the sick girl's future with the one in her own past, the death of Ray Kennedy and the insurance money that funded her stay in Chicago. Within the individualist ethos, every success is got at the expense of another failure, and although the trains are filled with "young people who meant to have things" (190), many of them will get nothing. If Cather were to leave the narrative at this point, she would have created a tale of simple aspiration, but the chapter continues to build on the image of its fast-moving trains.

Thea is heading to Moonstone for the visit that will convince her that she can no longer consider that place her home. En route on the Denver Express, however, her mind is filled with the mythic significance of a migratory population. Thea, like her mother, "believed in immigration," believed in the central ideology that in America one is "given another chance" (191). Turning her thoughts to her sense of home, Thea "was glad that this was her country." She believes that the land possesses a destiny that is new to the world. Her thoughts then turn to her dead friend and sponsor, Ray Kennedy, and Cather finally names the feeling that has animated Thea on the Denver Express train: "He, too, had that feeling of empire," Thea reflects. The logic of chapter 8, then, moves along a simple, direct track. It begins with individual, restless ambition (the emblem of which is migration) and moves to a sense of physical and intellectual superiority based on the simple good fortune of survival. The track then terminates in a feeling of empire. The implication here is that what unites Americans of consequence (Cather is clear about such distinctions and is never sentimental over losses) is this specific feeling that Ray retained, "as if all the Southwest really belonged to him because he had knocked about over it so much." According to Thea, "that feeling . . . was the real element of companionship between her and Ray" (192). This is the attitude of possession displayed by Cather's major figures (Outland and St. Peter, Alexandra Bergson, Jim Burden), the sense that by being here, by coming here, working here, and thinking here, the "Spirit of the Great Divide" yields the rights of dominion—for a little while. In Cather any such possession is always transitory, subject to subsequent transaction.

The cultural logic of imperialism suggested by Willa Cather implicates every American gesture toward individual distinction as contributing to the American empire. Every act of immigration, every continental migration, each man and woman's attempt to succeed by endorsement, critique, or attack on the social order, is in and of itself an advance of the national culture as a whole toward an imperial position. Thea is not thinking simply of the purity of art as she advances her career. She is not committing herself solely to beauty or to voice or even to song. Her ambitions are clearly animated by such aesthetic devotions, but Cather explains that it is much more than this that motivates Thea Kronberg. Thea is rising from nowhere, from the comically named, lowbrow town of Moonstone, from a preacher's family that, in Cather's treatment, is a prototype for Sinclair Lewis's more baldly satirical depictions of the Midwest. But Thea draws strength from the old faces of withered and wasted immigrant men and women at her father's church, faces that are "mysteriously marked by Destiny" and decline in her memories of them (115). In the same way that Alexandra's countenance was the first to look on the Great Divide and see agricultural wealth, Thea's is the first face to look on those "who have worked hard and who have always been poor" (113) and see cultural wealth, her own potential for greatness, and the seeds of empire.

There are two Catherian great facts in *The Song of the Lark*, one fleeting and the other perpetual. Early in the novel Dr. Archie looks on the summer moon and thinks: "For the time being it was the great fact in the world" (36). In the context of Dr. Archie's Moonstone, the full moon represents a settled existence, an established practice in an established town. He does not believe in it, however, and throughout the novel he looks for something more. Why is he in Moonstone? Why are any members of his generation there? "It isn't as if we'd been born here," he tells Thea, and it is not as if he has any commitment to the place; he just happens to have shown up there for the time being, like a phase of the moon. "The railroad is the one real fact in this country," he eventually concludes. "That has to be; the world has to be got back and forth" (72). The solid fact of *The Song of the Lark* is embodied by the railroad, moving the course of empire westward, paralleled by the telegraph and its imperial message. The railroad not only has brought them all to Moonstone but represents as well deliverance from the various phases of settlement. Thea takes the railroad back to Chicago, then to New York, and eventually to international dominance. The railroad gets the plot of the novel back and forth and gets Thea out of Moonstone for good. The railroad is the avatar of U.S. transit.

Crucial to the novel are Thea's complex emotional relations to family and friends in Moonstone who believe in and help her. The people of Moonstone who recognize greatness in Thea conspire to get her out of the town, remain available to sustain her in times of personal and economic crisis, and know also that the exchange is not an even one. Thea's belief in her self-sufficiency is sharply qualified in the novel, for Cather makes it clear that one does not climb without stepping on something or someone. Although Thea tells Ray Kennedy that "everybody's up against it for himself, succeeds or fails—himself," the novel bears out not her words but Kennedy's response. Kennedy tells her that "there are a lot of halfway people in this world who help the winners win, and the failers fail" (108). Cather will underscore this man's sense of the mechanics of ascendancy when the insurance on his life funds Thea's first trip to Chicago, financing the initial step of her success. It marks the supreme wit of Cather that Ray Kennedy is trammeled by the novel's emblem of ambition and empire, the railroad engine. Ray becomes a victim of another man's helpful negligence. The narrative makes it clear that to achieve greatness, Thea must believe that only she is capable of cultivating what she possesses; whether she knows it or not, however, she cannot succeed alone. Thea's illusion of self-sufficiency is ideological. It is no fault of hers but rather a condition of her success.

Those who aid Thea on her way know that they will receive nothing in return. At the same time, Thea can take from them the full realization that although gratitude is appropriate, repayment is contingent on success and convenience. All Thea's loyalties are provisional. On her deathbed Thea's mother articulates the sense that the best of one's children, "the bright ones," as she says, "get away from you" (343). Mrs. Kronberg's death marks a decisive Catherian crossroads for Thea. Had she returned to her mother's side when her mother called for her, Thea's artistic career would have stalled, if not derailed. A compassionate daughter would have gone home; an ambitious one would not. Thea's success depends on her own comprehension that loyalty has its limits, including fidelity to home, to lovers, and to her own mother.

The novel makes absolutely clear that Thea's rise to prominence is built on an inner, illusory sense of complete self-sufficiency. She feels beholden to Ray Kennedy, surely, and she is also grateful to Dr. Archie for his help and to Fred Ottenberg, her parents, and her town, but none of this gratitude is equivalent to a willingness to qualify her ambition or influence her next move in any way. Thea is, if we place ourselves at a distance, away from the narrator's obvious affection for her, a ruthless woman. Because she is truly talented, there are many who will underwrite her and live vicariously through her successes, but Thea is under no obligation, felt or imposed, to repay or to sacrifice for others. In fact, she associates such burdens with self-destruction. Thea communicates the necessity of avoiding volitional dependence on others in the story she tells Fred Ottenberg about the jealous husband who danced his adventurous wife "over the edge of the cliff" to their death (243). Thea must take help from others, but she will be destroyed if she allows herself to be led by the desires of these others. Cather can make this no clearer than by having Thea refuse to answer her mother's deathbed request for her presence.

Thea's is an ambition that brooks no interference, that interprets the world around itself in terms of obstacles and opportunities but never as causes or burdens. As one who "believes in immigration," Thea learns a vital lesson from her migratory forebears: "The past closes up behind one," she says at one point, "one can't go back" (286). More than that: even in cases where one *can* return, one does not have to; in fact, one must not. Implicit in the great crossing from one continent to another, and then from one sense of self to the next, is the obliteration of past loyalties and all the confining, sentimental obligations surrounding the idea of home. Thea's mode of thought about the past, her obligations, and the burden of history are an intriguing Catherian projection of an American ideology. To believe in immigration is likewise to disbelieve in settled allegiances and to devalue any past that does not "close up behind one." A persistent past is an interfering past, one that must be let go or thrown over. An empire with no history to serve, no obligations and no home, is an empire that exists only in the future. No wonder, then, that most do not recognize it from the inside.

It is important to see beyond Thea's articulation of artistic commitment to her fierce determination. Her artistic pronouncements, especially those realized in Panther Canyon, provide her the ideals she must have to sustain her radical break with home, family, and passion. Similar to Jim Burden's belief in Ántonia, the inspiration that Thea takes from the ancient cliff dweller women compensates for the detachment she has from her own origins. In Panther Canyon she emigrates intellectually from her Kronberg ancestry and bonds herself to a tradition of artistry ("a long chain of human endeavor" [264]), learning the rhetoric of aesthetic creation that can support her ambition. Among the ancient people Thea fulfills her migratory destiny: "There was certainly no kindly Providence that directed one's life; and one's parents did not in the least care what became of one, so long as one did not misbehave and endanger their comfort. One's life was at the mercy of blind chance. She had better take it in her own hands. . . . Yet she had clung fast to whatever was left of Moonstone in her mind. No more of that! The Cliff-Dwellers had lengthened her past. She had older and higher obligations" (266). Just as the migratory man and woman break ties to family, home, and community and enter an "older and higher obligation" to human mobility, so too does Thea realize that her familial loyalties are only a small part of her humanity. This is, after all, what it means to believe in immigration: ties to family and home are provisional and can be overridden by higher obligations, such as those represented by art, religion, profession, or simple flight. The list is really endless once one accepts as fundamental the role of migration in human existence. Under such circumstances, staying home is the departure from the norm, and permanent residence is only a temporary fact, like a phase of the moon.

The American eagle's presence in the midst of Thea's reveries of inconstancy ties her ambition again to its wider, imperial significance. The appearance of the symbolic national bird validates Thea's migratory self-confidence and connects her at once both to an ancient civilization and to a burgeoning contemporary empire. Cather's Thea is not simply an exceptional woman but rather is portrayed as a woman of emblematic success and achievement, a heroic type, like the great farmer-speculator Alexandra Bergson or the great scholar-mythographer Godfrey St. Peter. Thea is a woman of ambitious drive who, simply by going about her private story of success, contributes to a highly politicized, national story of empire. As she lies in the sun, content with the realizations she has come to among the dwellings of the ancient people, an eagle, "tawny and of great size," passes overhead. Thea's mind is then filled with a sense of "endeavor, achievement, desire," a sense of oneness with the desires of races, peoples, and selves (277). The configuration of historical, continental, natural, and imperial forces amounts to an aesthetic statement of considerable ideological weight. It is common in the twentieth century to separate peoples from governments and to assign imperial activities to the latter, absolving the populace from such endeavors. Willa Cather suggests otherwise in this novel, connecting individual consciousness to the formation of empire in a gesture of literary correspondence. In the Panther Canyon configuration Cather assigns to individual responsibility the shape of world history, denying the possibility of distinguishing the local from the global.

A configuration of opposite forces appears in the novel's two tramp incidents. To a migratory people, the homeless tramp resonates as a sinister representation of the threat of destinationless migration, of futility and failure, much as the homeless population figures within national media assessments today. Migrants without destination (or vagrants) are often vilified, according to Paul Carter, because they represent repressed desires, the fear and the shame of a displaced people (7). Mrs. Kronberg gives the tramps a half-dollar to vacate the place where she wants to picnic, but their presence menaces her. "She hated to think how many of them there were, crawling along the tracks of that vast country" (106). The second tramp, the one that haunts Thea's mind, looms larger still. When Thea was a child "the dirtiest and most utterly wretched-looking tramp she had ever seen" had passed by her house, and she covered her nose to block "the terrible odour about him" (119). She regrets this display of disgust because the tramp notices it and is embarrassed. The degenerate condition of this man is drawn further by what he must do for money, dressing in a clown suit and handling rattlesnakes for popular amusement, offering to eat one for a dollar. He is eventually arrested and forced out of town because there is "no provision to grubstake vagrants" in Moonstone (120). The saloonkeeper kills the tramp's rattlesnakes (his source of income). In response the tramp writes an obscenity on the town's water tank, marking it as his gravestone before jumping inside to his death. Typhoid fever spreads as a result, six children die, and Thea spends a good deal of time "trying to make herself realize what pitch of hatred or despair could drive a man to do such a hideous thing. . . . How could people fall so far out of fortune?" (121).

The story of the water-supply tramp is among Cather's more resounding. The children who ingest the "bad water" from this man's highly inscribed suicide die, and their deaths lead the city council to pass tougher laws about tramps. Presumably, vagrants will henceforth be escorted out of town. To Thea, however, the tramp's story is the underside of her own ambition. Her achievements will sustain others as strongly as the tramp's signal accomplishment destroyed them. She tells her mentor, Howard Archie, that people should have helped the tramp instead of driving him out, but Archie's words correct any such charitable impulses: "Ugly accidents happen . . . always have and always will. But the failures are swept back into the pile and forgotten. They don't leave any lasting scar in the world and they don't affect the future." Archie concludes with words that Thea will later embody: "The people who forge ahead and do something, they really count" (122). At this crossroads Cather could have created out of Thea a servant of the people, a helpmate or a goodwife. Archie tells her to forget the tramp, but Cather's narrative suggests more than that. As Thea leaves Archie's office she is "happy, flattered, and stimulated," and throughout that summer she experiences "a desire to run and run about those quiet streets until she wore out her shoes" (123). The ambitious response to the tramp's death (and to the unlucky, thirsty children) is elation and desire, the satisfaction of survival. The text then endorses this response with Ray Kennedy's accidental death. Immediately following the tramp story is the train crash that sweeps Ray Kennedy back into the pile and enables Thea to forge ahead.

Thea goes on to make an unqualified success of herself, but her achievement is less satisfying than the terms on which Cather stipulates its possession. Nonetheless, the novel's final sections are crucial to its meaning. At the close of *The Song of the Lark*, in the section coldly titled "Kronberg," Thea is a hardened, solitary, wholly consumed artist. Howard Archie suggests that she lacks a "personal life, outside your work," to which Thea responds patiently that her work is her personal life. "It's like being woven into a big web" (380). The entanglement of her work, she says, her devotion to it, "takes you up, and uses you, and spins you out; and that is your life." There is no time left for lovers, conventional lives, or commitments to other human beings or institutions. All Thea's passion is devoted to her career; her loves and hates are bound up in her aesthetic ideals and in her will not merely to survive but to achieve greatness. The cliff dwellers taught her "the inevitable hardness of human life" (386) that justifies her fervent nature and the decisions she has made. Lasting marriage is impossible, and friends are maintained subject to their own willingness to endure. "I've only a few friends," she explains, "but I can lose every one of them, if it has to be" (389).

The chill of "Kronberg" is the air of imperial ascendancy. An empire, once formed, takes on its own perpetuation as its primary purpose. Thea speaks in her final textual appearances with unchallenged authority. She has dwarfed her mentor, Howard Archie, she has withstood with unparalleled dignity the affair with Fred Ottenberg, and she has survived a near marriage to Nordquist. As artist and as the textual personification of empire she is untouchable. She is her own reason for being, and by each word uttered and with every gesture committed she articulates and defines what that greatness is. Thea decides as well what she will remember and what she will discard, recalling only what contributes to her ascendancy, forgetting the things that may drag her down. At one point, earlier in the novel, she induces fear in Fred Ottenberg by the "elevation" in her eyes, a look described by Cather as one that "had no memories" but was purely "unconscious" (314). Thea refers to it as "an animal sort of feeling" (386). Cather's Thea Kronberg is not simply talented or gifted, a woman of genius; she is also, quite significantly, in possession of tremendous power.

The one great fact in *The Song of the Lark* is the railroad: "The world has to be got back and forth." The American social order depicted in the novel is one of "general scramble" (160) where ambitious people grab at and exploit one another for gain. It is a world of fortuitous accident and unfortunate error, a milieu dominated by an ideology of individualism and provisional loyalty. Ambition and empire are its great watchwords, the simultaneous enactment of a continuity in American culture at the levels of self and social order, tied together by the bonding force of migratory consciousness. In the novel's epilogue Thea has become an icon in Moonstone, bringing comforting, compensatory memories to the old, and to the young, dreams. In Thea's story is invested considerable value, and on her example is built a social system that implicitly rewards mobility, provisionality, and mutability. Traditional homage to home, fidelity, and stability are voiced as compensation for losses, but these notions hold little motivational value to the ambitious. The successful ones at all levels, from simply "staying afloat" to world domination, move away from these values as easily as they migrate away from their sources—origins, families, and "permanent" residences.

Thea's angst at the end of the novel is real enough, but it is not the stuff of melancholy or regret. The fulfillment that her performances bring to others is "the only commensurate answer" to the question of her purpose and value. Outside of that function, she may indeed wonder about "the good of it all" (399). At the novel's close she serves on the stage the same idea that had motivated her and those who produced her in the past, the idea that "closed roads" are to be opened and all "the gates dropped" (398) that stand between stasis and movement. *The Song of the Lark* can be read as the story of female empowerment and voice, but only narrowly. In the context projected by Willa Cather's migratory aesthetics, the success story of individual female ambition becomes an imperial gesture, a definition of how and why out of this country and at this time the eagle soared and the empire reared its head.

One of Ours

My good knights . . . I shall tell you the plain truth.
Whoever remains in one spot stands to lose.
—*The Poem of the Cid*

One of Ours (1922) is not a conventional war novel, neither a narrative in the classic tradition of heroic deeds and eternal gestures toward greatness nor a novel in the modern war tradition of lost innocence and grand futility. Cather is not concerned with grace under pressure, with masculine transformation, or with issues of command, loyalty, courage, or conscience. The novel does not try to become war fiction in the classic

manner, by making sense of a man's war experience, or in the modernist tradition of using the conditions of war as a metaphor for society
as a whole. Rather, *One of Ours* traces the historical logic that follows
when the destination country of the immigrant becomes an economic
and military world power. This war novel has been recognized as one
in which Willa Cather "shifted her vantage point toward the relationship of America to its European heritage" and toward the formation
of an "American consciousness" out of the combination of frontier and
immigration experiences (Rosowski, *Voyage* 97). *One of Ours* centers on
the productivity of the United States: wheat fields that feed the world,
industries that power the machines, and the main focus, a culture that
produces eager, devoted soldiers willing to die for all of it. The novel is
Cather's most political book for its overt concentration on the American turn toward active, global militarism. Jim Burden's wheat fields feed
the world; "that feeling of empire" transfixes the nation; thousands of
Thea-like women and men restlessly conceive of the world as their personal theater of operations—the globe, in short, becomes an American
possession.

Claude Wheeler is a Thea Kronberg mass produced in wholesale
quantities. He possesses none of her talent but all of her dissatisfaction
with the status quo. He feels that he deserves something more than his
middlebrow, farmer-class origins can deliver. He is a small man with
big plans, a limited, conventional mind with delusions of greatness.
He is also, however, in command of tremendous resources. He has a
very wealthy national benefactor known as his Uncle Sam, who finds
him "worth the watchfulness and devotion of so many men and machines, this extravagant consumption of fuel and energy" (230). Mul-
tiply Claude Wheeler by hundreds of thousands and extend his mind
to the national culture as a whole, and what emerges is a clearly articulated sense of Cather's America: the birth of empire, the spread of
U.S. ideals on an international scale, packaged and delivered like canned
goods across oceans and continents, right to your door.

Back in Nebraska, in the first half of *One of Ours*, Claude senses a dead
end in the American dream. The business creed has left him spiritually vacant, puritanical sexual mores have left him high and dry, and the
prospect of farming for the rest of his life has created in him a brutish,
mulish solemnity. But to plow the land under the rhythms of empire!
To man the assembly line with the compensatory dream of international
dominance! Or better yet, to escape drudgery altogether and become

a soldier! While he is an American soldier in France, Claude's vision of empire compensates for his suspicions that the United States is producing a spiritually vacuous culture: "He had begun to believe that the Americans were people of shallow emotions . . . and if it was true, there was no cure for it. Life was so short that it meant nothing at all unless it were continually reinforced by something that endured; unless the shadows of individual existence came and went against a background that held together" (328). What enduring thing would serve to reinforce the short life of the average American? For Jim Burden it was Ántonia; for Professor St. Peter, Tom Outland. A nation cannot be constructed on the basis of individualized alternatives to mundane existence, however; at least, an *empire* cannot be so built. In *One of Ours* the enduring background underlying the nation is the persistent, national narrative of imperial ascendancy. Everyone should keep their suitcases under their beds, ready to answer the call of duty. The idea that will unite the immigrant nation, then, is the casting of its concerns and its values across the globe. The world will become, as Cather saw in her novel about the fallen soldier, an American place.

One of Ours situates itself on a liminal moment in American history and on a central dilemma in its culture. The moment is when the nation made its turn away from hemispheric isolation toward involvement in a major European war, thus introducing the term "world war" into the international vocabulary. Historically the process extended from the era before the Great War until the eve of World War II, continually refining and expanding the application of American interests abroad. Nonetheless, the terms of the transition are laid out clearly in the novel. It involves the unsolved "question of property" (68) and the closing of the American frontier (100), as Claude realizes. It also involves the adaptation for the United States of the conditions of "the great argument" of German expansion: "preparation, organization, inexhaustible resources, inexhaustible men." What Cather centers on is not simply a historical moment but also a recurring dilemma in American culture. What is the global role of the nation of immigrants? Is the United States a safe refuge from the world or the next stage in world development? From the former come the American isolationists; from the latter emerges the American mission. In isolation one can cultivate the arts of music and agriculture as ends in themselves, but a nation with a mission knows music as something to march (or dance) to and knows its farms as the wheat fields and cornfields that feed the world. America may be exempt from history, or it may represent the course of future historical development; in either case, a migratory consciousness will be convinced that the nation is not constrained by past examples of imperial failure. Its soldiers can march confidently over the ruins of a succession of historical empires.

Claude Wheeler, the novel's main focus, moves from being a circus-going, vain, isolated farm boy ridiculed by his father and pitied by his mother to an international war hero who has died for France in a kind of martial apotheosis. Before the war began, Claude defined Ameri-can life solely as "buying and selling, building and pulling down" (328). Until the war came, Claude tells his friend David, "the world seemed like a business proposition," controlled by small-minded men made emblematic by his brother Bayliss. "Until the war broke out, he had supposed they did control it; his boyhood had been clouded and ener-vated by that belief" (339). The force that animates the United States is the spirit of free enterprise, the businessperson's creed, but as an ex-pression of human spirituality the creed lacks both the grandeur and the sense of purpose that had built European civilization, erected the great cathedrals, and led to the construction of the Americas by Euro-pean interests. Once the businessperson's creed becomes a global force, however, winning wars through unprecedented rates of industrial pro-duction and sustaining universal influence through ideological sales-manship, then the vacuous spirit of enterprise is transformed into the century's new order, into the modernist politics of media leverage and population mobility. Grandeur and purpose are accomplished through military and economic vastness and through awesome levels of produc-tivity. In other words, in the American empire, spirit will follow power on the profit margin.

Much of Claude's soldier musings hearken back to the creation of an American ideology based on war-making capabilities. As he listens to the sound of the guns he hears the pounding articulation of a new ide-ology: "What they said was, that men could still die for an idea; and would burn all they had made to keep their dreams. He knew the future of the world was safe; the careful planners would never be able to put it into a strait-jacket. . . . Ideals were not archaic things, beautiful and impotent; they were the real sources of power among men" (339). In European culture power did flow from the force of ideas, from the ideas of Christianity, democracy, liberty, nationalism. In the U.S. culture that would supplant it, however, the relationship between power and ideas is reversed. The empire of the United States, in Cather's projection, will produce a culture based largely on the expression of force. Claude thinks to himself that ideas are the sources of power among men, but he comes to this realization only after witnessing the military power of his country. Claude's ideas about sources of power, then, emerge immediately from his exposure to the military capacity of the United States. In the American Century the military and economic might of the nation becomes the source of the ideas that will characterize its social order and its culture.

The ideal that Claude dies for, the idea that moves thousands of American Claudes off the prairie, onto the troop ships, and out to the trenches of the Great War, is the economic, military, and political capacities of the United States of America. The war proves to Claude's mind that Americans are not shallow thinkers. They are not an isolated breed of narrow-minded businesspeople, grabbing and taking, buying and selling. The war proves to Claude that they "cared about something else," something articulated not in market shares and crop acres but in the "distant artillery . . . choking to get something out" (339). Before the war the United States may have been a cheap, materialistic alternative to European culture, a destination for the poor and the failing, an unformed and awkward nation of second chances. Once the United States enters the war, however, it is clear that this nation is not only a destination in space but the very future of world history itself. The logic of this new empire is worked out in the rhythms of the battlefield.

Claude's fellow soldier David Gerhardt embodies a discredited alternative to the victorious middle-class ideal represented by Cather's hero. David is a violinist, an artist. If it were not for the war, Cather, author of *Song of the Lark*, might have written about him, but the war has put such innocently ambitious romantic endeavors in the past. The theoretical link between ambition and empire, emblematized by the appearance of the eagle in Panther Canyon, has become incarnate in the military power of America. The cost, however, is Thea herself: there will be no more room for her aesthetics in the new order. The new American empire will not be constructed around or even communicated in the language of art and music. Claude thinks David should be exempt from war, but David knows otherwise. "Oh, one violinist more or less doesn't matter! But who is ever going back to anything?" he asks (330). David then tells Claude that "the young men of our time had to die to bring a new idea into the world . . . something Olympian" (331).

Neither he nor Cather names what the men have died for, but it sounds imperial. David has given up his art for it (although, good boy that he is, he did make enough recordings, capitalizing on his uniform on the album cover, to provide economic support for his mother), and he and Claude will die for it, too. An entire literary generation will find itself lost to it, and Cather herself will sense that the world broke into two generations, those before and those after, around the threshold of this Olympian thing. The ideals of art are not worth dying for and will not motivate a nation. The ideals of war, on the other hand, of heroic deaths and open markets—these are the sources of greatness.

To those of us who have been raised on American wars and who have no conception of a United States without an army, navy, air force, marine corps, CIA, or NASA can hardly read *One of Ours* without some sense of bewilderment. The conclusions hardly seem surprising. The entire history of the nation as it has been taught to us, from the Indian-hating Puritans through the Persian Gulf War, has been a relentless expression of firepower. Of course, the historians who write the story of America in this way were born in the middle of this century, after the world broke into two Olympian pieces. Richard Slotkin, in three volumes of cultural analysis, has traced the history of American violence and warfare as an ideological force based in this central thesis: "The first colonists saw in America an opportunity to regenerate their fortunes, their spirits, and the power of their church and nation; but the means to that regeneration ultimately became the means of violence, and the myth of regeneration through violence became the structuring metaphor of the American experience" (*Regeneration* 5). In *One of Ours* the structuring metaphor of violence imbues the character of Claude and defines his range of opportunities in Nebraska, Colorado, and abroad. Indeed, Stanley Cooperman describes Claude as possessing the qualities of a war lover: "stimulation by violence; dutiful application of 'ideals' to sanctify violence; and . . . the translation of violence into erotic fulfillment" (169). Cather's novel reminds the reader that what has become, at the end of the twentieth century, a thoroughly naturalized structuring metaphor of American existence is a cultural design, the product of historical choices and the particular construction of the American state.

The national history as we know it today has been written by Claude Wheeler's heirs, by historians who have written under the sound of the guns. Millions of Americans have since shared the sentiment of Claude's orphan friend, Albert Usher, that "the U.S. Marines are my family. Wherever they are, I'm at home" (229). Indeed, Usher's feeling has been so convincing, so typical, that many other marines have experienced tremendous difficulties returning to civilian homes after the conclusion of their war assignments. Cather describes American troop ships as "simple and great thoughts, like purposes forming" in the United States to be fulfilled abroad (218). In the context of this novel the American military is among the culture's most profound ideas. It is often at the forefront of social change, especially in the arenas of civil rights. Its weapons research has poured into the marketplace a steady stream of consumer goods and services, including computer software, microwave ovens, and mobile phones. Historically, it is difficult to find great changes in the United States that did not either result from or coincide with war making of some sort: national independence, manifest destiny, emancipation of slaves, voting rights, Volkswagons and Toyotas, the internet, global empire.

When the immigrants and their descendants in *One of Ours* return en masse to Europe, they do so as a conquering army. Throughout the century Americans will return to past or future sites of immigrant origins in the uniform of the U.S. armed services. When the military fails, as it did in Vietnam, the nation experiences a kind of paroxysm, not because Americans cannot fathom failure, but because the culture cannot survive the exhaustion of its fundamental national doctrine. From a historical perspective, however, the military defeat in Vietnam is mitigated significantly by the thousands of Southeast Asians who have emigrated to the United States since 1975. These latest migratory Americans have been inspired largely by Americans in uniform. The source of Cather's inspiration in *One of Ours* is the meditation on this idea of a military culture. The U.S. military is the incarnation of the national spirit; its ties to the culture at large, to industry, and to production levels express an American national faith, "the real sources of power among men."

Cather's novel captures an ideological situation in which numerous sources of human power intersect to enact an empire of unprecedented dimensions. The means of American business (buying and selling) intersect with the frontier myth of regeneration through violence (the bloody tests of faith) to produce the common experience that will unite the Claudes and Davids of America into one powerful idea. The forces that Thea saw as her enemies (materialism, opportunism, capitalist hucksterism) will now combine with the idealistic vigor that sustained her (spirituality, ambition, confidence) in an unstoppable combination of materiel and spirit not seen on earth since the height of Christian internationalism in the thirteenth century. The war in *One of Ours* will also transform the rest of the world from its status as the raw material of America's immigrant population to the end product of U.S. culture. War may interfere with business and cause market failures, and business may interfere with war and confuse alliances, but if war and business are aligned, an empire of migration will crisscross the globe. Similarly, art and business may be contradictory, but war can unite them in such icons as David's wartime recordings of classic violin music, sold to soldiers' mothers by mail order. Throughout Cather's novel the forces that might have provided narrative tensions—the gender division represented by Claude and Enid, the generational division between Claude and his father, the division of ideals between Claude and Bayliss—are trivialized in the face of the incorporating force of the Great War. The war becomes the great fact in *One of Ours*, greater than the weather, greater than the railroad, providing explanatory meaning (to make war) to the question Ray Kennedy asks in *The Song of the Lark*, "why are we here?"

As Claude walks through the war ruins of the French countryside, he is disheartened by the destruction. The scene looks like "a great dump-heap," a disaster area resembling the results of a "cyclone or a fire." He is cheered up, however, when he comes on makeshift shelters constructed by the returning French population, "little wooden barracks made from old timbers and American goods boxes." The names on the boxes are familiar to him: "From Emery Bird, Thayer Co., Kansas City, Mo.," and "Daniels and Fisher, Denver, Colo." (307). Here is evidence of the global value of "building and pulling down." The image is repeated when Claude reaches his destination and visits the home of Mlle de Courcey. The woman claims that "this war has taught us all how little the made things matter. Only the feeling matters" (312). Cather's narrative contradicts her pre-Americanized sensibility, however. Mlle de Courcey proudly shows Claude her storeroom "stocked with rows of coffee tins, condensed milk, canned vegetables and meat, all with American trade names he knew so well; names which seemed doubly familiar and 'reliable' here, so far from home." She then tells Claude that "the town could not have got through the winter without these things," that "they made the difference between life and death" (311). Consequently, although Mlle de Courcey says that she believes made things to matter little, Claude thinks proudly to himself that "his country had a long arm" (311). Long after the war is over, Mlle de Courcey will still eat food from cans and keep her storehouse filled with American-style products. *One of Ours* is an acknowledgment of how much the made things do matter in the world of American construction. In the empire the idea of made things will inspire men and women into heroic action and will sustain a cultural style.

The very first scene in "Bidding the Eagles of the West to Fly On," the novel's war section, captures the transformative power possessed by the idea of made things. Claude has been separated from his command and is "utterly confused and turned about . . . with no idea where he was going" (261). He is found by Sergeant Hicks and a group of ten hungry American soldiers who are badgering a shopwoman for cheese, falling on her supplies "like wolves" (262). They pay her well (with "open palms full of crumpled notes"), confident that they are backed by "shiploads of money" en route to Europe (263). The shopwoman thus comes face to face with historical change:

> She liked them, but not the legend of waste and prodigality that ran before them—and followed after. It was superfluous and dis-integrating in a world of hard facts. An army in which the men had meat for breakfast. . . . Their moving kitchens and supply trains were the wonder of France. . . . Nobody had ever seen so much food before; coffee, milk, sugar, bacon, hams; everything the world was famished for. . . . All this was not war. . . . It was an invasion, like the other. The first destroyed material possessions, and this threatened everybody's integrity. (264)

The world's integrity is indeed threatened by the American invasion of soldiers, material goods, and consciousness. The world's character and identity will be changed forever by the shiploads of money, the "tinned provisions . . . piled like mountain ranges" on the French countryside. The idea of made things means that the trail of endless supplies, "ship-loads of useless things," will become cultural necessities because the world will be constructed around the functions that these made things possess—art through phonograph records and movie houses, information through radio broadcasts, food and sustenance through canned (mobile) goods. *One of Ours* is teeming with a cultural moment. We live not, as the shopwoman thinks, in a world of hard facts but in a world of manufacturing, movement, and change where the great facts come and go. The Catherian century of migration has arrived in her shop, and it devours (like wolves) the way the Old World was before the Americans began to move back to claim it as the possession of the New.

There are moments in history that expose tremendous transformations at work or reveal the hidden forces that underpin the movements of a culture. Events that expose the extent of U.S. military power are moments of awesome self-confrontation for many Americans. The transfer of thousands of troops and what was called "a city as big as Seattle" to the desert of Saudi Arabia during the Gulf War provoked one such instance of awe, an instance of national pride that was not at all contingent on the actual outcome of the war. Although the war achieved only part of its purpose, it was rightly called a symbolic victory because the stakes had less to do with the enemy state of Iraq than with the political and cultural vitality of the United States of America. There is another side to the fact of a military culture, however. In the early 1990s the United States experienced a severe economic recession. At the same time, the collapse of the Soviet Union, which put an end to the cold war, meant that for the first time in fifty years less money was necessary to meet perceived defense needs. As a result numerous army and navy bases in the United States were closed. What these events revealed, however, was not the boon of a peace dividend but the civilian economy's tremendous reliance on military spending. Over the course of their nightly broadcasts, the television news programs interviewed restaurant owners, barbers, storekeepers, and other American entrepreneurs who claimed that they would lose their livelihoods with the closing of the military installations. The closing of the bases in 1993 demonstrated a fundamental truth projected in *One of Ours:* the American economy, and U.S. culture as a whole, is propelled and animated by the idea and the hard facts that the military and its various incarnations produce.

The strength of Cather's novel lies in the steady unfolding of its narrative, through which it demonstrates the place of the military within the cultural logic of the United States. Everything in the novel, everything that happens to the Wheeler family, to Claude, to Claude and Enid, to Gladys, and to the local economy in Nebraska, leads inexorably to war culture and to an imperial American style. This cultural logic, however, was produced by the overt policy aims of the U.S. government and military services. The war effort of the Wilson administration was not confined to simple reactions to events in Europe, but included as well an impressive, successful domestic campaign aimed at the American populace. The German threat to France was as tangible as soldiers at the door, but the German threat to the United States was a matter of ideological construction. David Kennedy describes the function of such governmental agencies as the National Board for Historical Service, which distributed materials to high schools and colleges for courses in "War Issues." The primary purpose of this curriculum was to establish German blame for the war (57). "More than the other belligerent governments, the Wilson administration was compelled to cultivate—even to manufacture—public opinion favorable to the war effort." Kennedy thus describes the home-front campaign as "the deliberate mobilization of emotions and ideas," making the Great War in the United States "peculiarly an affair of the mind" (46).

Cather's novel projects a culture that is moving toward a conception of war as the ultimate articulation of national purpose, a conception as strong as any spiritual orthodoxy. This conclusion is reached on numerous levels—economic, religious, social—that converge in the fate and figure of Claude Wheeler. To Claude, enlistment appears like a vision: it is a natural, salvational gesture on his part. After the war the efforts of soldiers were granted mythic significance by postwar initiatives that have never subsided in the twentieth century. In 1919, before all the American troops had returned home, officers of the American Expeditionary Force in France founded the American Legion "to preserve the memories and incidents of our association in the great war . . . to consecrate and sanctify our comradeship" (Kennedy 217–18). The affair of the mind, then, began concurrently with troop mobilization in the Great War, but as an American idea it has never demobilized. The sacredness of war participation is a major component of American culture, embodied and articulated in monuments, holidays, and public rituals of remembrance and re-creation.

Cather does not focus on the efforts of either President Wilson or the American Legion in her novel. She does, however, describe the conditions under which men like Claude Wheeler came to accept the war as a natural occurrence and, more important, as a welcome relief from social and cultural stagnation. The success of the Wilson administration is measured not by the numbers of people persuaded by its propaganda but by the extent of the population unaware of its migration from one mode of consciousness to another. Although Cather does document the way in which Claude must change his thinking about Germans ("He had always been taught that the German people were pre-eminent in the virtues Americans most admire; a month ago he would have said they had all the ideals a decent American boy would fight for" [136]), the novel is not really concerned with war propaganda. *One of Ours* is less valuable as a historical document than as a cultural frame or a projection of a cultural process. There is little government in the novel, outside the state-supplied war information printed in the newspapers that are read by the Wheelers of Nebraska. There is a great deal of intellectual shifting that is tracked in the mind of Claude, however. In *One of Ours* Cather describes one particular quality of migratory consciousness, its natural susceptibility to external manipulation. It is a quality of mind— ambitious and egotistical, restless and politically resourceless—that we can begin to recognize as Cather's commonly patriotic American.

The population at large in *One of Ours* has no trouble modifying its thinking about Germans. It moves from the systematic assimilation of German immigrants to a vicious ostracism of them and from a conception of German culture as "pre-eminent in the virtues Americans most admire" to an equally sincere abhorrence of those qualities. "Even to these quiet, wheat-growing people, the siege guns before Liège were a menace," Cather narrates, "not to their safety or their goods, but to their comfortable, established way of thinking" (137). It is precisely their established way of thinking that is being transformed by artillery overseas. The pounding guns at Liège will be translated for them in the same way the artillery on the battlefield is made significant to Claude, as articulations of empire. The destruction of war is presented to and understood by most Nebraskans as "something new, and certainly evil . . . at work among mankind" (138). Political discussion in *One of Ours* is limited to the government news reported in local newspapers, and almost everyone accepts the Wilson administration's perspective on the war. Claude returns home from training camp, "a conspicuous figure" in his uniform, and travels through the countryside at harvest time, "the season when it is most itself" (199), when it fulfills its natural cycle. Claude the American is harvested as a soldier. The minds of his civilian compatriots are in turn harvested for the war effort. Wartime, to push the analogy one step further, is the season when the culture as a whole "is most itself," when its logic is fulfilled.

There are only a few exceptions to the general sense of the war as good versus evil. One is Ernest Havel, the intellectual who lives in "an atmosphere of mental liberty" (12), something that seems quite naturally to close him off from his fellow citizens. Claude finds him to be intriguing but also beyond his own intellectual grasp. Havel, however, does not depend on U.S. government sources exclusively for news of European conflicts. He sees the war as "the harvest of all that has been planted" (136), and Cather uses his character repeatedly to indicate her awareness of European politics. On the prairie, however, such intricate political arguments are not relevant. Another minor challenge to the Wilson administration is Troilus Oberlies, the increasingly unpopular local German farmer who favors Germany in the war. Cather's brief allusion to the disloyalty charges brought against him and another German farmer raises the issue of an immigrant nation's partisan involvement in warfare based on national rivalries. The hearings are set by Cather, significantly, in an American town named Frankfort. The Frankfort judge's advice to the two men is that they should not mean what they say and that they must not be loyal to any government aside from that of the United States (197). As the name of the town is transferable, so are political loyalties. The judgment is the only one possible to a migratory consciousness: do not forget where you are. Nonetheless, the sympathetic treatment that Cather gives to Ernest Havel and the two German immigrants indicates that she sees the progression of events and ideas, both spontaneous and manufactured, as depriving the American population of the full range of political alternatives available to the nation as it moved to influence European geography.

The title of the novel's opening section, "On Lovely Creek," signals the discontinuities that characterize the section as a whole. Lovely Creek is home to a social order where rustic turmoil is normal — fathers ridicule their sons, people marry the wrong mates, men of intelligence are ostracized, and men of mediocrity rise to economic power. The section is one of sustained disappointment for the prosaic Claude Wheeler. He is an unexceptional boy with exceptional desires. He is ambitious. He thinks of himself as being much greater than his circumstances, and he cannot settle for a life of farm drudgery. At the same time, he lacks any talent, resource, or conception of what it is he might do in the world other than be a disgruntled, sexually deprived appendage of some plow team.

Cather does a tour de force on Claude and dissatisfaction. He hates the way he looks ("a perfect block-head"), he despises his own name ("a 'chump' name"), he has "a sharp disgust for sensuality" produced by his father's masculine ethic, and he cannot seem to rise above the "clumsy, awkward, farmer boy" manners that seem to suit him for nothing but agricultural labor (16, 49, 85). He attends an inferior college not because he is unable to enter a better one but because his parents do not value the difference. He is marked as a sucker by tailors and salespeople.

Nonetheless, he knows himself well enough to know what he must fear: "accepting cheap substitutes," making "easy compromises," and "being fooled" (30). These are certainly the demons with which Claude must do battle. His countenance projects the look of one who has "a bridle-bit in his mouth," but his mind yearns for "something splendid about life" (46). When Cather wrote a version of this character type in "Paul's Case," it was a tale of desperation. For Claude Wheeler, however, the war provides a solution to all his discomforts, physical, social, and intellectual. It even relieves him from the onerous task of choosing his clothes.

The twentieth-century American adolescent Claude has a clear insight into the gap between what America promises and its social realities. He finds "the importance of making money or spending it" to be spiritually constricting (33); he sees that the love affair with machinery "could not make pleasure" (38) or substitute for it. His exposure to the more worldly Erlich family only emphasizes his sense of being trapped by small minds with petty concerns. "There had never been a man so strong or so good that he had escaped. And yet he sometimes felt sure that he, Claude Wheeler, would escape; that he would actually invent some clever shift to save himself from dissolution" (43). An ambitious yearning to escape the confines of home is vintage Cather. When the quality is possessed by exceptional minds like those of Thea Kronberg and Jim Burden, great art and powerful manuscripts are produced. Cather defines these aesthetic performances as natural expressions of desire. A cultural style is manufactured by the success stories of those who move on to achieve the ends that only spatial mobility can grant the American. But what about Claude and the millions like him, men and women who are not exceptional but who sense that they really ought to be, whose culture of individualism and self-sufficiency tells them that they really must be?

Like Tom Outland among the cliff dweller ruins, Claude Wheeler wants to "settle down into something that was his own"; he wants to possess something worth its pursuit, to "take hold of it with both hands, no matter how grim it was" (70). Also, like Tom Outland and Thea Kronberg, he sees little satisfaction in "working for money, when money brought nothing one wanted." In Claude's eyes money offers nothing but safety, the "perfect safety . . . required to kill all the best qualities in people and develop the mean ones." The realization of these immense dissatisfactions consumes Claude in the Lovely Creek section of the novel, as he becomes "aware that his energy, instead of accomplishing something, was spent in resisting unalterable conditions, and in unavailing efforts to subdue his own nature" (86). Cather would often pull from these conditions a heroic endeavor at artistic greatness or an irresistible attraction to one who is exceptional in order to aid and abet or simply witness greatness. Claude is Niel Herbert without Marian, Jim Burden without Ántonia, Thea Kronberg without talent and lovers, Tom Outland without tutors and facilitators. Claude has the Erlich family, but their brief presence in the narrative only emphasizes the absence of something necessary to Claude's development.

In this section Cather produces an impossible situation. Claude is maddening; he is a hopeless example of a young American man. In the later twentieth century he will be refined into a type, providing a rite of passage for every adolescent to experience. He is the prototype of the rebel without a cause, the hipster, the rock-and-roller sneaking around with illegal beer and whisky and contraband marijuana. An entire industry has evolved in the United States to house the millions of Claude Wheelers that pass through its census rolls every year, young men and women who are trained to continue the business of American culture while marching to the industrial beat of rebellion and safe insurgency. Cather's sense of compensatory ideology has no better example than in contemporary youth culture. Millions of Americans come to seemingly independent conclusions that there is nothing to do but grow up and join the "real world," thus safely relegating intellectual challenges to the contingencies of youth culture, to the sanctioned status of adolescent passage. If adolescent rebellion is something everyone goes through, then it is safely transformed from a potentially destructive force to a social requirement. Even excessive obedience is suspect. College students in the 1980s were often berated for their passivity and conservatism. In *One of Ours* Cather describes the phenomenon of youthful dissatisfaction in preparation for the acceptance of cultural codes as a natural force—birds of generational passage in temporal flight.

Claude Wheeler sees the coming of the war and his service in it as an acceptable substitute for the unacceptable options available to him in the United States. Indeed, life as he has known it makes military service a godsend. The only civilian option that he finds attractive—to have no purpose at all, to believe in the value of nothing—is off-limits to him. The problem that Claude poses to his local community is thus a serious one, because his adolescent angst is uncategorical. His father is

afraid that Claude is "one of those visionary fellows who make unneces-
sary difficulties" in life. His mother "thought the trouble with her son
was that he had not yet found his Saviour." Bayliss thinks that Claude
"was a moral rebel" with "dangerous opinions." The Wheeler's neighbors "liked Claude, but they laughed at him." Claude, finally, agrees
with everyone "that there was something wrong with him" for his discontent (86). The narrative, however, is unconvinced that Claude is a
freak. By creating rather grim choices for him, but also insisting on his
mediocrity, the narrative produces a profoundly disturbing situation.
Cather makes the options open to Claude narrow and spiritually constricting, thus painting his character into a slowly dissolving space. His
salvation will be the infantry.

Claude's preparations to become an imperial soldier are not complete until he experiences the emptiness of sexual existence with a
woman of similar ambitions and discontents. Book 2 of *One of Ours* is
ominously titled "Enid," the name of Claude's wife, a woman of even
less sexual presence than Claude himself. Although the section gets
Enid's name, it is dominated by war news and by the war's growing
relevance to the local economy. "Enid" opens on a Frederick Jackson
Turner note. Claude is in Denver, looking at the statue of Kit Carson,
noting that although the statue faces westward, "there was no West, in
that sense, any more." This situation strikes Claude as a personal "waste
of power," because unlike his father, Claude had no "new country" to
run away into, no place to vent his own "restless" youth (100). Cather's
American culture depends on rebellions against it for its vitality; without such space (a reversal of Turner's safety-valve frontier) it may self-
destruct. Claude's meditations before Kit Carson on horseback form
the question and "Enid" provides the response: no more West, but
plenty of globe for American cultural expansion.

Enid is as restless as Claude. In her first narrative appearance she
announces her dissatisfaction at being trapped in Nebraska. "The only
thing I really want to do is to go out to China and help Carrie in her
work" (105), Enid says, forecasting her eventual fate. Carrie, her sister,
is engaged in another imperial task, missionary work. (The connection
between Kit Carson, American empire, and Christian missionaries is
muted here but explored fully in *Death Comes for the Archbishop*.) Enid's
ambitious desires mean little to Claude, who asks why she cannot be
a missionary in the United States. He may as well ask himself why he
cannot run away into a new country right there in Nebraska. Claude's

question to Enid indicates how far his mind is from empire formation and what a prime candidate he is for enlistment. He fails to see that Enid is already the soldier that he must go through training to become:

> She was not a girl who would depart lightly from conventions that she recognized as authoritative. He remembered her as she used to march up to the platform for Children's Day exercises with the other little girls of the infant class; in her stiff white dress, never a curl awry or a wrinkle in her stocking, keeping her little comrades in order by the acquiescent gravity of her face, which seemed to say, "How pleasant it is to do thus and to do Right!" (120)

The little martinet grows up to become a nightmare of a wife for Claude, refusing sexual relations with him while attending to his dress and toilet needs with an efficiency that "unmanned him" (162).

Claude thinks of marriage in the way that he will be taught, as an imperial soldier, to think of war: as a solution in itself to what may be wrong with his life. This, once more, makes him a prime candidate for the cannon fodder he will become. He is completely unconscious when it comes to his own sexual inclinations. One cannot help but notice Cather's mockery of him throughout "Enid," a derision that leads Jean Schwind to see Claude as duped by the romantic ideals of both love and war (56, 61). From his bedridden courtship through the wedding-day shoes that are too tight on his feet, Claude's masculinity is ridiculed. Although Claude has doubts about his marriage prospect, he decides to go through with his plans. According to Cather, "He believed in the transforming power of marriage, as his mother believed in the miraculous effects of conversion" (145). Neither of these human events works for Claude, however. Only going to battle possesses the mystical status of a religious experience or the transformational value of marriage. By the time the narrative is finished with Claude, he will die believing in the transforming power of war service and his mother will be convinced that her son was saved from suffering by his war death.

The fact that Claude is blind to the phenomenon of regenerative warfare until it happens to him, that is, until he is about to die, raises important issues concerning the narrative itself in *One of Ours*. Throughout the marriage plans in "Enid," signs of the miracle of war abound on the prairie, fertilizing Claude's mind, so to speak, to accept his fate as soldier. For reasons important to Cather's text, however, Claude does not become conscious of the miracle as it unfolds. He goes to war not to be rejuvenated or to find a purpose in life but to escape drudgery and to evade humiliation. Cather's narrative presents warfare as the logical outcome of the culture as it unfolds on the prairie. War is not simply one option for Claude; it is the only option. If he went to war for empire or even to save a France he knew something about, Cather's would have been a different novel. The will to empire in Claude does not flow from an external idea, not even from the love of glory or from the desire to be remembered; rather, it is the logical outcome of everything that has contributed to his character. Like the appearance of Jesus or the Virgin Mary to the devout Christian, for Claude the coming of war articulates his innermost desire to live a life of significance, to go somewhere, to do something. The war is a modern miracle.

One of Ours might thus be considered as a text concerned with the production of the American soldier in the service of empire. Metaphors of harvest abound in the novel, suggesting that raising an army is an organic product of the culture as a whole. The section of the novel entitled "The Voyage of the Anchises" is a meditation on the movement of American minds from one way of thinking to another, from a variety of former occupations to soldiers. The ones who cannot make the transfer are thrown overboard to lighten the load. Cather employs the metaphor of illness, or fever, a common image in her time for what happens to the world when it goes to war. The metaphor is another effort to cast the transformation of the idea of the United States from refuge to empire in naturalistic terms. Throughout the novel the dominant sense is that this metamorphosis is a kind of fulfillment, a harvesting, a logical culmination of the social order and an answer to the dilemma it had produced for itself. Claude articulates the national mission: "I've left everything behind me. I am going over" (251). The empire will indeed throw him over in the process of global ascendancy.

Mr. Wheeler has little to say to Claude in *One of Ours* until the war sends the price of wheat through the ceiling. After that, the father and son have a number of civil, nonsarcastic conversations about the market value of the family's crops. Apparently war proves good for the rather strained relations between these two men. Mr. Wheeler responds to the war in the way that Alexandra Bergson would have probably responded, seeing war as a good business prospect. For Claude, the uniform of the U.S. Army bestows on his life a meaning previously unavailable to him, but he does not think this through in the way that Cather has him think through his various discontents. It simply feels right to him when he becomes a soldier: his body becomes comfortable; his shoes fit.

The war makes all ambitious persons restless and brings individual anxieties into sharp focus. It is among the great facts of a Catherian existence in the novel and must be put to use. For Claude, the war heats up in direct proportion to the cooling of his sexual heels. By the time he is firmly ensconced in his oppressively platonic marriage, the Germans are threatening Paris and Claude is identifying with historic captives, people he calls "children of the moon, with their unappeased longings and futile dreams" (171). He is a man with "an uncertain, purposeless trail," and the war emphasizes his self-doubts: "what *was* the matter with him?" he asks himself (184). Enid, on the other hand, has fewer apparent anxieties about her sexuality and seems comfortable with herself. She is a typical Catherian heroine in that she sees what she wants and eventually obtains it. The combination of a sick sister in China and a general atmosphere of upheaval is her opportunity to pack her suitcases and move into the missionary world. She shows Claude that it can be done when she simply leaves home to go overseas under the auspices of the church.

As the war expands to include the United States, many things are clarified in Cather's Nebraska. The schoolhouse American flag, usually reserved for "the Fourth of July or a political rally," is now employed to signal the nation at war. Claude has never before witnessed this use of the flag, "no bands, no noise, no orators; a spot of restless colour against the sodden March sky" (189). The U.S. flag is being transformed before his eyes from national emblem to the symbol of empire. Furthermore, the things that Claude had always suspected were meaningless—such as the hauling of lumber—really "don't matter now" that Americans are at war (189). The war gives to Claude Wheeler what talent gave Thea Kronberg, what innate intelligence gave Jim Burden, and what charm and beauty gave Marian Forrester—a way out, a purpose, a natural significance. "You didn't get stuck here," Gladys tells him when he returns in uniform. War training puts the world, his nation, and his purpose in order: "this country that had once seemed little and dull to him, now seemed large and rich in variety." To Claude as soldier, his place of origin and the meaning of his childhood "came together before his eyes as a harmonious whole" (208).

The notion that America at war makes sense of what the nation sig-

nifies is a familiar one in the twentieth century. Reading Cather while
the United States prepares for war, or while military issues are foremost in current events, projects an irresistible frame of analysis across
time. The hoisting of the American flag on the aluminum fronts of
suburban homes, the bumper stickers vilifying the current enemy of
U.S. interests, yellow ribbons commemorating the latest cause for vehe-
mence, the mistreatment of previously inconsequential ethnic groups
connected with the day's foes—all these are projected in various ways
in Cather's narrative of the war's emergence on the American prairie.
War making in America is the one political act that is held sacred in the
United States. It is understood as an endeavor that transcends partisan
politics. To criticize the war strategy of the sitting president, for example, is an unacceptable practice, especially among those who desire
the presidency. There are exceptions to this general rule, but they serve
only to reinforce the overall sense that war is above politics, that war
is an expression of the general culture. Critics of war policy are nearly
always marginal characters in the American political arena. The activities of the military have become, in the twentieth century, sacred acts of
American authentication. To misunderstand this great fact of America
is to mistake the culture for something it is not; to accept it uncritically
is to become Claude Wheeler.

Claude's view of war's salvific qualities are seriously qualified by the
narrative in *One of Ours*. Cather makes clear that his view of things
is nothing less than deluded. "He believed that he was going abroad
with an expeditionary force that would make war without rage, with
uncompromising generosity and chivalry" (202). Claude is attracted to
the "facetious tone" used by his comrades to describe the way they
will "can the Kaiser" and so forth. Critics have welcomed Cather's
harsh treatment of Claude. Merrill Skaggs describes Claude as getting
"a happy death, as he deserves . . . a swashbuckling last gasp" for a
young man "who was born unlucky and still lived to see France" (44).
David Stouck emphasizes the implicit critique of the American social
order in the novel rising from the fact that for Claude, war is a "golden
chance" for significance, "an indication of just how sordid life was in the
United States" (*Cather's Imagination* 96). Finally, Blanche Gelfant sees
that Claude "dies young, happy, and deluded." Beyond noting Claude's
delusions, however, Gelfant finds the novel as a whole to be "a nihilistic
text in Willa Cather's canon. It describes a quest for an indescribable
something that ends with *nothing*." The novel does, nonetheless, carry a

colossal *something* in Gelfant's analysis: "In showing that war—rather than peace, prosperity, and family life—realized the highest ideals of humanity, it attributed a value that it was also impelled to deny, for war led its hero to death, although he believed it was giving him his life" ("What Was It" 87). This is precisely the point: Claude possesses more meaning dead than alive. Alive, he is a fool figure, a bumbler, a jerk. But he is much more when dead. After all, a sacred system makes sense of death, and by making sense of death it attaches meaning to life.

In *Fallen Soldiers: Reshaping the Memory of the World Wars* George Mosse describes "the Myth of the War Experience" as it developed throughout the twentieth century in Germany and in the United States. His definition is worth quoting at length. According to Mosse, the myth of the war experience looked back on war "as a meaningful and even sacred event." The myth developed most vitally in defeated nations but also in nations for whom victory was either qualified or questioned.

> The Myth of the War Experience was designed to mask war and to legitimize the war experience; it was meant to displace the reality of war. The memory of the war was refashioned into a sacred experience which provided the nation with a new depth of religious feeling, putting at its disposal the ever-present saints and martyrs, places of worship, and a heritage to emulate. . . . The cult of the fallen soldier became a centerpiece of the religion of nationalism after the war . . . how the war dead should be honoured and buried, what symbolism war monuments should project, and how both nature and Christianity might be used to assert the legitimacy of death and sacrifice in war. (7, 10)

This process is the focus of Cather's narrative: the transformation of a thoroughly useless young man, a loser by nearly any standard of measure, to heroic status through war death. Cather recognized at once the conflation of religious and militarist imperatives into an imperial style.

All the embarrassingly naïve pronouncements Claude and his fellow soldiers make on the voyage to France become aphoristic truths once Claude dies. On the *Anchises* Claude thinks of himself in possession of "ever-widening freedom" (248) got by "the rough-necks' own miracle" of war service (253). The ironies here are compounded when Claude dies on a length of ground ignobly called "the Snout." Once he is dead, however, his thoughts and the freedom he possesses as he is massacred along with thousands of others are irrelevant. The meaning of his life is attached to it by the mechanism of Mosse's war experience mythology. The first constructions are made by the surviving soldiers returning to the United States who gather over the superstructure of their ship. They agree that the better officers are the ones who have died, not the ones who have survived the war. They also agree that the men who do not get awards are the men who most deserve them. The process is well underway: the dead and the undecorated are made heroic, their loss is turned into secret triumph. At home in Nebraska Claude's mother has accepted the death of her son as a part of the cult of the fallen soldier. She knows that survival is worse than war death ("one by one" the survivors of war "quietly die by their own hand"), so that in dying Claude has been saved "some horrible suffering" (370). By casting his death in battle into a heroic achievement, his family is spared the truth that even Claude suspected prior to the war, that his life was essentially meaningless. War service has saved Claude from a nihilistic existence. For Claude, who is without talent, without purpose, and without religious conviction, the army is indeed his savior.

An empire, whether Christian or American, ancient Greek or Roman, depends on a sustained belief that a soldier's life is validated through military service and through death if necessary. *One of Ours* is strewn with references to previous imperial styles: to the pagan eras, Greek Olympian and Roman Augustan, and to the Christian variations, Spanish, German, and British. Events lead to the inevitable rise of a new empire, however, on transhistorical, transnational, American terms. Ruins of "Julius Caesar's fortified camps" are located by an English army captain in Spain (298); a French peasant girl in an occupied town persists in a love affair with a German officer (355); Germans taken prisoner want to emigrate to America as soon as the war finishes (342). The best news to one locality is the appearance of the American flag and the singing of the "Star Spangled Banner," events that bring a French town back to life: "excitement, change, something to look forward to at last" (350). If we piece together the incidents of the war section of *One of Ours*, the reasons for the American empire's success are made clear. Under the American style Caesar's international grasp is authenticated. With the Americans in charge the French girl can have the German lover, and the German POWs will find that people in America are "glad to see them" as immigrants, once the war hysteria passes.

Claude finds his home and his life in the American army. "The Americans were prone," Claude observes, "to make themselves very much at home" no matter where they were, a habit often interpreted as rudeness (327). Manners are defined by temporal powers, however, and power is shifting in *One of Ours*. The army expresses the culture as a whole, in which American migrations mean that home is literally anywhere and movable. In Cather's sense of America this is the direction of the social order in general and of the military as its vanguard expression. The culture will include an efficient, mobile imperial army as a great fact in the lives of American youth and in the cultural imagination of all others. When the soldiers of the immigrant receiver country return to Europe, they come in implicit disregard for national rivalries. Claude feels as if he is "completely understood" as a soldier in France, that he is "no longer a stranger" (316). He is, of course, part of an invasion force, and it is as conqueror that Claude feels he has found himself. The satisfaction is so great that Claude is ready to die for it, and his belief in his purpose is strong enough to compensate for his ignoble, inglorious slaughter.

One of Ours clearly articulates the contradictions and complexities inherent in the idea of the United States as an imperial military power. The tradition of war fiction is a minefield for the writer. Since the medieval era, "war heralds" have served to "ascertain brave deeds, assign credit," and tell what happened when the brave men fell. The tradition of war tales has elevated "prowess, not truth or justice or piety," as "the ultimate measure of behavior" (O'Connell 92, 93).

Claude is finally judged a good man because he died bravely, transforming what had been a disastrous life into the apotheosis of martyrdom. This, of course, begs the question of what made Claude such a failure in the first place. More than half of Cather's novel is devoted not to Claude as warrior but to the making (or the unmaking) of Claude the citizen. The narrative records how Claude's social and cultural context, his time and his place in the United States, systematically strips away any significance that his life may possess and any promise he might develop. His lack of intellectual resources or acceptable role models keeps him from insisting on a liberal education in Lincoln rather than at the more parochial Temple university. His belief that idleness is inherently evil makes it impossible for him to properly heal after his accident with the mules. The social pressure on Enid to get married and be a helpmate to Claude leads her to marry him against her wishes and leads him to propose to her even when he knows of her serious doubts.

All these conditions persist into the present era, making Cather's novel a classic study of war culture from the citizen's perspective. College students who accept Army Reserve commitments in return for college scholarships; criminal adolescents given the choice of prison or army duty; women and minorities expecting equal (and therefore relatively preferable) treatment under the auspices of the military code; the use of American soldiers in providing natural disaster relief, quelling urban rioting, or feeding starving people around the world—in each of these examples the function of the American military expands to encompass the culture. The mission of the U.S. military in Somalia in 1993, for example, threatened to make apolitical humanitarian organizations such as the Red Cross anachronistic. None of these examples represents an evil; in fact, each of them illustrates a version of the good. It was also good that Claude found service in the army, for otherwise he would have spent his life alone in his honeymoon house waiting for Enid to return, living a long life as a local oddity rather than a short one as a national hero. Nonetheless, what attracts Cather's attention is not the military per se but the conditions that have evolved to authenticate the military alternative as redemptive. In contemporary terms, it is good that the U.S. Army fed the Somalians, but what does it mean for the world to depend on the American military as the last resort for its food and shelter?

One of Ours projects an empire. More than the other war fiction writers of the 1920s (Hemingway, Dos Passos, Faulkner), Cather connects the American participation in the war not to individual styles or masculine codes of behavior but to the emergence of an American military and cultural empire. The death of Cather's soldier becomes the "centerpiece of war as a human drama" (Mosse 32). All permissible excesses of human feeling and all resources of Christian symbolism will rush into the iconography of war death like cold air rushing into a vacuum. Jesus is missing on the prairie, but Claude is there to take his place on the cross, along with the hundreds of thousands of Claudes who have hanged there since. These are the men whose lives were empty enough to find the prospect of death in battle preferable to life in their time and place in America.

Willa Cather takes the emergence of the American empire seriously as the material out of which a narrative art must be forged. To ignore the empire would be tantamount to either making one's art irrelevant or, if one possessed genius, contributing directly to the empire's status. Standing around on the superstructure of the troop ship, the returning soldiers express their alienation from the process they have just completed. So, too, does *One of Ours* contain a pervasive sense of distance, stepping back, and examination. Such is the detached sensibility that comes naturally to the migratory mind. In it we can almost hear the novelist musing behind the text, asking what should be made of this. The next book Cather would write, *The Professor's House*, is very much concerned with the relation of writer to subject matter and with the autonomy of textual material. As an object of study *One of Ours* concerns itself with what "we" produce as "ours," what Americans call their own, their sons and daughters, their culture, their empire. Ours is the great fact of America, the empire of migration. In *Death Comes for the Archbishop* the significance of this migratory consciousness is projected not just to the culture of the United States but to the West, the world, and the cosmos.

Death Comes for the Archbishop

> The eagle, the one and only eagle, here in the far corner
> of the earth, where the shadow of his great wings falls, the
> one bird more terrible in history than all the rest of brute
> creatures put together. . . . Yet they say that even the most
> remote of his descendants are doomed, that all who echo
> his tongue and bear his blood must perish.
> —WILLA CATHER AT ARLES, 1902

To Willa Cather, the phenomenon of human transit and the development of the United States as the product of migratory origins meant considerably more than the transmission of human beings from old countries to new. It is not simply human beings who migrate from one place to another throughout history; it is also human thought that moves around the globe, leaving paths called influence. This latter phenomenon is less readily tracked, however, particularly within historical eras of intense nationalism when emphasis is placed on indigenous distinctions and national traditions. Seriously tracking the migratory patterns of consciousness implies a human connectedness that transcends national boundaries and that would, by implication, call into question the legitimacy of such boundaries. According to historian Gilbert

Highet, "the history of the world could . . . be written as a history of the movement of ideas from one group of human beings to another" (10). Such a project would require a fundamentally different conception of world history, however. It would be a history concerned less with national origins and more with global, intellectual transactions. Perhaps geography would supplant history, and intellectual meteorologists would chart the high- and low-pressure zones of human consciousness. "To consider the movement of thought throughout the world is, in a way, like making a new map in which we can see distant countries connected by invisible tides, intellectual currents moving by strange paths around the whole globe" (Highet 28). Cather describes the troop ships that took men like Claude Wheeler to war in Europe as "simple and great thoughts" (218), transmitting the consciousness of an American empire across an ocean, back to origins that have become destinations. *Death Comes for the Archbishop* (1927) projects these simple and great thoughts of transmission as the seeds of empire in the United States.

Historians understandably have been more successful at tracking physical motion than they have been at mapping intellectual currents. Although agreement can be reached regarding physical migration, national rivalries come into play when the sources for such phenomena as revolutions, discoveries, and cultural movements are discussed. Was the U.S. Constitution the product of Locke and Rousseau? Scottish philosophies? Iroquoian ideas of federation? Was the Renaissance a rebirth of Italian culture or the result of the emigration of intellectuals from Constantinople to Florence? The great medieval synthesis, culminating in the work of St. Thomas Aquinas, unified the thinking represented in ancient philosophical systems with Christian theology, but how did the substance of ancient thought get to Aquinas? The physical movement of a library is not equivalent to the movement of the ideas contained in the collection, which may have preceded the movement of texts or may not be accomplished for years following the transferal. If Aquinas were taught ancient philosophy, or had his reading directed by his instructors, why did he and not they accomplish the synthesis of knowledge? Clearly, the simple reading of a text is not equivalent to the transferal of its substance from one mind to another, nor is the migration of a person equivalent to the successful migration of any particular idea or mode of thought.

There have been historical instances, however, in which the transmission of particular forms of knowledge can be traced. The movement of Enlightenment ideas from northern Europe to the American colonies in the late eighteenth century provides one example, together with the return of these ideas to Europe, especially to France, as a revolutionary program. These ideas returned to Europe in another form, however, after merging with Native American and African influences in the New World. This particular transmission of ideas can be located in specific migrations made by such figures as Thomas Paine, Benjamin Franklin, and Thomas Jefferson. In the twentieth century the relocation of German Jewish scientists to the United States is evidence also of the transmission of knowledge and expertise from one place to another. The simple and great thought of the hydrogen bomb was among the results of this more recent transmission. These are dramatic examples of the movement of ideas.

In 1789 Samuel Slater served as an apprentice spinner to Richard Arkwright in Belper, England. Slater turned twenty-one that year and decided that he would attempt to make something of himself as a textile manufacturer in the newly independent United States of America. The royal statute of 22 George III, chapter 60, however, made it a punishable offense to export from England "any machinery, models, or mechanical drawings" and even forbade "the migration of artisans." But putting a stop to the migration of ideas is not so easily accomplished. To get around the old mercantilist statute, Slater memorized Arkwright's "entire series of wheels and bands and rollers with precise dimensions," disguised himself as an indigent migrant, and readily passed under the watchful eyes of English customs officers. After arriving in New York he made contact with Moses Brown of Rhode Island and founded the Pawtucket, Rhode Island, cotton manufacturing mills (Dixon Fox 10–11).

We have made icons of the man with the ax and the man with the musket, the heroes who felled trees, hunted game, and established wilderness homesteads that become the outposts, towns, and cities of the nation. The original migrations to America, however, consisted of more than a succession of hunters and farmers. Fox calls men like Samuel Slater "pioneers of ideas and special competence," migrants "with the book, the scalpel, the compass." Through such movement we might trace the way in which "professional competence was transplanted to America," the process whereby the American way was constructed by ingenuity and theft (4). On the other hand, one might consider the entire colonization and settlement of the New World by migrants from Europe as a massive transfer of both intellectual content and intellectual spirit. Seeing historical migration in this way, we would be less concerned with trade routes and balances of payments and more likely to focus on intersections of consciousness, of mind with mind and mind with natural surroundings. It is part of the rhetoric of the late twentieth century to speak of the colonization of consciousness by powerful sources, as if the process of intellectual movement and influence were ever a parlor game. More often, transactions of consciousness are characterized by steady encroachments or simple larceny, and independence is rarely accomplished save at the cost of escape or isolation. The choice of the American eagle for the Great Seal of the United States reflected the classical emblem of the Roman republic, but the image is also the eagle of Exodus (19:4) and Revelation (12:14), "an image of escape and emigration" (Sollers 44).

The image of Samuel Slater carrying in his mind an entire industrial system and applying that knowledge to his new surroundings in the United States captures what Willa Cather projects in the text of *Death Comes for the Archbishop*. The concept of ideas in transit, the mechanics involved in the projection and migration of an idea across an ocean and a continent, and the relationship between consciousness and materiality are central concerns of this novel. Cather writes of intellectual colonists when she writes of her missionaries; Latour and Vaillant wish to plant ideas and colonize the minds of the Mexicans, the Americans, and (to a lesser extent) the indigenous peoples. The troop ships in *One of Ours* embodied the idea of the United States evolving from nation to empire, returning to Europe as the force that would shape the destiny of the world throughout the twentieth century. In the same way, the thousands of immigrants who have come to the United States have embodied the idea that no particular place is necessarily home to any human being and that as a species, human beings are movable and take well to being transplanted. The idea of movement is the idea of America as represented by the eagle, the bird of prey that will make its home on any rock high enough to provide a clear vision. The eagle settles on the rock only to await its next move. An empire of migratory values, of transactions of power and focus, and of the adaptation of old ideas to contemporary necessity is the concern of Cather's novel about an itinerant French bishop sent to the Spanish American Southwest by French and Italian cardinals to spread the faith of Rome among the Mexican and American people and, with luck, among the Navajo, the Ácoma, and the Laguna.

Gillian Bottomly has argued that "the centrality of migration in history" compels the contemporary observer to confront "the fluidity of cultural forms, despite the association of the modern concept of culture as defining a specific and separate (national) identity. Obviously, with so many people constantly on the move throughout world history, there can be no such thing as a 'pure' culture, let alone a 'pure' race" (42–43). *Death Comes for the Archbishop* demonstrates the accuracy of Bottomly's argument. The novel begins in 1848, with three Roman Catholic cardinals perched like eagles overlooking Rome, on a terrace "famous for its fine view." One cardinal is French (he is also described by Cather as Norman), one is Italian (described likewise as Venetian), and the third cardinal, the host, is referred to as being Spanish (but with a face "much modified through his English mother"). The physical presence of these three multicultural cardinals bears witness to the historic migrations that formed Europe long before the invention of nation-states and to the marriages that continue to complicate the idea of integral national identity. The cardinals' terrace "was a mere shelf of rock, overhanging a steep declivity," beyond which "was the drop into the air, and far below the landscape stretched soft and undulating; there was nothing to arrest the eye until it reached Rome itself" (3). The cardinals are men of vision, in possession of the long view of history associated with Catholicism. In the opening pages of the novel Cather brings a number of global phenomena into alignment: the migrations that formed Europe, the annexation of Texas and the southwestern territories by the United States after the war with Mexico in 1848, the idea of the Roman empire, the universal focus of the Catholic church, and a mode of consciousness capable of sustaining the alignment of disparate historical influences.

Cather describes the view beneath the terrace as one in which the late afternoon sun "suggested motion." "The light was full of action and had a peculiar quality of climax—of splendid finish." The cardinals are "talking business" together, namely, the business of Catholic influence in North America. Father Ferrand, a Baltimore missionary "Irish by birth, French by ancestry," is lobbying for the creation of an apostolic vicarate in the newly annexed territories in the United States. The "splendid finish" associated with the sunset suggests the transfer of the locus of Western civilization from Rome and Europe to the United States, "the beginning of momentous things," according to the American bishop (6). Indeed, the entire prologue to the novel may be read as a meditation on the transfer of consciousness to which Jean Latour will contribute, the transmission of the center of the West to the New World. The Spanish cardinal relates an anecdote that serves as an emblem to the process dramatized in the novel. Years ago, a missionary from New Spain visited his great-grandfather, asking for monetary donations and anything else that could be spared to contribute to his efforts among the indigenous population. The missionary asked also for a painting from the grandfather's collection to adorn the mission church. The cardinal's grandfather agreed and told the missionary to choose any one, assuming that the rustic American's lack of sophistication would lead him to choose something of little value. "But not at all," explains the cardinal, "the hairy Franciscan pounced upon one of the best in the collection" and took a magnificent El Greco painting with him back to America (12). The Spanish cardinal is shrewd in the telling of this tale, expressing his awareness of the historical process in which he participates. It is not always members of the very "best" class of Europeans who migrate to America as settlers or as missionaries; nonetheless, the very best in terms of ideas, inspiration, and consciousness is gathering in the New World. When the American returns to Europe, as did "the hairy Franciscan," and as did the soldiers in *One of Ours*, it will be to continue the transmission of power to America begun by immigration.

Death Comes for the Archbishop is a further projection of the idea of American empire, paying particular attention to the quality of ideas on which the empire originated. Cather sets the opening of the novel in 1848, a pivotal year in the territorial expansion of the United States, and concludes it near the end of the nineteenth century, at the end of the century of manifest destiny. But Cather is not concerned with the usual tale of homesteads, forts, Indian wars, and gold rushes—although these material phenomena all figure in the background to the novel's events. Rather, *Death Comes for the Archbishop* centers on the business of transmission, the way in which intellectual capital—ideas, spirituality, modes of thought—is carried from one place to the next. The novel also makes clear that the modes of transmission or the structural phenomena that form the transactions of intellectual and spiritual migration will become the most fundamental basis of the empire. In other words, the temporary condition of migration becomes, in the United States, a permanent condition of psychic, national existence. Cather calls it America's business. The great fact of movement, the belief in a detachable people, is the faith that builds the nation and that undergirds the idea of America.

Jean Latour, the missionary, is a practical man. "We missionaries wear a frock-coat and wide-brimmed hat all day, you know," he writes to his brother in Europe, "and look like American traders." Latour's letter reveals a good deal about his function in the newly acquired territories, as he explains how "for so much of the day I must be a 'business man'! . . . And all day I am an American in speech and thought—yes, in heart too. The kindness of the American traders, and especially of the military officers at the Fort, commands more than a superficial loyalty. I mean to help the officers at their task here. I can assist them more than they realize. The Church can do more than the Fort to make these poor Mexicans 'good Americans' " (35-36). Jean Latour's letter draws an implicit parallel among the activities of traders, missionaries, and soldiers, establishing on the local level the global, imperial scope projected by the Roman prologue. Although the narrative will observe later that in looking at Latour and Vaillant, "no one could have mistaken these two men for hunters or traders" (65), the novel will nonetheless insist on the coincident missions of barter, religion, and military orders. The first episode of book 2, "Missionary Journeys," for example, begins and ends with trading images. Father Vaillant is attempting to build a congregation at Santo Domingo by "canvassing from house to house and offering medals and religious colour prints to all who came to church" (53). Later he trades "a good many prayers" for Manuel Lujon's soul in return for Lujon's prize mules. The trade is Cather's use of Southwest humor as if in the service of God. Lujon does not really wish to give away his property, but he is out-traded by Vaillant when the shrewd missionary implies that his soul is on the trading table. "Father Vaillant had forced his hand," Lujon thinks to himself, "yet he bore no resentment." His belief in Vaillant's mission assuages his material loss, and his Catholic faith will be bolstered by the idea of his mules in Vaillant's service. "Every time you think of these mules," Vaillant says to Lujon, "you will feel pride in your good deed" (63). This is missionary business, and Vaillant is among the best traders. When a gold rush brings thousands of souls to Pike's Peak, Latour knows that it is Vaillant who fits the bishop of Leavenworth's call for one who is "not only devoted, but resourceful and intelligent, one who would be at his ease with all sorts of men," as any good trader must be (245).

Joseph Vaillant became a priest only after giving up his first ambition, which was to enlist in the French army as a soldier (224). When he and Jean Latour discuss the progress of the empire over soup, entertaining visions of future vineyards on the shores of Lake Erie, they wonder about the size of the territory that falls under Latour's charge. "The Commandant at the Fort seems as much in the dark as I," says Latour. Then he introduces a historical figure into the fictional narrative: "He says I can get some information from the scout, Kit Carson, who lives at Taos" (40). Kit Carson plays a crucial role in *Death Comes for the Archbishop*, a shadowy authentication of Cather's projection and a reminder of its textual fictionality. As Vaillant embodies the combination of business practices with missionary journeys, the figure of Kit Carson suggests the way in which the conversion and conquest of native peoples intersect as common purposes.

The placement of historically verifiable characters into fiction is an arresting technique. Kit Carson, Indian fighter and frontier scout, has a continuous, recurring presence in *Death Comes for the Archbishop*. It is a matter of some moment when he and Latour meet, when the bishop "felt a quick glow of pleasure in looking at the man." The narrative implies a commonality between them, "standards, loyalties, a code which is not easily put into words but which is instantly felt when two men who live by it come together by chance" (75). They become friends and remain so throughout Latour's life, even though the bishop will refer to him as "his own misguided friend" (291) for his career of massacre. "Carson was a soldier under orders, and he did a soldier's brutal work," according to the narrative (292). Despite the apology for and denigration of Carson's actions, his job is presented as a great fact of history. The point is that the friendship between Latour and Carson persists, like an alliance of purpose along divergent means.

The military presence in *Death Comes for the Archbishop* is a muted one. Telling the story from a twentieth-century sensibility, Cather seems intent on making the military function discernible but not dominant. In other words, although this new civilization is not eclipsed by its militarism, it is the army that makes possible what the culture accomplishes. When Don Antonio Olivares announces that he will pay for the construction of Latour's American cathedral at Santa Fe, he does so in the presence of "the officers at the Post" whom his wife is entertaining. The moment is a significant one in the story of the American nation and in the development of its military. It is New Year's 1860, and the commandant of the fort has been "called back to Washington," while another popular soldier, an Irish Catholic lieutenant, is being sent "further west" to fight Native Americans in Arizona (180). Characteristically, Cather does not make explicit the historical developments that have split the military's purpose in two at this juncture, between the political struggles in Washington that will make civil war possible and the ongoing war policy to subdue the plains dwellers. Nonetheless, at the end of his life Father Latour voices his gratitude for the two military achievements that occur as a result of the juncture: "the end of black slavery" and the treaty reached between the United States and the Navajo (290).

The military has more than a simple physical presence at the 1860 New Year's party. As he listens to the "savage" sounds of American banjo music, Latour sees once again the way in which his ambition is connected to the progress of empire. He senses a commonality in "the recklessness, the call of wild countries which all these men had felt and followed in one way or another. Through clouds of cigar smoke, the scout and the soldiers, the Mexican *rancheros* and the priests, sat silently watching. . . . Father Latour was thinking how each of these men not only had a story, but seemed to have become his story. Those anxious, far-seeing blue eyes of Carson's, to whom could they belong but to a scout and trail-breaker?" (182) The figure of Kit Carson again signals the intrusion of historical documentation into Cather's fiction and serves as a reminder, once more, of empire formation.

Latour's sense of affinity with the far-seeing Carson extends also to Carson's rival in the novel, Don Manuel Chavez, himself an intriguing character. "Chavez boasted his descent from two Castilian knights who freed the city of Chavez from the Moors in 1160" (183). The parallels between the Spanish Reconquest in the fifteenth century and the nineteenth-century American-Indian wars, campaigns that gave rise to similar literary developments, have been explored in detail by Spanish literary critic Manuel Broncano. Chavez, the direct descendant of Spanish Moor fighters, is an Indian fighter. He is "jealous of Carson's fame" and claims "that he had seen more Indian warfare before he was twenty than Carson would ever see" (183). In any case, it is Bishop Latour's awakening sense of common purpose with such men that situates the meaning of Cather's novel. Latour clearly disapproves of killing Native Americans, but never in the novel does he overtly object to the methods of Carson, Chavez, or the U. S. Army. *Death Comes for the Archbishop* depicts an array of simultaneous enactments of empire, scouts and soldiers, rancheros and priests, who "in one way or another" are writing the same story across the continent.

The story is the narrative of a conquering civilization, the common purpose of Bishop Latour and Kit Carson that transcends their divergent methods. Both men bring the news, good and otherwise, that the culture of migration, of traders, missionaries, and Indian fighters, has arrived in the Southwest territory. The news is never more apparent than at the end of the novel, when Cather, through Bishop Latour, confronts the inevitability of Native American removal. Latour knows that the treaty with the Navajo will not hold and that "there would never be an end to the Indian wars while there was one Navajo or Apache left alive. Too many traders and manufacturers made a rich profit out of that warfare; a political machine and immense capital were employed to keep it going" (290). Part of Latour's melancholy at the end of his life is probably due to the knowledge that he is also a part of the machinery of empire that is displacing a civilization. Throughout his career in the Southwest, Latour has moved from one place to another representing his faith. He is far from his original home in Auvergne, France, and far from his first position as parish priest on Lake Ontario. His career is testimony to the idea that it does not matter where he lives; as an American missionary, he makes his home where he happens to be. His mobility, his missionary journeys and the simple fact that his faith is transplantable, contributes to the destruction of the indigenous cultures of America. Latour is nearly always on the move in the novel, making continual journeys across the continent and overseeing trips made by his assistant, Joseph Vaillant. This mobility is more significant to the formation of empire than is any idea, faith, or belief that the missionaries preach.

At the end of the novel, near the end of his life, Archbishop Latour is asked by the Navajo chief Manuelito to intervene on behalf of the Navajo in Washington. "They asked nothing of the Government, he told Father Latour, but their religion, and their own land where they had lived from immemorial times. Their country, he explained, was a part of their religion; the two were inseparable" (292). In the context of Latour's missionary journeys, however, and in the context of the novel's imperial scope, Manuelito's request is far from nothing. The idea of the United States is directly at odds with Manuelito's request: in America, place and belief, land and religion, are not and cannot be connected by sacred links. In a culture of mobility consecrated ties to specific parcels of land are unthinkable. Manuelito says that the Canyon de Chelly is a sacred place. "Their gods were there, just as the Padre's God was in his church" (293). According to Navajo legend, the Shiprock, just north of the canyon, "was once a ship of the air" that flew from a mysterious place of origins and brought "the parents of the Navajo race" to this desert, where the gods wanted them to settle for all time. Latour travels to bring his god to New Mexico, America, and beyond, but the Navajo gods brought the Navajos to America to stay put. To the Navajos, travel is associated with origins; it defines their relation with the past. To Latour, the sacred journey is part of the present; it is the act that defines the future. Latour traveled thousands of miles to build a cathedral under the auspices of a religion based on an abstraction. The Navajo cannot "go three hundred miles away and live in a strange land" and therefore must have their canyon. In these sentiments Cather expresses the conflict of consciousness that would lead to the demise of Native American cultures.

The confrontation between whites and native peoples on the American plains pitted a culture of migration and transferal (paradoxically represented by "settlers") against a culture in which places and landscapes are sacred (represented, paradoxically, by nomadic peoples). It is interesting that late twentieth-century environmentalism is often seen as a return to the values of Native Americans regarding the lands and waterways. This is an inaccurate parallel. The environmentalist movement is based not on the idea of sacred places but on the imperative that all lands and waterways be preserved and cleansed so that no matter where Americans move, the environment will be healthy. Contemporary Green politics endorses the abstract idea of universal ecological balance, but not the sense of consecrated lands in which dwell the deities of the human race. A closer parallel to the Navajo sense of sacred territory motivated Theodore Roosevelt, who established the national park system during his presidency so that Americans could participate in rituals of hunting, camping, and "roughing it." Nonetheless, it was never the land itself that was sacred; rather, the act of moving through it, with a rifle, a bible, or a box of samples in hand, was a matter of consecrated ritual.

The archbishop's cathedral is an emblem of the American conception of home. Cather's American idea of home is an abstract idea, not equivalent to the word *house* or *apartment*. There are even aphorisms ("home is where the heart is") in the language to convince the wary that it really is all right to be homeless. According to Cather in *Death Comes for the Archbishop*, what separates the Indian from the American mind is in the application and use of such abstractions as home. The American possesses an idea of cathedral, for example, an abstract idea of a sacred place. The idea motivates movement and is continually applied to material conditions, but it is not necessarily contingent on its incarnation. Furthermore, the idea is not contingent on any particular cathedral, and there are in fact thousands of consecrated Christian churches in the United States. On the other hand, the Navajo possess a physical place, an actual rock. The place motivates abstraction, such as dreams and visions, that cannot be removed from the holy site. To the American mind, the abstraction precedes its material incarnation; to put it in current language, abstract thinking is privileged with the status of origination. In the Navajo mind the process is reversed. The material object precedes (and may even produce) the abstraction — the voice, the vision, the dream. To the American, the physical site, the cathedral, is evidence of the veracity of the abstract faith. Navajo consciousness considers the abstraction, the vision, as evidence of the sacred status of the physical place. Bishop Latour suspects that this kind of thing is superstition, magic, and is not to be trusted. When he confronts it, he is awed and even horrified.

Cather repeatedly emphasizes the idea of the rock as the symbol of the human desire for stability. In the chapter called "The Rock" Cather juxtaposes Jean Latour's Gothic desert vision with the idea of the Ácoma holy site, the rock on which their civilization existed. Latour compares the Christian idea of the rock as "the utmost expression of human need," the symbol of the Church of his mission in America, with the "strange literalness" of the Ácoma rock: "The Ácomas, who must share the universal human yearning for something permanent, enduring, without shadow of change, — they had their idea in substance. They actually lived upon their Rock; were born upon it and died upon it" (98). This literalness and intractability are contrasted to Latour's visionary impulses and his mobility. It is the intransigence of the native mind that dooms it before this new idea of malleability represented by missionaries, traders, and soldiers.

For all the association of Native Americans with cliffs, rocks, ledges, and other images of stability and endurance, Cather does not present their cultures as rooted in permanence. Instead, her narrative marvels at their ephemerality. "It was the Indian manner to vanish into the landscape, not to stand out against it." In contrast, the manner of the European was to "assert himself in any landscape, to change it" or "to leave some mark of memorial of his sojourn." Not only that, but whereas Europeans sought to "arrange and re-create" their surroundings, the "Indians disliked novelty and change" and wished to leave no trace of their existence. Father Latour dreams of constructing a Romanesque cathedral at Santa Fe, a far cry from the Indian desire to "pass unseen and unheard through a country" (232–34). Latour is deeply moved by the secret faith of the slave woman, Sada, who is prohibited by her American Protestant owners from entering the Catholic church. Nonetheless, she worships "while her watchers slept." As she hurries away, Latour is mesmerized by "the line of black footprints his departing visitor had left in the wet scurf of snow" (218). Footprints, "some mark of memorial," a visible record—these are the qualities recognized by Latour and his culture as significant evidence of being. When Latour and Eusabio are passed by two Zuñi runners on the open plain, the latter two men "coursed over the sand with the fleetness of young antelope, their bodies disappearing and reappearing among the sand dunes, like the shadows that eagles cast," leaving no tangible record of passage (234). The confrontation of these two cultures is really no confrontation at all. Between the one that wishes to leave a record and the one that does not, the record will show the clear footprints of the victor while the vanquished simply disappear.

Archbishop Latour never fully articulates an awareness that he carries a culture of sustained migration with him on his missionary journeys. At his death, however, he does possess a vision indicating both that Cather is aware of what he carries and that Latour subconsciously knows what he has accomplished. As he dies the archbishop experiences a sense of "standing in a tip-tilted green field among his native mountains, and he was trying to give consolation to a young man who was being torn in two before his eyes by the desire to go and the necessity to stay. He was trying to forge a new Will in that devout and exhausted priest" (297). The new will that is forged in Father Latour is the will and ambition forged in *Death Comes for the Archbishop*, the will and ambition that transform the landscape from historical, sacred place to the spatial setting for an empire of migration. This is the will that is the subject of the mythmaking dimension of the novel. In *One of Ours* the voyage of the *Anchises* that carried Claude to his imperial destiny, his martyrdom for the American presence, was written with more than a hint of irony. In

Death Comes for the Archbishop, however, the irony is replaced by a rather solemn examination of the origins and implications of the transfer of world power from the Old to the New World.

In a useful definition of historical mythmaking, Michael Howard points to "the creation of an image of the past, through careful selection and interpretation, in order to create or sustain certain emotions or beliefs." Such is the business of historians, according to Howard, "in order to encourage patriotic or religious feeling or to create support for a dynasty or for a political regime" (188). Cather's program in *Death Comes for the Archbishop*, by her emphasis on the business of empire shared by traders, soldiers, and priests, is to focus on the common idea that motivated the disparate activities leading to the creation of the United States' dynasty. The novel is not a simple act of nationalistic apologia, however. The title itself points to a second, parallel purpose, invoking a fatality. Furthermore, the choice of subject matter, Latour's spirituality and the repeated emphasis on miraculous events, complicates the historical meaning of the novel as well as its significance as a literary production in the secular sense.

The fatality of the mythmaking process was sensed by one of Cather's favorite poets, from whose words she had already lifted one title for a novel. Walt Whitman's "O Pioneers!" clearly influenced Cather early in her career. Cather may also have shared Whitman's sense of a "fatal environment" in the West, as expressed in "A Death Sonnet for Custer," originally published in the *New York Tribune* on July 10, 1876. Richard Slotkin has taken Whitman's line as the title of his study of frontier myths and has explicated the meaning of the term. Whitman uses the term in saying that George Armstrong Custer entered a fatal environment of plains Indians who surrounded and outnumbered his forces. The term may also be used less literally, however, to refer to "a meaningful myth-historical design," the very frame of mind possessed by Custer, compelling him to presume victory despite the odds. According to Slotkin, "myth, as much as any other aspect of reality . . . , creates the 'fatal environment' of expectations and imperatives in which . . . a whole political culture may be trapped" (*Fatal Environment* 10, 20). The fatal environment is a perceptual field that provides meanings that precede events or circumstances. It was the fatal environment of prewar propaganda that convinced Claude Wheeler, for example, that he was going to war for ideals and not for business, while all around him, clear to the reader but not to Claude, were signs of war business and war profit making. At the front, while Claude dreams of ideals and glory, the reader sees the canned goods, the construction projects, and the machinery that flood the European markets in wartime.

The fatal environment of *Death Comes for the Archbishop* is more complex than the relatively simple ironies of *One of Ours*. Jean Latour carries a sense of the real with him to the Southwest, and Cather dramatizes the way in which his vision affects the landscape in his mind as he travels from Laguna to Ácoma: "In all his travels the Bishop had seen no country like this. From the flat red sea of sand rose great rock mesas, generally Gothic in outline, resembling vast cathedrals" (94). The capability of seeing Gothic in the American landscape indicates a transmission of meaning from France to the desert that will prove fatal to the indigenous inhabitants of the region as well as determine subsequent developments there. It is this way of seeing that leads W. J. T. Mitchell to connect the genre of landscape painting to "the discourses of imperialism" ("Imperial Landscape" 9). Cather comments on the European mind inherent in landscape vision, noting that "the early missionaries might well have forgotten the poor Ácomas, that tribe of ancient rock-turtles, and believed themselves in some cloister hung on a spur of the Pyrenees" (102). The act of intellectual transmigration will accomplish the success of the empire, and it is the transmission itself that the text describes as miraculous.

Cather has written extensively on the idea of perception and possession. Jim Burden's private image of Ántonia is the best-known example, where his love for this immigrant farm girl transforms a decidedly unfortunate life into a heroic, mythic ideal of fecundity and earthy nationalism. The same process is examined closely in *The Professor's House*, with the idea of Tom Outland serving as the locus of various intellectual struggles. In *One of Ours* Claude's mind had to be sufficiently drained of any organic sense of purpose before it was reinfused with the motivation of martyrs and romantic soldiers. Similarly, in *The Song of the Lark*, the question of Thea's talent is meaningless without the perception of that talent in her (and not in Lily Fisher, for example) by influential sponsors and mentors like Ray Kennedy and Harsanyi. The world, in Cather's texts, operates not of its own volition but by the will of its perceivers. Perception precedes actuality, and abstraction determines fact. In other words, meaning is not inherent but is discovered or applied by acts of signification. These acts of signification are what contemporary critics call mythmaking, and the process itself results in a fatal environment of predeterminant meaning.

Cather's critics have explicated the similarity between Father Latour and western heroes. John J. Murphy describes him as a combination of American heroic figures ("Leatherstocking, the Virginian, and even Huckleberry Finn") and classical figures, "particularly Aeneas, whose destiny was to shape a new culture in Italy by transplanting the home gods of Troy" ("Willa Cather's Archbishop" 161). The difference between *Death Comes for the Archbishop* and these ancient and recent prototypes is in the textual tension between Latour's sense of the miraculous and the narrative's sense of the intersection between historical and spatial modes of thought. In Cather's imagination medieval ahistoricism provided the closest parallel to American spatial consciousness. The medieval sense of a miraculous presence in nature, however, is replaced in the New World with the American sense of historical destiny, the miraculous nature of history.

What Whitman termed the fatal environment and what Slotkin explicated as expectations and imperatives are, in Cather's novel, equivalent to what were once understood and experienced as religious miracles, where one dimension of reality intrudes on or redefines another. In the modern conception of reality miracles are explained away either scientifically or historically, but the movement of historical events themselves remains mysterious. Is Latour's belief in his god more true than Jacinto's belief in the Navajo gods, and is that why Latour succeeds? Or is there a materialist, historical explanation for the transmission of the Christianity that replaced native religious systems in New Mexico? Cather's text implies overtly that it is a business transaction: Latour is trading his faith in return for improved material conditions (36). No doubt a great deal of meaning is abstracted from a food supply.

Nonetheless, the idea of the miraculous is central to the meaning of the novel. In the opening scene Father Latour prays to the Holy Mother to guide him when he is lost in the desert. As a result or as a coincidence, he finds his way to a remote homestead. "If Father Vaillant were here, he would say, 'A miracle.' . . . And it was a miracle, Father Latour knew that. But his dear Joseph must always have the miracle very direct and spectacular, not with Nature, but against it" (29). To Latour's modernist conception, miracles exist in the environment itself, in the unfolding of events and in the circumstances that accidentally occur. There is as well something miraculous in the ability of some to see the meaning of events, to read the signs correctly and to know when and where to move, physically or intellectually, to capitalize on what are to others unforeseen circumstances. Latour explains this to Vaillant when he describes the miraculous as "human vision corrected by divine love." "I do not see you as you really are, Joseph; I see you through my affection for you. The Miracles of the Church seem to me to rest not so much upon faces or voices or healing power coming suddenly near to us from afar off, but upon our perceptions being made finer, so that for a moment our eyes can see and our ears can hear what is there about us always" (50). This is the miracle of perception that has informed much of Cather's characterizations of human relations, the miracle that is also central to the modernist aesthetic. If there is a common faith among modernist writers, it is the belief in the authenticity of private vision. In Latour's formulation miracles come to those of ambitious perceptions.

The miraculous aspects of historical developments are found in the movements and migrations that have produced the present. Historical events themselves constitute the second part of Latour's sense of the persistence of mystery. The previously quoted definition of a miracle that he offers Vaillant comes at the end of the chapter entitled "A Bell and A Miracle." The miracle named in the title refers to the Virgin Mary's appearance at Guadalupe, resulting in the construction of a shrine to Our Lady of Guadalupe. The bell is equally miraculous, however, according to a modern understanding of the term. The exact details are not known, but someone brought to San Miguel a large silver bell forged in Spain and inscribed to St. Joseph in the year 1356. Latour explains to Vaillant that the Spanish learned the technology of silversmithing and bell making from the Moors during the Moorish domination of Spain in the medieval period. Christian bells, Latour explains, are "an adaptation of a Moslem custom." Vaillant suspects that this belittles Christians, but Latour corrects him with a modern sensibility. The bell is evidence of the miraculous transactions that occur though historical events, transferals that validate and make heroic the culture of migration that Latour represents. "I am glad to think there is Moorish silver in your bell," says Latour. "The Spaniards handed on their skill to the Mexicans, and the Mexicans have taught the Navajos to work silver; but it all came from the Moors" (45). Furthermore, it will culminate with the Americans, the result of the efforts of missionaries, traders, and soldiers.

The miracle of history is cultural migration: the movement of ideas, the business of transmission, and the trading of concepts, items, and ways of life that accomplish historical development. The focus of *Death Comes for the Archbishop* is not simply on faith or belief but on the ways that these qualities move, the ways that they are bartered, and on the processes of cultural incorporation and recombination. Stasis signals death in Cather. Culture moves through the strength of armies, clearly, but military success must be conjoined to the endurance of ideas. Animating the military presence that is always in the background of Latour's journeys is a sense of mobility's sacred status. After all, the military is there to protect the movement of traders and settlers into the new territories. The vitality of Latour's faith, of his mode of consciousness, is likewise rooted in its mobility. Philosophers have observed that "the mission of humanity through the ages has been to make an effort to create or recreate gods in order to transcend itself." This transcendent quality communicates across religious systems, as any holy site will remain moving centuries later "even if one does not really know its true nature" (Halbswachs 52). Cather modifies this sense to the degree that it is not so much the holy site that achieves poignancy but the transmission of the holy vision from one place to another. There are Native American holy places in the desert that have been there for centuries. In fact, these holy sites cannot be moved because they are actually equivalent to the landscape; they exist either as the land itself or within the topography. In Cather's view, however, it is this quality of stasis that dooms them in the face of the migratory culture of the United States.

Using Catherian terms one could say that America is settled by minds in which stability is an abstraction, in which national origins, religions, and ethnic identities are traded over time. The idea of permanence is not attached to spatiality; landscape, like history, is a dynamic phenomenon within migratory consciousness. Therefore, it is in the Native American Jacinto that Jean Latour discovers the limits of his missionary capabilities. The migratory model will not work with Jacinto, and there can be no intellectual transaction. "The Bishop seldom questioned Jacinto about his thoughts or beliefs. He didn't think it polite, and he believed it to be useless. There was no way in which he could transfer his own memories of European civilization into the Indian mind, and he was quite willing to believe that behind Jacinto there was a long tradition, a story of experience, which no language could translate to him" (92). Throughout Cather a transfer of memories has characterized the successful migrant, the mind able to move from one frame of reference into another. Jacinto does possess the pre-requisite physical mobility, being "as much at home in the Bishop's study as in his own pueblo—and he was never too much at home any-where" (93), but he does not possess the intellectual mobility that will make for a Catherian survival. Jacinto represents an affront to the mi-grating faith, the singular heresy, and at his death Archbishop Latour will lament his faith's inability to incorporate the challenge symbolized by the native mind. He cannot incorporate what he finds repulsive.

Latour is physically sickened in the face of a Native American holy site at Stone Lips. Although he sees the sacred cavern as "somewhat like a Gothic chapel," the effect of his entrance into the cave with Jacinto is far from ethereal. He suffers "an extreme distaste for the place," a visceral reaction, and he detects "a fetid odour, not very strong but highly disagreeable" (127). When he emerges the next morning, he is "convinced that neither the white men nor the Mexicans in Santa Fe understood anything about Indian beliefs or the workings of the Indian mind" (133). Latour is intrigued by his conclusion and cannot, as a mis-sionary, rest with it. He visits a man who Kit Carson claims knows Native Americans, a trader named Zeb Orchard. Orchard tells Latour that although the Native Americans may become Catholics, they will never be separated from their beliefs. His assessment is stark: "The things they value most are worth nothing to us" (135). In this formula-tion Cather is typically precise regarding the contest for North America between European migrants and indigenous populations. As a clash of ideas, the struggle was more a holy war, such as that between fifteenth-century Moslems and Spaniards, than a simple political expansion. At stake, in other words, was not only land and minerals but also a system of thought, a mode of consciousness. Those who will not move, those who will insist on the sanctity of one spot, stand to lose. The price is extracted brutally from indigenous populations and is continually de-manded as the price of survival in America.

Bishop Latour's vision culminates in his plans to build a Midi Romanesque cathedral at Santa Fe. He will not take from the landscape what meanings it may yield (he is repulsed by indigenous significance) but will transfer to the landscape "something nearer home," something he brings with him in his mind, an imperial transmission. His success may be contrasted to the dramatic failure of Padre Martínez, who tried to root the Christian church in the landscape of the Southwest, blend-ing nativist traditions with Catholicism. "We have a living Church here, not a dead arm of the European Church," Martínez declares to Latour. "Our religion grew out of the soil, and has its own roots. . . . Rome has no authority here." Furthermore, Martínez advises Latour "to study our native traditions before you begin your reforms" (146, 147). However, Cather's narrative reserves for Martínez a rather ignoble death after a long, bitter feud with another priest, Father Lucero, a man who has hoarded local money and is known as "the miser." Clearly, Martínez's methods are the methods not of a migratory faith but of one attempting to root itself, like the Shiprock, once and for all. From the perspective of Latour and of the novel as a whole, this is a gluttonous form of apostasy. At his death Father Lucero has a Dantesque vision of Martínez in hell: " '*Comete tu cola, Martínez, comete tu cola!*' (Eat your tail, Martínez, eat your tail!)" (171).

"When I look up at this rock," Jean Latour tells Joseph Vaillant at the site of his proposed cathedral, "I can almost feel the Rhone behind me" (239). Latour is not rooting his faith in the soil to build a new church, and he is not extracting ideas from the landscape. Rather, he is transposing his church from a European setting to an American one, proving the mobility of his faith. Paul Carter describes the true subject of all explorer writings as the transfiguration of historical space, "the plotting of a track along which historical time might later flood in on a tide of names" (22). Latour's church does not grow out of the desert plains but is written on to the desert, just as the plow inscribes the marks of immigrant ambition by making scratches on the plains in *O Pioneers!* Latour then voices the idea of a common future that will bind him to the landscape, the emblematic American community of purpose. "But the Cathedral is not for us, Father Joseph," he says. "We build for the future," not knowing who will have arrived there when the cathedral is completed and not needing to know (242). Latour's successes are acknowledged in Rome, and in the novel he achieves all that he has set out to achieve. His cathedral, on completion, possesses evocative power similar to the troop ships in *One of Ours* ("like simple and great thoughts") or to the great fact of the railroad in *The Song of the Lark*, getting the world back and forth. As the material expression of an idea, as an avatar of U.S. transit, the cathedral declares "a purpose so strong that it was like action" (269).

Other ideas echo in the landscape at the same time: "the whistle of a locomotive" (271) and "a great industrial expansion" in which Father Vaillant has elevated himself from a trader to "a promoter" (284–85).

The soldiers, traders, and missionaries have accomplished their business. The transmission has been completed. Miracles now occur regularly on the plains, and legends of "a mysterious stranger" and "a young
horseman" have supplanted nativist tales of great serpents and gods beneath the caverns (277). Christian symbology is not confined to the
lands in which it began or to the lands conquered by the early faith. In
America "a humble Mexican family" will be called on as the incarnation
of eternal Christian forms, as the Holy Family "after so many centuries
of history and glory . . . return to play Their first parts" among "the
lowliest of the lowly, the poorest of the poor,—in a wilderness at the
end of the world, where the angels could scarcely find Them!" (280–
81). Of course the angels can find them, because the angels are what the
missionaries carry in their packs. It is the idea of this migration that
will hold the culture like a rock to the manifestations of sacred faith,
the ideology of ambition and empire, of migration.

The significance of *Death Comes for the Archbishop* lies in Cather's
location of a fundamental aspect of American ideology in the figure
of a French priest traveling on a Roman mission through the Southwest territories of the United States in the middle of the nineteenth
century. The migratory idea faces its antithesis in confrontation with
a culture of stability. John McDermott locates the roots of the distinctively American philosophy of pragmatism in this "culture of transiency. It was born as a result of an exploring journey and its history is
one of continual trekking." Faith in exploration has given rise to such
distinctively American cultural styles as "a pluralistic version" of pressing questions and a suspicion "of any single, intractable, assured vision
of the human condition." Moreover, McDermott finds relativism firmly
rooted in this faith. Americans possess "a deep sense of multiple possible interpretations" that allows them to entertain contrary ideas on
crucial matters of policy and morality (60–61). The one idea that can
not be tolerated, however, is an uncompromising hold to a single idea,
place, or totalizing faith—such as that held by the Ácoma and Navajo
of *Death Comes for the Archbishop*, or what Americans commonly refer
to as the "cults" of fanatics, or the doctrinaire politics of ideologues.
In the novel, examples of failed missionaries range from the lax apostasy of Father Gallegos (a lost vision) to the tyranny of Father Baltazar.
Latour's success comes through migration and flexibility. Latour's life
is prototypically American in that, to put it in McDemott's terms, his
"life is basically a journey, transient and worthy of meaning for its own

sake" (60). The success of Archbishop Latour lies in his migrations to and from Santa Fe, Baltimore, and Rome, interacting with traders and soldiers and the church hierarchy, always representing the idea of transmission. The Romanesque cathedral is his mark of triumph not as a symbol of stability but as the symbol of transiency.

A culture of ambition and empire unites the individual desires of citizens with the larger movements of state. In *Death Comes for the Archbishop* the simple faith of the missionary traveler and the integrity and solemnity of his belief in God are tied explicitly to the parallel business of ambitious trading and imperial soldiering. As a whole, this novel, together with *One of Ours* and *Song of the Lark*, links common cultural practices of Americans (such as careerism, militarism, and wide varieties of religiosity) to the empire that they have created in the twentieth century. Every change-of-address card filed with the United States Postal Service is a gesture of empire, an expression of migratory consciousness, linking the moving van, the troop ship, and the cathedral.

At the conclusion of his famous frontier thesis, Frederick Jackson Turner refers to the "restless, nervous energy" of Americans and asserts that "the expansive character of American life" has not disappeared with the frontier territories. Regarding "the character of American life," Turner argues that "movement has been its dominant fact" (27). The standard interpretation of this statement has been a physical one, stressing the class and territorial mobility of the American citizen. Mobility has also passed into the culture as an ideological great fact of American existence, however. The philosophy of pragmatism, as McDermott explains, is based on the disbelief in absolute positions and the incredulous reaction to fixed dogma or intransigence of any kind. As movement becomes a quality of mind, all ideas and belief systems are leveled by the common experience of crossing, of having let go of some prior idea and moved into another. Such is the single requirement for inclusion in the American system as projected by Cather's fiction. It does not matter what you believe in as long as you recognize that all beliefs are the product of crossing from some previous idea or situation into another. America transforms anti-essentialism into an essentialist principle.

The very first image that confronts Jean Latour in the desert of the Southwest is the cruciform tree, symbolizing both his Christian faith and the American journeys that he will accomplish. Those who accomplish the Catherian act of crossing do so by selectively remembering the past; at the same time, they are not blinded by their origins. In addition, they adapt to the landscape but do not succumb to its terrors. When Latour prays before the cruciform tree, he prays with the faith in crossing that informs his ambition and with his faith as a young missionary priest. He prays as well (and unwittingly) to the empire to which his successful aspirations contribute. The novel documents the "winning of the West" by a number of forces, including independent Indian fighters, military installations, traders, railroad companies, gold rushes, and missionaries, but each is the incarnation of a single idea. The faith that conquered America, as Cather saw it, held that within the very quality of movement exists an inherent progression of the human condition. "We're over," as the soldiers say in *One of Ours*, we have come here, and because we have crossed over, we achieve authenticity. The idea of America is accomplished through migration from one place to another, intellectually, physically, and spiritually. When Thea Kronberg thinks of herself in her relation to others, she envisions that "each of them concealed another person in himself, just as she did," and that everyone had "to guard them fiercely." The sense of spatialized multiplicity, allowing transactions among various potential selves, characterizes a culture of movement and migration. Thea considers her life progress "as if she had an appointment to meet the rest of herself sometime, somewhere. It was moving to meet her and she was moving to meet it" (189). At the end of his life Archbishop Latour, "soon to have done with the calendared time," is described as being situated, spatially, "in the middle of his own consciousness; none of his former states of mind were lost or outgrown" (288). Even Claude Wheeler, before dying, articulates a sense of "beginning over again," possessing another life as a soldier in the Grand Army of the Republic (332). The crisis that afflicted Godfrey St. Peter, recall, was made emblematic by his reluctance to move from one place to another. Movement is essential in Cather's America—moving among potential selves, migrating into new territories, transmitting ideas across frontiers.

The empire of migration will throw over anyone or any culture incapable of movement or spiritually opposed to crossing. The price of admission into the empire is to abdicate any unchangeable, principled existence that will not yield to the business of migration. Intractability is the national heresy. Americans must learn early that they contain multitudes or they will be, in some fashion, destroyed. Thea could detach herself from her sponsors and mentors by claiming that it was another self whom they saw, not her own self. Claude relegated his dreary boyhood in Nebraska to another life entirely. And Latour sees his states of mind as compass points on a map of his travels, all available to the simultaneity of his spatial consciousness. Thus Cather's heroes, those who die a glorious death or come to some sense of accomplishment, are those who realize that they have emerged out of tremendous motion into a space that can be possessed only in passing. The empire thrives on a consciousness that locates in historical passage not loss but the foundations of future migration.

The Empire of Migration

There's no place like home,
There's no place like home.
—DOROTHY, *The Wizard of Oz*

In *The Wizard of Oz* Judy Garland articulates what Salman Rushdie calls "the anthem of all the world's migrants" when, as the Kansas farm girl Dorothy Gale, she sings "Somewhere, over the Rainbow." The overt message of this American movie is that "there's no place like home," but Rushdie rightly insists that this message is completely undercut by the production as a whole. In the rainbow song Dorothy "expresses . . . the human dream of *leaving*, a dream at least as powerful as its counter-vailing dream of roots. At the heart of *The Wizard of Oz* is a great tension between these two dreams," but the stronger argument presented by the movie is the one that compels migration to another place. As a whole the film is "about the joys of going away, of leaving the greyness and entering the color, of making a new life in the 'place where there isn't any trouble'" (*Wizard of Oz* 23).

The continuous appeal of *The Wizard of Oz* lies in its presentation of a core anxiety shared by Americans. This anxiety is expressed by Father Latour's deathbed ambivalence, "the desire to go and the necessity to stay," out of which a new will must be forged (297). Because "some people go this way, some people go that way," as the Scarecrow explains at the crossroads, the situation of the American is not whether to go but which way. People come and go quickly, yellow brick roads exist to be followed, and if we think we are forever safe in our houses, think again. The tornado that carries Dorothy to Oz is the strong wind of events be-yond our control—tornadoes, bank failures, job losses, and job offers—by which a house is lifted up and carried off, as if in a dream. Unlike the gods who empower the Navajo Shiprock, however, the supernatural Glinda advises Dorothy not to stay in her house and worship the dead gods of Oz but to leave the house behind and to follow the road. Like so many of Cather's migrants, Dorothy must travel to get home again. She must uproot to become rooted. But of course she will never be rooted. The memory of having traveled so far will prevent her from ever feeling settled. She will never again see the three farmhands or the traveling salesman in the same way, much less Miss Gulch. The new will that has been forged on the American continent is the Catherian sense of ambition and empire, of courageous homelessness, of the settled values of migration and uprooting.

What has Dorothy been telling American children each generation since 1939? Why did CBS television find a ratings gold mine in broadcasting the movie year after year during the era of the cold war's imperial style? American families in the 1950s and 1960s watched *The Wizard of Oz* on television while the Department of Defense built the interstate highway system throughout the United States. The movie explains why Americans have journeyed and why they must keep on moving from place to place, searching for somewhere over the rainbow, somewhere "over there," to settle. What Dorothy discovers is the meaning of Father Latour's missionary journeys, the meaning of Claude's reverse migration, and the essence of Thea Kronberg's rise to stardom. In the American conception of things the world has to be got back and forth. Glinda tells Dorothy that she always had the power to go home, just by clicking her heels and saying "there's no place like home." Glinda could not have given Dorothy the message, however, before Dorothy had migrated away from her fallen, sepia-tone house to the colorful Oz and before she had killed off the castle-dwelling witch. In other words, to an American audience home makes sense only as a location to which one has traveled. Home is not origins; home is destination. Father Latour makes a home—that is, he builds a cathedral—in Santa Fe. Dorothy had to leave Kansas to make an elaborate journey to her home, a home essentially transformed and renewed because she can now see it as a migrant does, as does one who knows all those around her as characters from other places.

The message of Dorothy Gale, the homeless girl who transforms the countryside, is the cultivation of migratory consciousness. Dorothy Gale learns to be at home in transit. The quest for home is described as a physical journey, and the place where she wants to go is made equivalent to an abstract quality. In the empire of migration one has a home in the same way that one has a heart, courage, or brains. Home is not property so much as intellectual or emotional space; the idea of it precedes its establishment. After all, Dorothy was already at home, or at her house, when she decided to follow the yellow brick road to Oz. Why not go back inside the sepia-tone farmhouse, out through the back door and into the root cellar, where Auntie Em and the others are hiding? The answer is the same as that to another question: if Dorothy wanted to be home, why did she run away? Because it makes no sense, in the American understanding, to stay home. Dorothy cannot be at home until she migrates. As Jim Burden would have said, she cannot settle down if she stays there. And so, like Father Latour, who dies of having lived, Dorothy stays home by having migrated.

Willa Cather was concerned throughout her career as a novelist with intersections and crossings: home and journey, memory and desire, settlement and migration, past and future. The crossroad is a complex symbol in Catherian aesthetics, and in all its ramifications it encapsulates the great fact of American culture as a global phenomenon. The crossroad is an emblem both of the empire of great migrations, transoceanic and transcontinental, and the empire of national movement, from town to town, job to job, and state to state. The novels of Willa Cather provide a context for seeing the way in which these migrations and intersections compose U.S. culture. In the national rhetoric of the mass media Americans are more often distracted by the divisiveness of a culture of crossroads. With every intersection—bilingual education, multicultural classrooms, refugees off the coast in crowded boats—Americans face again the tragic crossroads of origins. Every American has either left something behind in the name of moving on or succeeding or has achieved stability thanks to the willingness of some forebear to risk everything and make the crossing. Each subsequent transaction is a reminder of what has been discarded but not forgotten.

Willa Cather's short novel *My Mortal Enemy* (1926) presents the gradual undoing of a woman who has lost her sense of the future and has come to identify her destiny in her past. Myra's youth was consumed by desire, and "her runaway marriage" (3) achieves legendary status in her hometown. As she grows older, however, Myra is engrossed by a sense of loss, of having somehow betrayed her origins. This novel is Cather's American nightmare. The migratory American who comes to Myra Henshawe's conclusion, "I should have stayed. . . . We've thrown our lives away" (62), is indeed living out the fate of Cather's most haunted victims. The worst thing that can happen in Cather's empire of migration is to believe in a wrong move, to become displaced, to fail to lighten the load or to throw over what cannot be transported. Henshawe's anguish is no doubt similar to what Mr. Shimerda was thinking before he committed suicide in the Nebraska winter.

Myra Henshawe is afflicted with the sense that she had made a mistake in running away with Oswald. Instead of emulating her uncle, who would risk personal ruin "to crush an enemy" (67), Myra married hers and ran off on the Chicago express with him. The future then becomes an affront to her, as wealth and her "fortune" lie unreachable in the past. Her uncle established a home for female "refugees," homeless women and unclaimed orphans, the casualties among a migratory people. There are many such men and women in Cather's fiction, tramps, outcasts, victims of a migratory culture that has no place for those who will not accept the abstract nature of home and origins. Fortunes are worked out in migration, but not all fortunes are good ones. As she ages Myra does become what her forebears put into her: an orphan, "cut . . . off without a penny" (67, 12). God has blessed Myra Henshawe with only one kind of memory, the kind that will not forget and cannot discard.

"Why must I die like this, alone with my mortal enemy?" (78). Myra is alone when she dies, but not with her husband and enemy, Oswald. She dies facing the ocean dawn, symbol of the future, the sunrise she had associated with forgiveness. She gets to the seashore by her own volition, demonstrating a vestige of the "insane ambition" that had led her to cut all material ties to her origins. At her death her enemy is a confluence of ideas and images, including Oswald, the dawn, the desire to run away, and the need for forgiveness. A people that defines itself by the future, by what has yet to be accomplished or by the place that has yet to be possessed, will sustain an ambivalence toward time, a mixture of hostility and nostalgia. We want to be assured that what we have done is all right with the gods, with history, while at the same time reassuring ourselves that we have moved sufficiently, into the future, to justify the space we occupy.

Cather's empire of migration is a culture in transit, where intellectuals and laborers alike keep their suitcases under the bed, on the verge of packing up and moving on. Critics of this culture point to the nation's lack of core beliefs, to its vulgar materialism, to the absence of tradition. These qualities are symptoms, however, not sources. Myra's sense was that "in religion, desire was fulfillment, it was the seeking itself that rewarded" (77). The same is true of her social order as a whole. Accomplishment is suspect in America; witness the ritualistic destruction of heroes, the unstoppable leveling of any achievement, the pleasure in seeing base motives revealed at the highest echelons of power and prestige. Those who disappear into the future are truly the heroes of this culture. "Myra Henshawe, never, after her elopement, came back but once"; such is the source of her mystique, compensating for the "monotonous" life of the narrator, Nellie, and her friends (3). On closer examination Cather's text reveals that Myra Henshawe has lived the life of an American crucible, moving from a willful disavowal of heritage and origins to a self-created future and the profound sense of loss that accompanies all such crossings.

James Baldwin, in an essay on the nationalist identity of the American, contemplates "the terms on which he is related to his country, and to the world." Baldwin is struck by the American belief in an existence "apart from all the forces which have produced him." Such an assumption, however, flows directly from the nation's history, particularly from the history of its population, "which is the history of the total, and willing, alienation of entire peoples from their forebears" (115). An entire nation predicated on the belief in origins *elsewhere* is a homeless nation. The national ideology is one where homelessness is compensated for in terms of an American dream of home ownership and where the absence of familially based points of reference is balanced by the rhetoric of family values. The fact is that homelessness is simply unthinkable as the basis for historical, national, settled existence. Because of this, as Cather demonstrates, Americans busily create compensatory, spatialized ideologies of home, history, and community. What Americans share as a people is migratory consciousness, the natural ability to move among contingencies and provisionalities, to lighten the load when necessary and to gather at will. Willa Cather projects in her novels the centrality of cosmic homelessness, the empire of migration, and raises both to the level of an aesthetic ideal. In her hands it is no defect, no sign of a "nervous" people or an "unsettled" culture, but a defining characteristic, a mode of consciousness and the sine qua non of American existence.

American culture, in the context of Willa Cather's writing, exists as a finished object in the future alone, in the form of spatial imagination, national purpose, and migration into possibility. American hostility toward history, toward the past as the image of completion, is the migrant's resentment for the settled, the traveler's suspicion of the entrenched. Hence American revisionist history, as an institution, ritualistically denies the objective status of the past. The two kinds of memory Cather wrote of—the will to sustain and the will to forget (or to revise)—display the mobility of American historical consciousness across temporal and spatial frontiers. Cather's fiction has sustained and increased its relevance to the American scene in the half-century since her death because it projects these central cultural crossings. Cather wrote of migratory consciousness, exploring its various manifestations as a historical force, as the ambitions of individual men and women, as a cultural trait, and as the mythos of empire. The novels of Willa Cather project the great fact of a migratory people: in the culture of displacement, removal is the highest expression of being American. There really is no place like home, and we keep our suitcases under the bed, ready to go there.

Bibliography

Aichinger, Peter. *The American Soldier in Fiction, 1889–1963: A History of the Attitudes toward Warfare and the Military Establishment*. Ames: Iowa State University Press, 1975.

Anderson, Benedict. *Imagined Communities: Reflections on the Origin and Spread of Nationalism*. Rev. ed. New York: Verso, 1993.

Angus, Ian, and Sut Jhally. *Cultural Politics in Contemporary America*. New York: Routledge, 1989.

Arnold, Marilyn. "The Integrating Vision of Bishop Latour in Willa Cather's *Death Comes for the Archbishop*." *Literature and Belief* 8 (1988): 39–57.

Auerbach, Carl A. "Freedom of Movement in International Law and United States Policy." In *Human Migration: Patterns and Policies*, ed. William H. McNeill and Ruth S. Adams, 317–35. Bloomington: Indiana University Press, 1978.

Baldwin, James. *Notes of a Native Son*. New York: Bantam, 1964.

Bercovitch, Sacvan. *The American Jeremiad*. Madison: University of Wisconsin Press, 1978.

———. *The Rites of Assent: Transformations in the Symbolic Construction of America*. New York: Routledge, 1993.

Berger, John. *Ways of Seeing*. New York: Penguin, 1977.

Berger, Peter L., with Brigitte Berger and Hansfried Kellner (joint authors). *The Homeless Mind: Modernization and Consciousness*. New York: Random House, 1973.

Blair, John G. *Modular America: Cross-Cultural Perspectives on the Emergence of an American Way*. Westport, Conn.: Greenwood, 1988.

Bloom, Edward A., and Lillian D. Bloom. *Willa Cather's Gift of Sympathy*. Carbondale: Southern Illinois University Press, 1962.

Bottomly, Gillian. *From Another Place: Migration and the Politics of Culture*. New York: Cambridge University Press, 1992.

Braudel, Fernand. *On History*. Trans. Sarah Matthews. Chicago: University of Chicago Press, 1980 (1969).

Broncano, Manuel. "From Frontiersmen to Imperial Army: The Case of the United States and Spain." Lectures, Bryant College, Smithfield, R.I., January 1993.

Callander, Marilyn Berg. *Willa Cather and the Fairy Tale*. Ann Arbor: UMI Research Press, 1989.

Caraher, Brian G. "Introduction: Intimate Conflict." In *Intimate Conflict: Contradiction in Literary and Philosophical Discourse: A Collection of Essays by Diverse Hands*, ed. Brian G. Caraher, 1–34. Albany: SUNY Press, 1992.

Carlin, Deborah. *Cather, the Canon, and the Politics of Reading*. Amherst: University of Massachusetts Press, 1992.

Carlson, Robert A. *The Americanization Syndrome: A Quest for Conformity*. New York: St. Martin's, 1987.

Carter, Paul. *Living in a New Country: History, Travelling, and Language*. Boston: Faber and Faber, 1992.

Cather, Willa. *Death Comes for the Archbishop*. New York: Vintage Classics, 1991 (1927).

———. *The Kingdom of Art: Willa Cather's First Principles and Critical Statements, 1893–1896*. Ed. Bernice Slote. Lincoln: University of Nebraska Press, 1966.

———. *A Lost Lady*. New York: Vintage Classics, 1990 (1923).

———. *Lucy Gayheart*. New York: Vintage, 1976 (1936).

———. *My Ántonia*. Boston: Houghton Mifflin, 1988 (1918).

———. *My Mortal Enemy*. New York: Vintage Classics, 1990 (1926).

———. *Not under Forty*. Lincoln: University of Nebraska Press, 1988 (1922).

———. *The Old Beauty and Others*. New York: Vintage, 1976 (1948).

———. *One of Ours*. New York: Vintage Classics, 1991 (1922).

———. *On Writing: Critical Studies on Writing as an Art*. New York: Knopf, 1953.

———. *O Pioneers!* New York: Signet, 1988 (1913).

———. *The Professor's House*. New York: Vintage Classics, 1990 (1925).

———. *Sapphira and the Slave Girl*. New York: Vintage, 1975 (1940).

———. *Shadows on the Rock*. New York: Vintage, 1971 (1931).

———. *The Song of the Lark*. New York: Penguin, 1991 (1915).

———. *Willa Cather in Europe: Her Own Story of the First Journey*. Ed. George N. Kates. New York: Knopf, 1956.

———. *Willa Cather in Person: Interviews, Speeches, and Letters*. Ed. L. Brent Bohlke. Lincoln: University of Nebraska Press, 1986.

———. *The World and the Parish: Willa Cather's Articles and Reviews, 1893–1902*. 2 vols. Lincoln: University of Nebraska Press, 1970.

Cather, Willa, and Georgine Milmine. *The Life of Mary Baker G. Eddy and the History of Christian Science*. Introduction and afterword by David Stouck. Lincoln: University of Nebraska Press, 1993 (1909).

Collins, Jim. *Uncommon Cultures: Popular Culture and Post-Modernism*. New York: Routledge, 1989.

Cooperman, Stanley. "The War Lover: Claude." In *Critical Essays on Willa Cather*, ed. John J. Murphy, 169–76. Boston: G.K. Hall, 1984.

Cowley, Malcolm. *Exile's Return: A Literary Odyssey of the 1920s*. New York: Viking, 1951.

Davidson, Cathy N. *Revolution and the Word: The Rise of the Novel in America*. New York: Oxford, 1986.

Dos Passos, John. *Manhatten Transfer*. Boston: Houghton Mifflin, 1953 (1925).

Douglass, Frederick. *Narrative of the Life of Frederick Douglass, an American Slave*. New York: Anchor, 1973 (1845).

Einstein, Albert. *Ideas and Opinions*. Trans. Sonja Bargmann. New York: Crown, 1954.

Ellis, William. *The Theory of the American Romance: An Ideology in American Intellectual History*. Ann Arbor: UMI Research Press, 1989.

Elshtain, Jean Bethke. *Women and War.* New York: Basic, 1987.

Falck, Colin. *Myth, Truth, and Literature: Towards a True Post-Modernism*. New York: Cambridge University Press, 1989.

Fisher-Wirth, Ann W. "Dispossession and Redemption in the Novels of Willa Cather." *Cather Studies* 1 (1990): 36–57.

Fox, Dixon Ryan. *Ideas in Motion*. New York: Appleton-Century, 1935.

Fox, Robin Lane. *Pagans and Christians*. New York: HarperCollins, 1986.

Freedberg, David. *The Power of Images: Studies in the History and Theory of Response*. Chicago: University of Chicago Press, 1989.

Fryer, Judith. *Felicitous Space: The Imaginative Structures of Edith Wharton and Willa Cather.* Chapel Hill: University of North Carolina Press, 1986.

Fuchs, Lawrence H. *The American Kaleidoscope: Race, Ethnicity, and the Civic Culture*. Hanover: University Press of New England, 1990.

Gelfant, Blanche H. "The Forgotten Reaping Hook: Sex in *My Antonia*." In *Willa Cather: Modern Critical Views*, ed. Harold Bloom, 103–21. New York: Chelsea House, 1985.

———. " 'What Was It . . . ?': The Secret of Family Accord in *One of Ours*." In *Willa Cather: Family, Community, and History* (The BYU Symposium), ed. John J. Murphy with Linda Hunter Adams and Paul Rawlins, 85–102. Provo, Utah: Brigham Young University Humanities Publications Center (and Willa Cather Education Foundation), 1990.

George, Benjamin. "The French-Canadian Connection: Willa Cather as Canadian Writer." In *Critical Essays on Willa Cather*, ed. John J. Murphy, 269–79. Boston: G.K. Hall, 1984.

Giannone, Richard. *Music in Willa Cather's Fiction*. Lincoln: University of Nebraska Press, 1968.

———. "Willa Cather and the Unfinished Novel of Deliverance." *Prairie Schooner* 52 (Spring 1978): 25–46.

Girgus, Sam B. *Desire and the Political Unconscious in American Literature*. New York: St. Martin's, 1990.

Gitlin, Todd. *The Whole World Is Watching: Mass Media in the Making and Unmaking of the New Left*. Berkeley: University of California Press, 1980.

Gleason, Philip. *Speaking of Diversity: Language and Ethnicity in Twentieth-Century America*. Baltimore: Johns Hopkins University Press, 1992.

Graff, Gerald. "American Criticism: Left and Right." In *Ideology and Classic American Literature*, ed. Sacvan Bercovitch and Myra Jehlen, 91–121. New York: Cambridge University Press, 1986.

———. *Literature against Itself: Literary Ideas in Modern Society*. Chicago: University of Chicago Press, 1979.

Grafton, Anthony. *New Worlds, Ancient Texts: The Power of Tradition and the Shock of Discovery*. Cambridge, Mass.: Belknap, 1992.

Grinberg, Leon, and Rebecca Grinberg. *Psychoanalytic Perspectives on Migration and Exile*. Trans. Nancy Festinger. New Haven, Conn.: Yale University Press, 1989.

Halbwachs, Maurice. *On Collective Memory*. Ed. and trans. Lewis A. Coser. Chicago: University of Chicago Press, 1992 (1952).

Handlin, Oscar. *The Uprooted*. 2d ed. Boston: Little, Brown, 1973.

Hansen, Marcus Lee. "The Problem of the Third Generation Immigrant." In *American Immigrants and Their Generations: Studies and Commentaries on the Hansen Thesis after Fifty Years*, ed. Peter Kivisto and Dag Blanck, 191–203. Urbana: University of Illinois Press, 1990.

Harrell, David. *From Mesa Verde to The Professor's House*. Albuquerque: University of New Mexico Press, 1992.

Herberg, Will. *Protestant-Catholic-Jew: An Essay in American Religious Sociology*. Rev. ed. Garden City, N.Y.: Anchor, 1960.

Higham, John. "From Process to Structure: Formulations of American Immigrant History." In *American Immigrants and Their Generations: Studies and Commentaries on the Hansen Thesis after Fifty Years*, ed. Peter Kivisto and Dag Blanck, 11–43. Urbana: University of Illinois Press, 1990.

Highet, Gilbert. *The Migration of Ideas*. New York: Oxford University Press, 1954.

Hobsbawm, Eric J. *The Age of Empire: 1875–1914*. New York: Pantheon, 1987.

———. *Nations and Nationalism since 1780: Programme, Myth, Reality*. New York: Cambridge University Press, 1990.

Howard, Michael. *The Causes of War and Other Essays*. London: Temple Smith, 1983.

Hunter, James Davison. *Culture Wars: The Struggle to Define America*. New York: Basic, 1991.

Iser, Wolfgang. *The Fictive and the Imaginary: Charting Literary Anthropology*. Baltimore: Johns Hopkins University Press, 1993.

Jameson, Fredric. *The Political Unconscious: Narrative as Socially Symbolic Act.* Ithaca, N.Y.: Cornell University Press, 1981.

Jeffords, Susan. *The Remasculinization of America: Gender and the Vietnam War.* Bloomington: Indiana University Press, 1989.

Jehlen, Myra. *American Incarnation: The Individual, the Nation, and the Continent.* Cambridge, Mass.: Harvard University Press, 1986.

Kammen, Michael. *Mystic Chords of Memory: The Transformation of Tradition in American Culture.* New York: Knopf, 1991.

Kaplan, Amy. "Left Alone with Empire." In *Cultures of United States Imperialism*, ed. Amy Kaplan and Donald E. Pease, 3–21. Durham, N.C.: Duke University Press, 1993.

Kearney, Richard. *The Wake of Imagination: Toward a Postmodern Culture.* Minneapolis: University of Minnesota Press, 1988.

Kemp, Anthony. *The Estrangement of the Past: A Study in the Origins of Modern Historical Consciousness.* New York: Oxford University Press, 1991.

Kennedy, David M. *Over Here: The First World War and American Society.* New York: Oxford University Press, 1980.

Kettner, James H. *The Development of American Citizenship, 1608–1870.* Chapel Hill: University of North Carolina Press, 1978.

Kiefer, Christie W. *Changing Cultures, Changing Lives: An Ethnographic Study of Three Generations of Japanese Americans.* San Francisco: Jossey-Bass, 1974.

Kuberski, Philip. *The Persistence of Memory: Organism, Myth, Text.* Berkeley: University of California Press, 1992.

LaCapra, Dominick. *Rethinking Intellectual History: Texts, Contexts, Languages.* Ithaca, N.Y.: Cornell University Press, 1983.

Lauter, Paul. *Canons and Contexts.* New York: Oxford University Press, 1991.

Lee, Hermione. *Willa Cather: Double Lives.* New York: Pantheon, 1989.

Leed, Eric J. *No Man's Land: Combat and Identity in World War I.* New York: Cambridge University Press, 1979.

Lentricchia, Frank. *Criticism and Social Change.* Chicago: University of Chicago Press, 1983.

Levy, Helen Fiddyment. *Fiction of the Home Place: Jewett, Cather, Glasgow, Porter, Welty, and Naylor.* Jackson: University Press of Mississippi, 1992.

Lewis, Edith. *Willa Cather Living: A Personal Record.* New York: Knopf, 1953.

Longfellow, Henry Wadsworth. *The Complete Poetical Works of Henry Wadsworth Longfellow.* Boston: Riverside, 1915.

Lutwack, Leonard. *The Role of Place in Literature.* Syracuse, N.Y.: Syracuse University Press, 1984.

McDermott, John J. *Streams of Experience: Reflections on the History and Philosophy of American Culture.* Amherst: University of Massachusetts Press, 1986.

Marcel, Gabriel. *Homo Viator: Introduction to a Metaphysic of Hope.* Chicago: Henry Regency, 1951.

Marshall, S. L. A. *Men against Fire: The Problem of Battle Command in Future War.* New York: William Morris, 1947.

Martin, Calvin Luther. *In the Spirit of the Earth: Rethinking History and Time.* Baltimore: Johns Hopkins University Press, 1992.

Martin, Terence. "The Drama of Memory in *My Antonia.*" In *Willa Cather: Modern Critical Views,* ed. Harold Bloom, 87-101. New York: Chelsea House, 1985.

Marty, Martin E. "Migration: The Moral Framework." In *Human Migration: Patterns and Policies,* ed. William H. McNeill and Ruth S. Adams, 387-403. Bloomington: Indiana University Press, 1978.

Matthews, Fred. "Paradigm Changes in Interpretations of Ethnicity, 1930-1980: From Process to Structure." In *American Immigrants and Their Generations: Studies and Commentaries on the Hansen Thesis after Fifty Years,* ed. Peter Kivisto and Dag Blanck, 167-90. Urbana: University of Illinois Press, 1990.

Middleton, Jo Ann. *Willa Cather's Modernism: A Study of Style and Technique.* Rutherford, N.J.: Farleigh Dickenson University Press, 1990.

Miller, Wayne Charles. *An Armed America: Its Face in Fiction: A History of the American Military Novel.* New York: New York University Press, 1970.

Mills, Nicolaus. *The Crowd in American Literature.* Baton Rouge: Louisiana State University Press, 1986.

Mitchell, W. J. T. *Iconology: Image, Text, Ideology.* Chicago: University of Chicago Press, 1986.

———. "Imperial Landscape." In *Landscape and Power,* ed. W. J. T. Mitchell, 5-34. Chicago: University of Chicago Press, 1994.

———. *The Politics of Interpretation.* Chicago: University of Chicago Press, 1983.

Monroe, William. "Stories as 'Equipment for Living'—and Dying." In *Willa Cather: Family, Community, and History* (The BYU Symposium), ed. John J. Murphy with Linda Hunter Adams and Paul Rawlins, 301-10. Provo, Utah: Brigham Young University Humanities Publications Center (and Willa Cather Education Foundation), 1990.

Morrison, Peter A., and Judith P. Wheeler. "The Image of 'Elsewhere' in the American Tradition of Migration." In *Human Migration: Patterns and Policies,* ed. William H. McNeill and Ruth S. Adams, 75-84. Bloomington: Indiana University Press, 1978.

Morrison, Toni. *Playing in the Dark: Whiteness in the Literary Imagination.* Cambridge, Mass.: Harvard University Press, 1992.

Mosse, George. *Fallen Soldiers: Reshaping the Memory of the World Wars.* New York: Oxford University Press, 1990.

Munsterberg, Hugo. *The Americans.* Trans. Edwin B. Holt. New York: McClure, Phillips, 1904.

Murphy, John J. "Cather's New World Divine Comedy: The Dante Connection." *Cather Studies* 1 (1990): 21–35.

——. "The Missions of Latour and Paul: *Death Comes for the Archbishop* and the Early Church." *Literature and Belief* 8 (1988): 58–64.

——. "Willa Cather's Archbishop: A Western and Classical Perspective." In *Willa Cather: Modern Critical Views,* ed. Harold Bloom, 161–69. New York: Chelsea House, 1985.

Murphy, Joseph. "Cather's Re-Vision of American Typology in *My Antonia.*" In *Willa Cather: Family, Community, and History* (The BYU Symposium), ed. John J. Murphy with Linda Hunter Adams and Paul Rawlins, 214–19. Provo, Utah: Brigham Young University Humanities Publications Center (and Willa Cather Education Foundation, 1990).

Newton, Judith Lowder. "History as Usual? Feminism and the New Historicism." In *The New Historicism,* ed. H. Aram Veeser, 152–167. New York: Routledge, 1989.

Nugent, Walter. *Crossings: The Great Transatlantic Migrations, 1870–1914.* Bloomington: Indiana University Press, 1994.

O'Brien, Sharon. *Willa Cather: The Emerging Voice.* New York: Oxford University Press, 1987.

O'Connell, Robert L. *Of Arms and Men: A History of War, Weapons, and Aggression.* New York: Oxford University Press, 1989.

Ostwalt, Conrad Eugene, Jr. *After Eden: The Secularization of American Space in the Fiction of Willa Cather and Theodore Dreiser.* Lewisburg, Pa.: Bucknell University Press, 1990.

Paglia, Camille. *Sexual Personae: Art and Decadence from Nefertiti to Emily Dickinson.* New Haven, Conn.: Yale University Press, 1990.

Pierson, George W. *The Moving American.* New York: Knopf, 1973.

Quirk, Tom. *Bergson and American Culture: The Worlds of Willa Cather and Wallace Stevens.* Chapel Hill: University of North Carolina Press, 1990.

Randall, John H., *The Landscape and the Looking Glass: Willa Cather's Search for Value.* Westport, Conn.: Greenwood, 1960.

Reising, Russell J. *The Usable Past: Theory and the Study of American Literature.* New York: Methuen, 1986.

Robey, Bryant. *The American People: A Timely Exploration of a Changing America and the Important New Demographic Trends around Us.* New York: E.P. Dutton, 1985.

Robinson, Phyllis C. *Willa: The Life of Willa Cather.* New York: Holt, Rinehart and Winston, 1983.

Romines, Ann. *The Home Plot: Women, Writing, and Domestic Ritual.* Amherst: University of Massachusetts Press, 1992.

Ropers, Richard H. *The Invisible Homeless: A New Urban Ecology.* New York: Human Sciences, 1988.

Rosowski, Susan J. *The Voyage Perilous: Willa Cather's Romanticism.* Lincoln: University of Nebraska Press, 1986.

———. "Willa Cather's *A Lost Lady:* The Paradoxes of Change." *Novel* 11 (1977): 51–62.

———. "Willa Cather's Subverted Endings and Gendered Time" *Cather Studies* 1 (1990): 68–88.

———. "Writing against Silences: Female Adolescent Development in the Novels of Willa Cather." *Studies in the Novel* 21, no. 1 (1989): 60–77.

Rowlandson, Mary. "The Sovereignty and Goodness of God." In *Puritans among the Indians: Accounts of Captivity and Redemption, 1676–1724*, ed. Alden T. Vaughn and Edward W. Clark, 29–75. Cambridge, Mass.: Belknap, 1981.

Rushdie, Salman. *Imaginary Homelands: Essays and Criticism, 1981–1991.* New York: Viking, 1991.

———. *The Wizard of Oz.* London: BFI, 1992.

Rutherford, Andrew. *The Literature of War: Five Studies in Heroic Virtue.* London: Macmillan, 1978.

Ryder, Mary Beth. *Willa Cather and Classical Myth: The Search for a New Parnassus.* Lewiston, N.Y.: Edwin Mellen, 1990.

Schlissel, Lillian. "The Frontier Family: Dislocation and the American Experience." In *Making America: The Society and Culture of the United States*, ed. Luther S. Luedtke, 83–94. Chapel Hill: University of North Carolina Press, 1992.

Schwind, Jean. "The 'Beautiful' War in *One of Ours.*" *Modern Fiction Studies* 30 (1984): 53–72.

Sergeant, Elizabeth Shepley. *Willa Cather: A Memoir.* Lincoln: University of Nebraska Press, 1953.

Shaw, Patrick W. *Willa Cather and the Art of Conflict: Re-Visioning Her Creative Imagination.* Troy, N.Y.: Whitson, 1992.

Shils, Edward. "Roots—the Sense of Place and Past: The Cultural Gains and Losses of Migration." In *Human Migration: Patterns and Policies*, eds. William H. McNeill and Ruth S. Adams, 404–26. Bloomington: Indiana University Press, 1978.

Simpson, Lewis P. *The Brazen Face of History: Studies in the Literary Consciousness of America.* Baton Rouge: Louisiana State University Press, 1980.

Skaggs, Merrill Maguire. *After the World Broke in Two: The Later Novels of Willa Cather.* Charlottesville: University Press of Virginia, 1990.

Slotkin, Richard. *The Fatal Environment: The Myth of the Frontier in the Age of Industrialization, 1800–1890.* New York: Atheneum, 1985.

———. *Gunfighter Nation: The Myth of the Frontier in Twentieth-Century America.* New York: Atheneum, 1992.

———. "Myth and the Production of History." In *Ideology and Classic American Literature*, ed. Sacvan Bercovitch and Myra Jehlen, 70–90. New York: Cambridge University Press, 1986.

———. *Regeneration through Violence: The Mythology of the American Frontier, 1600–1860*. Middletown, Conn.: Wesleyan University Press, 1973.

Smith, Paul. *Discerning the Subject*. Minneapolis: University of Minnesota Press, 1988.

Soja, Edward. "History: Geography: Modernity." In *The Cultural Studies Reader*, ed. Simon During, 135–50. New York: Routledge, 1993.

———. *Postmodern Geographies: The Reassertion of Space in Critical Social Theory*. New York: Verso, 1989.

Sollers, Werner. *Beyond Ethnicity: Consent and Descent in American Culture*. New York: Oxford University Press, 1986.

Sophocles. *Oedipus Rex*. Ed. R. D. Dawe. Cambridge: Cambridge University Press, 1982.

Stouck, David. *Willa Cather's Imagination*. Lincoln: University of Nebraska Press, 1975.

———. "Willa Cather and the Russians." *Cather Studies* 1 (1990): 1–20.

Stout, Janis P. *Strategies of Reticence: Silence and Meaning in the Works of Jane Austen, Willa Cather, Katherine Anne Porter, Joan Dideon*. Charlottesville: University Press of Virginia, 1990.

Stowe, Harriet Beecher. *Uncle Tom's Cabin; or, Life among the Lowly* (1852). Ed. and with an introduction by Ann Douglas. New York: Penguin, 1986.

Swift, John N. "Cather's Archbishop and the Backward Path." *Cather Studies* 1 (1990): 56–67.

Trachtenberg, Alan. *The Incorporation of America: Culture and Society in the Gilded Age*. New York: Hill and Wang, 1982.

Tuan, Yi-Fu. *Space and Place: The Perspective of Experience*. Minneapolis: University of Minnesota Press, 1977

Turner, Frederick Jackson. "The Significance of the Frontier in American History." In *The Turner Thesis: Concerning the Role of the Frontier in American History*, ed. George Rogers Taylor, 3–27. Lexington, Mass.: D.C. Heath, 1972.

Twain, Mark. *Adventures of Huckleberry Finn*. Berkeley: University of California Press, 1985 (1885).

Welty, Eudora. "The House of Willa Cather." In *Willa Cather: Modern Critical Views*, ed. Harold Bloom, 145–59. New York: Chelsea House, 1985.

Winters, Laura. *Willa Cather: Landscape and Exile*. Selinsgrove, N.J.: Susquehanna University Press, 1993.

Wise, Gene. *American Historical Explanations: A Strategy for Grounded Inquiry*. 2d ed. Minneapolis: University of Minnesota Press, 1980.

Woodress, James. *Willa Cather: A Literary Life*. Lincoln: University of Nebraska Press, 1987.

Index

JOSEPH R. URGO is an associate professor of English and humanities at Bryant College. He is the author of *Faulkner's Apocrypha: A Fable, Snopes, and The Spirit of Human Rebellion* (1989) and *Novel Frames: Literature as Guide to Race, Sex, and History in American Culture* (1991), as well as numerous essays on American literature and culture.